Peacebuilding

Further praise for *Peacebuilding*

"This timely and intellectually stimulating volume offers a theory embedded approach to designing and implementing more effective policies to tackle complex world issues such as terrorism, North–South relations, and good global governance. Essential reading for students, researchers and policymakers."

Nimet Beriker, Sabanci University

"Dennis Sandole's book promotes a holistic model in response to the complex realities of conflict prevention and peacebuilding in the post 9/11 era. A must for US policymakers and academic readers alike."

Thania Paffenholz, Centre on Conflict, Development and Peacebuilding, Switzerland

"A tour-de-force study of peacebuilding that offers long-term, sustainable solutions in a world of complex and interrelated challenges."

Janie Leatherman, Fairfield University

"This bold and wide-ranging book outlines how the U.S. and its partners can avoid the Iraq's and Afghanistan's of the future by using available tools of problem-solving and conflict analysis/resolution and applying more deliberately the known lessons from international successes in multi-dimensional conflict prevention and post-conflict peace building – rather than defaulting to piecemeal, unilateral, stove-piped programs that are often ineffective and may worsen the problem. Relating conflict resolution techniques to practical challenges in confronting conflicts, terrorists, and failed states and to the current "whole of government" discourse, this tour de force argues the advantages of a self-interested but pro-active "new realism" in achieving mutual security in our post-9/11, globalized world."

Michael S. Lund, Senior Associate for Conflict and Peacebuilding, Management Systems International

Peacebuilding

Preventing Violent Conflict
in a Complex World

DENNIS J. D. SANDOLE

polity

First published in 2010 by Polity Press

Polity Press
65 Bridge Street
Cambridge CB2 1UR, UK

Polity Press
350 Main Street
Malden, MA 02148, USA

ISBN-13: 978-0-7456-4165-2
ISBN-13: 978-0-7456-4166-9 (pb)

A catalogue record for this book is available from the British Library.

Typeset in 10.25 on 13 pt FF Scala
by Toppan Best-set Premedia Limited
Printed and bound in Great Britain by MPG Books Group Limited, Bodmin, Cornwall

The publisher has used its best endeavours to ensure that the URLs for external websites referred to in this book are correct and active at the time of going to press. However, the publisher has no responsibility for the websites and can make no guarantee that a site will remain live or that the content is or will remain appropriate.

Every effort has been made to trace all copyright holders, but if any have been inadvertently overlooked the publisher will be pleased to include any necessary credits in any subsequent reprint or edition.

For further information on Polity, visit our website: www.politybooks.com

Contents

Acknowledgements

The genesis of the idea for this book began with an exchange of e-mail messages between Dr Louise Knight, editorial director for Polity Press in Cambridge, England, and me a few months before the annual convention of the International Studies Association in San Diego, California, in March 2006. Dr Knight had determined that both she and I would be in attendance at that conference – she as an exhibitor and I as a presenter – and that we should meet to discuss how we might be able to work together. At the conference we had a pleasant discussion. I informed her how impressed I was with Polity's second edition of what was fast becoming a classic: *Contemporary Conflict Resolution* by Oliver Ramsbotham, Tom Woodhouse, and Hugh Miall. She told me about some other new ideas she had for Polity, including one in which I might participate, Polity's series on "War and Conflict in the Modern World." When I told her that one of the courses I had recently designed which could be relevant for books in that series was on peacebuilding, she invited me to contemplate doing a brief volume on that theme, which I could subsequently use as a text for the course. I accepted her invitation and the results are in the pages that follow.

In addition to Dr Knight, I have worked with her colleagues Rachel Donnelly, Emma Hutchinson, David Winters, Neil de Cort, and Caroline Richmond, each of whom has assisted me in making the transition from idea to completed product more likely. That transition became especially problematic when a period of illness intervened to throw all my plans to the wind. Nevertheless, despite multiple, successive "estimated dates of completion," none of which came to fruition, the volume was finally completed and submitted!

That eventual success can only be attributed to my life partner, Ingrid Sandole-Staroste (PhD), who gave up on her own life to ensure that mine remained viable. Ingrid also read through each chapter and the entirety of the manuscript to ensure that, among other things, painkilling medication was not also killing off attention to detail, coherence, and all the other qualities that we take for granted when writing for professional publication.

Saira Yamin, my graduate research assistant, who is completing her doctoral dissertation at ICAR on failed states, also read through the chapters individually and the entirety of the manuscript, plus worked on the index with me. Everything about Saira, including her Pakistani origins, outstanding participation in one of my peacebuilding courses, and work on state failure for her dissertation, made her especially helpful in this regard.

To all these good people, plus Dr Knight and two anonymous reviewers, I owe gratitude, but responsibility for what follows falls on me alone!

This book is dedicated to the new generation of post-zero-sum, post-Machiavellian problem solvers who recognize that, in the postmodern world, national interest is global interest and global interest is national interest and that those who fail to adjust to the "new reality" with an appropriate "new realism" become a part more of the problem than of the solution.

Prologue

Shortly after the terrorist attacks of 11 September 2001, which arguably "changed the world" in irreversible ways, I entered the office of my physician in Northern Virginia with the view that, since he was a native New Yorker, he would be profoundly affected by the destruction of the World Trade Center as well as by the more immediate destruction of parts of the Pentagon. When I raised the issue, his response was more reflective than visceral: "Well, we obviously have to learn to do some things in the world differently!" This volume, part of Polity's series on War and Conflict in the Modern World, is an effort to explore and spell out just what that might mean.

Framed as such, this volume represents an admittedly ambitious opportunity to shape the thinking and policies of the political leadership of the world's powers post-9/11, as well as to offer an introduction to peacebuilding for, among others, university students – two intended audiences that are actually not that far apart considering the record of peacebuilding efforts to date (see chapter 3). Complementing research in the immediate aftermath of 9/11 to understand the motivations of those who are prepared to kill themselves in order to kill others (see chapter 4), the effort to influence the thinking and behavior of national, international, and transnational policy-makers was accelerated by the run-up to the passionately contested 2008 US presidential elections.[1]

Projects to influence political leadership, often by former insiders, have a colorful pedigree, reflecting a "public–private partnership" model associated with Niccolò Machiavelli and others before him (e.g., Kautilya in India and Sun Tzu in China). In his classic *The Prince* (*Il principe*, written in 1513), Machiavelli described how successful leaders actually behaved (and, therefore, as they should, *a posteriori*, behave)[2] in what has come to be regarded by some as unethical and noxious, yet for others brilliant policy guidelines for political leaders. For example, his advice to "a Prince on the Subject of the Art of War" includes the following sentiments:

> A prince ought to have no other aim or thought, nor select anything else for his study, than war and its rules and disciplines; for this is the sole art that belongs to him who rules, and it is of such force that it not only upholds those who are born princes, but it often enables men to rise from a private station to that rank. And, on the contrary, it is seen that when princes have thought more of ease than of arms they have lost their states. (Machiavelli, [1532] 1998)

Underlying Machiavelli's recommendations were not only his reading of Greek and Roman history but also his personal experiences with, and observations of, the political leadership of his native Florence and elsewhere in medieval Europe during the late fifteenth and early sixteenth centuries. These included his own arrest and torture by the Medicis after they returned to power – the very same people for whom Machiavelli had written and dedicated his book (specifically, Lorenzo "the Magnificent").

A fundamental difference in tone between this volume and Machiavelli's, however, is that this book is about sustaining life on a fragile planet – notably the life of the planet itself. It is not, therefore, just about keeping one ruler or group of rulers in power or maintaining the privileged hegemony of one country through a series of zero-sum actions and reactions which, by definition, are at the expense of others. By implication, this volume is also designed for the concerned citizen – the "local" – as a correlate of the university student, in part to generate "bottom-up" pressure on "The Prince" to do what is practical (which may have been part of Machiavelli's original purpose),[3] as well as to stimulate empathy for the policymaking enterprise and interest in eventually joining its ranks.

The aftermath of 9/11, including the epiphenomenal "Global War on Terror" and the US-led military campaigns in Iraq and Afghanistan, drove US policy at the expense of nearly all other issues during most of the eight years in office of former President George W. Bush. It also tested the moral staying power of the "indispensible" nation's commitment to the rule of law and human rights. America-watchers world-wide have been monitoring the impact of the "Bush legacy" on Barack Obama's foreign policy agenda since his inauguration in January 2009 as America's 44th and first African American president (see chapter 5). Their objective has been to explore to what extent Obama (and other leading policy-makers) will do the "right thing" with regard to climate change, poverty, state failure, the proliferation of weapons of mass destruction, terrorism and other elements of the global problematique, among them the worst financial and economic crises since the Great Depression.

One example of the complexity inherent in the current global problematique is that "doing the right thing" with regard to the financial and economic crises may mean reaching widespread consensus on the proposition that "global problems require global solutions." By contrast, on the more traditional front of national security, doing the right thing may mean yielding to the Hobbesian magnetism of "every man for himself," motivating even the "high priests" of the European Union toward virulent nationalism and protectionism (see Sandole, 2002b).

I decided to enter the fray to help distill coherence out of chaos, to assist in laying the foundation for a primer on survival which focuses on survival in a broader sense than that envisioned by Machiavelli. The means identified for achieving this ambitious goal include making the case that policymakers must tackle all aspects of the global problematique if they want to deal successfully with any one of them. The means also include mining peacebuilding theory and practice to identify and provide concerned citizens and introductory students, as well as policymakers, with the vision, frameworks, and other tools ("checklists") necessary for constructing a "post-realist" problem-solving paradigm – a "new" or "cosmopolitan realism."[4] The underlying premise is that the postmodern world is increasingly characterized by complex, interconnected problems that cannot be solved by a single actor. Attempts to deal unilaterally with any one pressing issue at the expense of others with which it is interconnected only reinforces the phenomenon of "unintended consequences." The perception of increasing empirical validation of the primary proposition of complexity theory – "that everything is connected to everything else" (Waldrop, 1992) – has been assuming a surreal, law-like regularity.

Accordingly, if the prime minister of a country plagued by civil war wants to invite the concerned international community to help design and implement a "post-conflict peacebuilding" intervention in her country, she will have to work with colleagues who deal with, among other issues, conflict transformation, interfaith dialogue, trauma healing, gender relations, local security, reconciliation, poverty management, disease eradication, economic and social development, infrastructural reconstruction and, yes, global warming.

The arguments, frameworks, and insights in this volume may be compelling and persuasive for many, even to the point of seriously undermining their cherished beliefs and values.

The potency of prevailing paradigms can be such, however, that a modern-day Machiavellian might pay attention to the global problematique and the various linkages connecting its elements and still wind up in a zero-sum world of enemies and friends, win–lose strategies and tactics. As a consequence, he may never appreciably "feel" the core anomaly in Machiavellianism that "national interest is global interest" and, conversely, "global interest is national interest."

The "residual Machiavellian" will not, therefore, be persuaded by any effort to advance the agenda of "cosmopolitanism" or "new realism" (see Sandole, 2006a) in order finally and resolutely to supersede "classical realism." Classical realism, whose origins can be traced to Thucydides and his chronicles of the Peloponnesian War between Sparta and Athens over two thousand years ago, is, if nothing else, resilient. For example, at one point in the well-documented negotiations between Athens and the island state of Melos in 416 BC, the Athenian ambassadors declare to their Melian interlocutors: "The strong do what they can and the weak suffer what they must" (Thucydides, 1951, p. 331). These sentiments have resonated with many political leaders since then, among them the occupant of the Oval Office during the first decade of the twenty-first century.[5] They will continue to have their adherents, as has been clear in the acrimonious debates, including within the European Union, on how to deal best with financial and economic crises.

On the assumption that my physician was on the right track with his realization that, after 9/11, "We have to learn to do some things in the world differently," we now move on to chapter 1 to address peacebuilding and the complex world within which it is contemplated, designed, and implemented – a world beyond the imaginations of Thucydides or Machiavelli, although the likes of Saddam Hussein and Osama bin Laden, among others, would have made sense to them. We examine this world (or "these worlds") because that is the dynamic context which impacts policymaking at all levels and which, in turn, is impacted by it. It is with regard to the constantly shifting parameters of this dynamic setting that this book will try to make the case that peacebuilding – comprehensively defined – *must* inform complex global problem solving via appropriate global governance, *and* vice versa.

CHAPTER ONE

Peacebuilding and the Global Problematique

Introduction

Everyone is beset with problems, some more stressful than others (e.g., foreclosed mortgages, loss of employment, catastrophic diseases, caring for aging relatives, imprisonment, living in the midst of natural disasters or active war zones)! Furthermore, through still ongoing revolutionary advances in communications technology, we are in constant touch with our and others' problems via cell phones, the Internet, and other satellite-based systems. For example, as I first began to write these lines in June 2007, I was regularly shifting back and forth on the Internet to discern the latest developments in London involving two parked Mercedes Benz automobiles loaded with explosives, plus the attempted firebombing of the passenger terminal at Glasgow Airport in Scotland.

What was not clear to me at the time was why the apparent culprits in this case, young male Muslim physicians, originally from India and the Middle East but later resident and working in the United Kingdom, would want to perpetrate acts of terrorism against their British hosts. More importantly, many of us are not aware of how interconnected these actions are or can be with other developments. This is not merely a conceptual issue where, in PhD dissertations, published works, and research reports, we have to identify possible and actual linkages, but an operational issue as well. As former US Secretary of State Madeleine Albright put it (2008, pp. 6–7): "the problem with most advice is that it is better on the 'what' than on the 'how.' . . . Presidents appreciate being told what they might do, but they need people around them who can show them how to do it."

To solve Problem A, therefore, we may also have to take into account, operationally as well as conceptually, problems B, C, R, W, and Z (noting linked factors within as well as between the various areas). Otherwise, our problem-solving efforts – good intentions and sound intelligence to the contrary – may make us more a part of the problem than of the solution (Anderson, 1999). This is especially likely with peacebuilding, which deals with complex problem solving locally, nationally, regionally, and globally, often with nuanced linkages within and across multiple levels.

Peacebuiding: A Comprehensive Approach to Complex Problem Solving

So, "What is peacebuilding?" Moreover, how do we do it when, among others, global warming, poverty, WMD proliferation, state failure, terrorism, and the financial and economic crises are impacting the situation we wish to address through some peacebuilding project?

On first glance, "peacebuilding" seems to break down nicely into the "building" of "peace." But what kind of peace? Conflict and peace studies tell us that there are at least two types: negative peace and positive peace (Galtung, 1969). Negative peace is what most people outside the field mean when they discuss or think of "peace": the absence of hostilities, usually between states but between other units as well. This absence can be achieved through either prevention of likely violence (proactive) or suppression of ongoing violence (reactive). Thus, ceasefires are experiments in often temporary negative peace which may or may not lead to peace settlements, which would be more substantive approaches to negative peace.[1]

Regrettably, with the exception of conflict and peace studies scholars, students, and activists (e.g., Gandhi, King), rarely does one think of peace in the "positive" sense. This is one of the major problems with the world as we confront it today: national decision-makers, even of major states (including the American superpower and its rising Russian rival), tend to become stuck in the domain of *Realpolitik*-prioritized negative peace. Unless they can frame options outside the negative peace "box," they will never be able to achieve them.[2] In other words, with the exception of serendipitously stumbling on to something, we have to be able to conceive or "think" of it before we can actually take steps to achieve it.

While negative peace might be a necessary condition of positive peace, it tends not to be a sufficient condition, although some might claim that, over an extended period of time, positive peace could conceivably arise out of negative peace (Sandole, 2007a, chs 5 and 9). Nevertheless, aiming for negative peace, through either proactive prevention or reactive suppression, would certainly be a laudable goal in and of itself. I personally wish we had more negative peace in the world instead of the violence of Rwanda in 1994, Srebrenica in 1995, or Darfur at present. Negative peace is not, however, an optimal condition, because it stops short of dealing with the underlying, deep-rooted causes and conditions of the conflict which might escalate, or has escalated, to the violence that negative peace measures would address. The negative peace in Bosnia-Herzegovina, for example, which has endured for nearly fifteen years since its imposition by the Dayton Peace Accords, is now closer to a collapse into violent conflict than it is to a tipping point toward positive peace (McMahon and Western, 2009; Whitlock, 2009b).

This is the utility of positive peace measures: at least "in theory," they deal with the underlying, deep-rooted causes and conditions of a conflict which might develop, or has developed, into manifest violence. While stopping a war would certainly be helpful in creating conditions conducive to determining what its causes were, one could, nevertheless, endeavor to achieve positive peace goals in the absence of negative peace. The probability of achieving positive peace, however, would be low unless negative peace was first secured.

Here, we confront a puzzle: while everything that we have said thus far would suggest that peacebuilding usually means building positive peace, only what has come to be called maximalist peacebuilding would do that. By contrast, minimalist peacebuilding, which does not deal with underlying causes and conditions, means building negative peace, although perhaps with some elements of positive peace (Call and Cousens, 2008).[3]

The fact that "positive peace" is often not denoted by "peace" may help explain why maximalist peacebuilding is a relatively rare (and recent) phenomenon. Indeed, there were few references to it as an option until former UN Secretary General Boutros Boutros-Ghali (1992) included it in his seminal report to UN heads of state and government as the brutal wars in former Yugoslavia were getting underway.

Another reason why maximalist peacebuilding is rare is because of its complex, multi-actor, multi-level nature, whether one is responding to a specific situation either before or after violence has been brought to an end. Few of us have the patience or the complex problem-solving skills to coordinate persuasively third-party inputs from a multitude of interveners over a period of twenty or more years (see Nan, 2003; Lederach, 1997). So, rather than risk failure, we may not even attempt complex responses to complex problems at all, thereby reinforcing the tendency toward minimalist peacebuilding, which does not address underlying causes and conditions.

This raises the issue of the ways in which third-party interveners can respond to likely or actual conflicts. Using the metaphor of a "burning house" common to diplomats and the military, third-party interveners could, depending upon the likely or actual intensity of the "fire" (Fisher, 1997, ch. 8; Fisher and Keashly, 1991), do any or all of the following:

- *Preventive diplomacy* (*violent conflict prevention*): Take steps, based upon early warning, to prevent a house from "catching on fire" in the first place (*proactive*);
- *Peacekeeping* (*conflict management*): When the house is on fire, either because of the failure of violent conflict prevention efforts or through avoidance of their use, taking steps to prevent the fire from spreading (*reactive*);

and

- *Peacemaking*: When attempts to prevent the fire from spreading have failed, then attempt either:
- *Coercive peacemaking* (*conflict settlement*): Suppressing the fire (*reactive*)

and/or

- *Noncoercive peacemaking* (*conflict resolution*): Dealing with the underlying causes and conditions of the fire (*reactive*), which establishes a basis for:
- *Peacebuilding* "writ small" (*conflict transformation*), or what John Burton calls *conflict prevention*: Working with the survivors of the fire on their long-term relationships so that, the next time they have a problem, they do not have to burn down the house, the neighborhood, or the larger commons in the process of dealing with it (*reactive/ proactive*).

An alternative to this neat, linear progression from preventive diplomacy to peacebuilding "writ small" is for potential third parties to adopt a holistic peacebuilding perspective "writ large" at the outset of their engagement with a particular conflict system (see Burton, 1997). At the same time, they would consider conducting other third-party interventions within its parameters and, in the process, be strategically proactive. Over the course of an intervention, this would include maximalist as well as minimalist peacebuilding.[4]

Peacebuilding, therefore, is a dynamic approach and process, comprising a number of third-party interventions, with different actors performing different tasks at the same time and/or different points in time (see Diamond and McDonald, 1996). The underlying assumption is that, given the complex nature of conflicts in the post-Cold War/post-9/11 worlds, only some combination and sequence of approaches – in contrast to any one of them – is necessary to capture the complexity of conflict in any given situation.

The challenges for potential third parties, explored in this volume, include dealing with significant ontological, epistemological, and methodological issues surrounding the analytical differences, but also the substantive overlap and possible linkages between (a) violent conflict prevention, (b) conflict management, (c) conflict settlement, (d) conflict resolution, and (e) conflict transformation. The objective in each case is to determine the appropriate "mix" of reflective, two-way interaction between theory and practice necessary for achieving and sustaining maximalist peacebuilding. Otherwise the threat of collapse into a resurrected violent conflict situation is always present (see Sandole, 2009a; Sandole, 1999).

As already indicated, peacebuilding tends to be reactive (hence, "postconflict peacebuilding"). This occurs when third parties attempt an intervention only after the emergence of an actual violent conflict involving significant human rights violations – after "the house has been set alight" (e.g., as in Bosnia-Herzegovina during the early 1990s). In ad hoc reactive peacebuilding, members of the international community focus initially on one particular type of intervention (in Bosnia, conflict management through the United Nations Protection Force, UNPROFOR). However, if that fails, they may move on to other types. In Bosnia, this consisted of conflict settlement through NATO bombing of Serb forces and then, following the Dayton Peace Accords (see Holbrooke, 1998), peace enforcement with the Stabilization Force (SFOR), followed by the Implementation Force (IFOR), and eventually the European Union Force (EUFOR – "Althea"). Ad hoc reactive peacebuilding can, through successive "trial and error," develop into one possible trajectory toward conflict transformation (in Bosnia, through the conflict parties taking the steps necessary to achieve eventual membership in the European Union; see chapter 3 of this volume).

By contrast, proactive peacebuilding is what third-party interveners would attempt before a violent conflict occurs. In this case, interveners would design and implement an intervention to achieve violent conflict prevention – to prevent "the house from catching on fire." This is what Alger (2007, pp. 312–15) means by "long-term peacebuilding," which includes Lund's (2009) comprehensive use of conflict prevention. If that fails, interveners may decide on a strategy of partial ad hoc reactive peacebuilding – i.e., selecting one or more options and then, for example, moving first to conflict management (preventing the fire from spreading) and, if that fails, to conflict settlement (coercively suppressing the fire). If, however, their initial effort at proactive prevention succeeds – for example, as it did with the United Nations Preventive Deployment Force (UNPREDEP) in Macedonia (see Sokalski, 2003 and chapter 3 of this volume) – they may then decide to go forward with a strategy of comprehensive proactive peacebuilding: employing the full array of multi-sectoral, multi-actor interventions in which all categories of intervention are designed and implemented from the outset of an engagement with a particular violent conflict system within a conflict transformation framework (see Sandole, 2007a, ch. 3).

Comprehensive peacebuilding is a major source of effective regional and global governance, especially (but not only) in and across Africa, Asia, Latin America, the Middle East, Southeastern Europe, and the former Soviet Union – what conflict resolution pioneer John W. Burton (1990, 1997) refers to as conflict *prevention* and Oliver Ramsbotham, Tom Woodhouse, and Hugh Miall (2005) as cosmopolitan conflict resolution. It constitutes, "in theory," the ultimate antidote to the theory-policy deficits in our collective efforts to understand and deal with the deep-rooted causes and conditions of global terrorism – to move beyond minimalist into maximalist peacebuilding.

The major premise underlying this framing of peacebuilding is that "national interest" is global interest and vice versa, especially within the current parameters of globalization and the foreign policy agenda of President Obama (see chapter 5 of this volume). Moreover, to achieve any objective along the conflict prevention–transformation gradient at the local, state, interstate, or regional levels, policymakers must pay attention to the global level as well. As Ramsbotham et al. (2005, p. 115), put it: "Conflict formations run through our political communities *at all levels*, from the global to the national to the local. Moreover, these conflict formations are *intertwined* . . . [Accordingly,] there is no possibility of addressing local and regional conflicts without also taking the global and international setting into account" (emphasis added).

This volume reminds us that peacebuilding – whether reactive or proactive, ad hoc (single objective) or comprehensive (multi objective), minimalist (negative peace) or maximalist (positive peace) – is a multilateral and not a unilateral process (even for the world's sole surviving superpower).

Peacebuilding's Essential Context: The Global Problematique

Whatever framing of peacebuilding is attempted will depend in large part not only on the internal situation in any likely, active, or "post"-conflict situation, but also upon elements of the global problematique with which the effort must interact and deal. In order better to manage the complexity inherent in the global problematique, I have crafted the "Four Worlds Model of Perception and Action" (Sandole, 1987) as an initial point of departure for conducting analysis as a precondition to understanding and explaining a given situation, and to taking effective action with regard to it. The "four worlds' model" (4WM) comprises two external (exosomatic) domains – the (a) natural and (b) human-made worlds – and two internal (endosomatic) realms – the (c) mental/psychological and (d) biological/physiological worlds. Three of these "worlds" derive from the work of Sir Karl Popper (1972): the natural world (World 1), the human-made world (Popper called this "the man-made" world) (World 3), and the mental world (World 2). I contributed the biological/physiological world (World 4) to complete what I perceived as a possible gap in Popper's otherwise revolutionary work.[5]

The "Four Worlds" of complex problem-solving and global peacebuilding

Anytime an individual engages his or her external environment, Worlds 1 (natural) and 3 (human-made) generate stimuli which are then, upon activation of any of the senses, processed by the individual's internal domains, Worlds 2 (mental world) and 4 (biological/physiological world). Among the complex global problems which could then be "seen" are:

World 1 (Nature)

    1 climate change (see Gore, 2006; Abbott et al., 2007, ch. 2; Sachs, 2008, ch. 4; Shapiro, 2008, pp. 278–84; Yohe, 2007)

    2 deforestation (see Folmer and van Kooten, 2007)

    3 land degradation (see Coxhead and Øygard, 2007)

    4 air pollution (see Hutton, 2007a)

    5 biodiversity loss (see Biller, 2007; Sachs, 2008, ch. 6)

    6 natural disasters (see Flynn, 2007; Pielke, 2007)

    7 population growth (see Pearce, 2010; Sachs, 2008, chs. 7–8; Shapiro, 2008, ch. 2)

    8 hunger/malnutrition (see Behrman et al., 2007)

    9 water stress (see Hutton, 2007b; Sachs, 2008, ch. 5)

  10 resource abundance vs. scarcity (see Shapiro, 2008, pp. 268–78; Abbott et al., 2007, ch. 3; Collier, 2007a, chs. 3–4).

Needless to say, many of the problems manifest in W1 may have, as part of their genesis, earlier developments in World 3, such as:

World 3 (Human society)

    1 intra- and interstate wars (see Collier, 2007a, ch. 2, 2007b; Hewitt, 2010a, 2010b)

    2 genocide (see Huth and Valentino, 2008)

    3 "clash of civilizations" (see Huntington, 1993, 1996; Sandole, 2005b; Avruch, 2009; Bertelsman Stiftung, 2010)

    4 terrorism (see LaFree et al., 2010; Shapiro, 2008, pp. 287–302; Flynn, 2007; Linotte, 2007)

    5 state repression (see Pate, 2010; Toft and Saideman, 2010)

    6 migration (see Greenwood, 2007)

    7 WMD/small arms proliferation (see Abbott et al., 2007, ch. 5; Dunne, 2007; Frantz and Collins, 2007)

8 corruption (see Collier, 2007a, ch. 5; Rose-Ackerman, 2007)

9 failed/failing states (see Collier, 2007a; Ghani and Lockhart, 2008; Hoeffler, 2010; Wilkenfeld, 2008)

10 structural inequities (see Abbott et al., 2007, ch. 4; Orazem, 2007)

11 poverty (see Sachs, 2008, chs. 9–11)

12 infectious disease (see Jamison, 2007)

13 living conditions of women and children (see Patrinos, 2007; Viswanathan, 2007)

14 illicit drugs (see Miron, 2007)

15 risks to and through cyberspace (Clarke and Knake, 2010; Deibert and Rohozinski, 2010)

16 financial crises (see David Smith, 2010; Sorkin, 2009; Shapiro, 2008, ch. 5; Henry, 2007; Soros, 1998).

Clearly, the items listed under W1 and W3, while analytically distinct, are not mutually exclusive. So, for example, "population growth" (W1) may be coterminous with "migration" (W3). Adding to the complexity, therefore, a problem manifest in W1 at any point in time could reflect a causal journey over time comprising successive W1 and W3 factors, any one of which, depending upon the researcher's preferred theoretical and temporal frameworks, could be viewed as the primary locus of occurrence (W1 *or* W3), with some being so close to both W1 and W3 that they suggest a hybridity of analytical categories (W1 *and* W3). For example, the conflict in Darfur in Western Sudan (W3) could be framed as reflecting the following causal narrative: long-term economic underdevelopment during British rule (W3); the onset of the second Sudanese civil war (1983) (W3); reduction in rainfall (W1), accompanied by growing population (W3/W1) and increased use of arable land (W3/W1), resulting in desertification (W3/W1); the failure of the Khartoum government to heed warnings of crop failure (W3/W1); famine (W1); the polarizing effect of "Arab vs. African" politics directed by Khartoum, which furthered the underdevelopment of the Darfur region (W3); Libyan intervention (W3), a spillover to Chad (W3), and US involvement (W3) (see Prunier, 2005; Johnson, 2003).

By clarifying the details of the causal mosaic – the interconnections among some of these problem areas – we get a glimpse of what elements of W1 and W3 are involved and, more importantly, stretched and stressed in any conflict situation, plus what environmental aspects might continue to be affected in solving the problems that have generated the conflicts. In other words, an initial 4WM analysis provides a basis for determining "ontological complexity" (e.g., W1 and W3, instead of W1 or W3) in select aspects of the global problematique. By exploring relationships between epistemologically and methodologically driven sources of the problem and the recommendations deemed necessary to solve it, we facilitate effective problem identification and problem solving by sensitizing ourselves to the fact that, in order to solve "A," we may also have to deal with "B," "C," "R," etc. This realization is, in our world of increasing complexity and unintended consequences, quickly assuming the status of a categorical imperative or "universal law" (Kant, 1993, p. 30).[6]

This raises the issue of the perception of elements of the "global problematique" – how do Worlds 2 (mental) and 4 (biological/physiological) interact to "engage" Worlds 1 (nature) and 3 (human society)? While World 2 consists of our long-term memories, beliefs and values, and what Thomas Kuhn (1970) calls paradigms – in effect, the world views that shape our perceptions – World 4 consists of our central nervous system, brain, senses, and everything else that Leonardo da Vinci studied hundreds of years ago in what have emerged as history's first medical drawings. It is the (discharge potentials of the) senses that are triggered upon contact by energy from Worlds 1 (natural) and 3 (human-made), allowing for the transition from stimuli to information to be encoded, via synaptic connection, from neuron to neuron, until information reaches those parts of the brain where World 2 can decode it into perceptions and "definitions of the situation" (see Thomas, 1923).

Once information has been decoded, it can take one of at least four forms.

1 *Bare sensation*: a vague sense that something ("Y") is "out there"!
2 *Recognition and identification*: a clear sense of what that "thing" ("Y") is.
3 *Analysis and explanation*: a clear sense of the reason for, or "cause" ("X") of, the "thing" ("Y").
4 *Interpretation*: understanding the "X–Y" relationship within a larger body of meaning (e.g., a conflict theory), plus determining how best to respond to the "thing" ("Y") (e.g., conflict resolution praxis).

Between (1) "bare sensation," and (2) "recognition and identification," some challenges could develop as the perceiving actor attempts to make sense of her or his natural and/or human-made environments. First of all, "cognitive blindness" may occur, when an actor is not able to perceive something at all, or in a way comparable to how someone else might be perceiving it, because of the absence of an appropriate paradigm, theory, model, or concept in the actor's World 2 (mental world) that would allow for such a perception to be made (see Sandole, 2006b, 2002b; Kuhn, 1970; Boulding, 1956).

Secondly, over time, against the background of some internalized need for homeostatic stability (see Cannon, 1939), the perceiving actor's information-processing apparatus may not be able to make the requisite changes necessary to perceive what is, in effect, for him or her, a continuing anomaly: a deviation from his or her internalized expectations under the particular circumstances (Kuhn, 1970). In this case, the actor would be characterized by "cognitive resistance."

Thirdly, as a result of the anomaly remaining in the actor's perceptual field beyond some critical point, he or she may start to experience dissonance: a sense of "acute psychological discomfort" (e.g., anxiety) indicating that something is "out there" that should not be "there," which would clearly be a "conceptual experience" of bare sensation. Quite often, under the circumstances, the perceiving actor's defense mechanisms (e.g., denial, disguise, rationalization), which operate unknowingly to the actor, may return the actor to a state of "homeostatic stability" or equilibrium. This is an example of "evaluative-affective resistance (EAR) I" (see Boulding, 1956; Sandole, 1984), where the actor "nearly" notices the anomaly, but is nevertheless prevented by his or her internal defenses from perceiving it, thereby giving rise to maintenance of the status quo paradigm, theory, belief, or some other construct *qua* "standard operating procedure" (SOP) that may no longer be relevant to his or her survival.

Finally, in this particular conceptual system, we have "evaluative-affective resistance (EAR) II," where the anomaly somehow breaks through the actor's internal defenses and is perceived for "what it actually is," in which case the actor may be said to be experiencing a clear "thing" ("Y"), but not necessarily willingly or happily!

While the first three challenges operate at the unconscious level, only the fourth is experienced consciously. Once we experience the "thing" ("Y") clearly, then we can decide where it came from ("X"), why it came from where it did ("X–Y") and what we should do about it. The problem then, however, is that, although we may perceive the "thing" clearly, it may not be in agreement with someone else's "clear" perception of the "same thing."

In Thomas Kuhn's (1970) nontraditional account of the history of science, we are reminded time and again that two people, even the "high priests of truth" – scientists – may perceive the "same thing" differently, with profound implications for behavior, including shaping a nation's foreign policy toward other nations or non-state actors. Kuhn's work is revolutionary because he demonstrates not only how even natural scientists can live in "different worlds," but that those differences start to be expressed earlier than the dominant epistemological paradigm articulated over 300 years ago by René Descartes would have us believe – at the level of even "bare sensation" and not simply of "analysis and explanation" or "interpretation."

Accordingly, what determined whether former US President George W. Bush "saw" global warming ("Y") as a problem at all, and as one caused at least in part by human agency ("X"), may have depended not only on what he was "looking at" in World 1 (natural) through prisms provided by the knowledge in World 3 (human made), but also by what had been programmed into his World 2 (mental), assuming the available information could have made it through his World 4 (biological/physiological) to get to World 2 for decoding. And whatever he then saw or did not see would have determined what policies he decided to enact or not to enact, with profound implications for life on the planet!

One purpose of this volume is not only to articulate elements of the global problematique that may or may not be perceived in various ways, especially by actors in positions to make a difference. The objective is also to find ways to cut through actors' defenses via evaluative-affective resistance (EAR) II-based debates with a (re)framing of the problem that lends itself to (a) a recognition of the problem "for what it actually is"[7] and (b) a resolute will to do something about it that constitutes both the right and practical thing to do under the circumstances (e.g., preventing or stopping an ongoing genocide).

"Rounding Up the Usual Suspects": The *Realpolitik* Hijacking of Global Problems

Given the dominance across time and space of *Realpolitik* as the paradigmatic lens through which global affairs tend to be perceived by publics and policymakers alike – at least since the Melian Debate (416 BC) chronicled by Thucydides (1951) – it would not be surprising if many people, when asked what comes to mind when they hear the term "global problems," would respond with "war, violence, and terrorism." Possible cases that might occur to them are the threat of a nuclear exchange between India and Pakistan over Kashmir; 9/11; the rush-hour attacks on the Madrid (March 2004), London (July 2005), and Moscow (March 2010) transport systems; the Rwandan genocide of 1994 and one of its offshoots, Africa's "first world war" in the Democratic Republic of the Congo (DRC); the continuing, yet character-shifting genocidal conflicts in Darfur, Western Sudan; thirty years of communal violence in Northern Ireland; renewed violence in Lebanon; the intractable, seemingly unending Israeli–Palestinian conflict; and the wars in Iraq and Afghanistan, with, perhaps, more to come involving Iran and North Korea – not to mention a renewed "Cold War" of sorts with a resurgent Russia and other Soviet successor states.

Millions of people have been killed in these and other violent conflict situations, and many more would lose their lives in violent conflicts involving North Korea and Iran, especially since these potential adversaries are either nuclear powers or on the path to possessing nuclear weapons. Whatever "rationality" foreclosed recourse to the nuclear option during the Cold War (e.g., "Mutually Assured Destruction," or MAD) may not be available in future conflicts with the Russian Federation and other Soviet successor states.

Whether the Rwandan genocide and "The Troubles" in Northern Ireland are viewed as examples of terrorism or internal war (or both), the loss of life attributable to terrorism is dwarfed by that resulting from warfare and other violent episodes. The Rwandan and Northern Ireland examples add complexity to efforts to achieve definitional clarity, since Rwanda involved a catastrophic loss of life in a comparatively short period of time (e.g., half a million killed during three weeks in April 1994), while Northern Ireland generated under 4,000 fatalities over a thirty-year period – fewer than American fatalities in the US-led war in Iraq.

Given the grim list above, if asked whether "war, violence, and terrorism" have increased or decreased during the past fifteen years or so, many people could be forgiven for assuming that they have increased. The reality, however, is different, resulting in another disconnect between thinking that is based on the dominant world view and developments as they "actually are." For example, in the 2005 edition of their biennial surveys, Monty Marshall and Ted Robert Gurr reported that ethno-national wars for independence, autocratic regimes, repression and political discrimination, and the global magnitude of armed conflict had continued to decline. Further, these gains were "the result of persistent and *coordinated* efforts at *peace-building* by civil society organizations, national leaders, non-governmental organizations, and international bodies" (Marshall and Gurr, 2005, p. 1, emphasis added).

These findings are compatible with those generated by the first edition of the *Human Security Report* (2005) (which also includes Marshall and Gurr's data):

> By 2003, there were 40 percent fewer conflicts than in 1992. The deadliest conflicts – those with 1,000 or more battle-deaths – fell by some 80 percent. The number of genocides and other mass slaughters of civilians also dropped by 80 percent, while core human rights abuses have declined in

five out of six regions of the developing world since the mid-1990s. International terrorism is the only type of political violence that has increased. Although the death toll has jumped sharply over the past three years, terrorists kill only a fraction of the number who die in wars.

What accounts for the extraordinary and counter-intuitive improvement in global security over the past dozen years? The end of the Cold War, which had driven at least a third of all conflicts since World War II, appears to have been the single most critical factor.

In the late 1980s, Washington and Moscow stopped fueling "proxy wars" in the developing world, and the United Nations was liberated to play the global security role its founders intended. *Freed from the paralyzing stasis of Cold War geopolitics, the Security Council initiated an unprecedented, though sometimes inchoate, explosion of international activism designed to stop ongoing wars and prevent new ones.*

Other international agencies [including, for example, the OSCE], donor governments and nongovernmental organizations also played a critical role, but it was the United Nations that took the lead, pushing a range of *conflict-prevention* and *peace-building* initiatives on a scale never before attempted. The number of U.N. peacekeeping operations and missions to prevent and stop wars have increased by more than 400 percent since the end of the Cold War. As this upsurge of international activism grew in scope and intensity through the 1990s, the number of crises, wars, and genocides *declined.* (Mack, 2005, emphasis added).

As if to validate the aphorism that "all good things must come to an end," however, the 2008 report of the Gurr survey (Hewitt et al., 2008) demonstrates that these downward trends have stalled, suggesting that, in part, the violent conflict prevention, resolution, and transformation efforts of the UN and regional security organizations (RSOs) – critical elements of peacebuilding[8] "writ large" (see discussion below) – have not been sufficient to continue their successful run:

> New evidence, and a closer look at old evidence, suggests that if there was a global movement toward peace in the 1990s and early years of the 21st century, it has stalled. Some positive trends are still evident but they are offset by new challenges.
>
> Has the magnitude of armed conflict declined? The answer is yes when judged by falling numbers of internal wars and their average death-tolls across the last 20 years. But when we tabulate the number of states engaged in armed conflicts, either their own or multilateral wars as in Iraq and Afghanistan, the long-run trend is up. A larger portion of the global community of states is involved now than in any other time in the past six decades. . . . And the historic low of 19 ongoing armed conflicts in 2004 was followed by an increase to 25 in 2005. (Hewitt et al., 2008, p. 1)

Another possible reason for the reversal in trend is that the traditional *Realpolitik* paradigm, which influences "definitions" of peace (negative) as well as of global problems ("war, violence, and terrorism"), leaves out so much that may play a role in war, violence, and terrorism (e.g., inequalities between the developed and developing worlds; global warming) that the resulting prescriptions become, again, a part more of the problem than of the solution, exacerbating rather than undermining the factors making for war, violence, and terrorism.

One reason for the continued dominance of *Realpolitik* is that it still seems easier to commit resources to deal with terrorism than to the risk of war (with Iran, North Korea, or Russia), let alone global warming, despite the fact that fewer deaths are attributable to terrorism than to warfare and, ultimately, to global warming. Indeed, according to former US Congressman Sherwood Boehlert, a Republican, "the majority of Americans fail to see climate change as a compelling political issue" (Eilperin, 2008). Hence, since 9/11, ad hoc terrorism is what has preoccupied the world's dominant superpower and driven its policies, taking a narrow, virulent form of *Realpolitik* to new levels. Further, former President George W. Bush guaranteed for himself continued public concern on the issue of terrorism by conflating 9/11 with the wars in Iraq and Afghanistan. Senator John McCain, building upon Mr Bush's deft achievement and having attempted to succeed him in office, even declared that it would be fine with him if American forces remained in Iraq for 100, 1,000, or even a million years (although, to be fair, only under conditions that did not lead to American military fatalities or injuries; see Corn, 2008).

Such hubris, however, does not facilitate effective global problem solving. There is a need, therefore, to incorporate into the global problematique framings of global problems associated with other paradigmatic lenses, which speaks highly for the 4WM as well as the "4 + 2" integration of best practices deriving from competing paradigms.[9]

The Complex Interplay among Global Problems: Peacebuilding's Challenge

Analytically, it is easy to frame problems as lists of single issues, as we did above in discussing the 4WM. Operationally, however, the "real world" is seldom as neat or parsimonious as the dominant paradigm would suggest. The empirical expression of behaviors corresponding to select dependent and independent variables and their interrelationships is far more messy – far closer to a "4+2" integration of best paradigmatic practices. Nevertheless, the ways in which policymakers tend to frame issues – which, given our discussion of the 4WM, can be influenced by many factors – determine whether and how issues are tackled. When he was campaigning for the US presidency, then Senator Barack Obama, for example, had characterized the global problematique as follows:

> This century's threats are at least as dangerous as and in some ways *more complex* than those we have confronted in the past. They come from weapons that can kill on a mass scale and from global terrorists who respond to alienation or perceived injustice with murderous nihilism. They come from rogue states allied to terrorists and from rising powers that could challenge both America and the international foundation of liberal democracy. They come from weak states that cannot control their territory or provide for their people. And they come from a *warming planet* that will spur new diseases, spawn more devastating natural disasters, and *catalyze deadly conflicts*. (Obama, 2007, pp. 2–4, emphasis added).

While Senator Obama's characterization of the global problems that he would deal with as president does not specifically address their interconnections, such is surely implicit in his references to "complex" problems; to "a warming planet that will . . . catalyze deadly conflicts"; and, later in his article (ibid., p. 13), to "warmer temperatures and declining rainfall [that] will reduce crop yields, increasing conflict, famine, disease, and poverty."

The interconnections are made clearer by the *Financial Times* chief foreign affairs commentator Gideon Rachman:

> The food, energy and water problems *all touch on each other*. America's pursuit of alternatives to oil has led to massive investment in biofuels made from maize. That in turn has cut the amount of maize being used for food production and so contributed to rising fuel prices. The production of bio-fuels is also very water-intensive. Meanwhile, increased demand for agricultural land to grow more food is leading to the clearing of forest in Brazil – which could worsen global

warming – leading to further stress on the world's water supplies.
The potential for political conflicts increases along with the rise in food, energy and water prices. (Rachman, 2008, emphasis added).

Accordingly, apropos the resource wars (see Klare, 2008) that Rachman sees eventually developing, Thomas Homer-Dixon argues "that resource stress always *interacts* in complex conjunction with a host of other factors – ecological, institutional, economic and political – to cause mass violence" (2008, p. 26, emphasis in original).

Global warming is clearly a "new" item that has been added to the global problematique – not something that would traditionally, at least until recently, accompany the concerns of policymakers of the *Realpolitik* persuasion, although some "realists" might claim otherwise. For former US Secretary of State Madeleine Albright, global warming did not make the first cut:

> four trends pose a clear and present danger to American interests – first, terror and the rise of anti-Americanism in the Arab and Muslim worlds; second, the erosion of international consensus on nuclear proliferation; third, growing doubts about the value of democracy; and fourth, the gathering backlash against globalization due primarily to the widening split between rich and poor. (Albright, 2008, p. 23)

Dr Albright refers to "a fifth potential danger that *could exacerbate* the other four" (ibid., emphasis added), namely American withdrawal from international engagement, thereby implying interconnections among the separate dangerous trends.

In his survey of ancient empires, modern states, and global governance, Strobe Talbott (2008a), Deputy Secretary of State under Madeleine Albright, highlights two "mega-threats" that the next American president must deal with – global warming and nuclear weapons proliferation – which are, indeed, interconnected:

> It is asking a lot of the world – and the next president of the US – to grapple simultaneously with proliferation and climate change, but it is not asking too much, given the consequences of failure. Greater public awareness of the way in which *these and other dangers are connected* might help galvanize support of the necessary remedies, sacrifices and trade-offs.
>
> As farmlands turn to dust belts or deserts, and as the sea engulfs heavily populated coastal regions, whole nations will be thrown into economic and political chaos – *portending both internal and cross-border violence.*
>
> Projections indicate that the most onerous effects of climate change will be felt in poorer parts of the world, where soaring temperatures, encroaching sands, and rising sea levels are likely *to cause or hasten the failure of fragile states.* In failing, they will teach us about the *link* between their misery and our insecurity: *failed states are often outlaw states, sources of regional instability, incubators of terrorism, and thriving markets for lethal technology.* (Talbott, 2008b, p. 2, emphasis added).

Clearly, for Talbott, the global problematique includes other dangerous issues, but climate change and nuclear weapons proliferation top the list; moreover, they constitute the framework within which other problems must be seen.[10]

For the Oxford Research Group, an NGO based in the United Kingdom, four "mega-threats" play this agenda-shaping role, constituting a framework within which other global problems must be seen in order for all problems to be effectively addressed. Their research identifies four interconnected fundamental threats:

1 climate change
2 competition over resources

3 marginalization of the majority world
4 global militarization.

These are "most likely to lead to large-scale loss of life – of a magnitude unmatched by other potential threats – *and have the greatest potential to spark violent conflict, civil unrest or destabilisation that threatens the international system as we know it.*" A major point here is that action taken against one of these four threats "can be undone by poor decisions made in relation to another" (Abbott et al., 2007, pp. 3–6, emphasis added).

The "goodness-of-fit" noted here between the comments of policymakers, journalists, and NGO researchers on the ontology of the global problematique is rather striking, hinting that the first post-Bush US president would be open to "non-ideological" ideas from those inside or even outside his immediate circle of advisors. In contrast to George W. Bush, who "consciously resisted" the proposition not only that global warming is a threat but also that humans play a role in its genesis, his successor has been more predisposed to lead the world in efforts to do something about this and other global problems.

Peacebuilding provides a conceptual and operational basis for designing and implementing interventions into complex environments where either potential or actual violent conflict co-exists with a number of interrelated causal factors, each of which is itself part of the global problematique. Recalling the onerous complexity of "unintended consequences," even if we want to deal with only one problem, to be effective, we must deal with them all.

Conclusion: Structure of the Volume

In chapter 2, "Complex Problem Solving in Violent Conflicts," we explore frameworks beyond the four worlds' model (4WM)

for facilitating the application of peacebuilding theory and
practice to complex global problems, including intractable,
identity-based conflict situations (e.g., the ethnic Albanian–
Serb conflict over Kosovo). The objective is to identify the
unique characteristics of select conceptual tools, suggesting
an integrated, holistic model "in the making" that could facilitate an upgrade in analytical capabilities of theorists, policymakers, and practitioners concerned with complex problem
solving and peacebuilding.

In chapter 3, "Improving the Record," we examine the
record of peacebuilding in general, plus some specific
cases, noting successes as well as failures that could, as
"lessons learned," be applicable elsewhere as "best practices."
The Yugoslav successor states of the Western Balkans
figure prominently in an exploration of the continued viability
of the European Union and other international and regional
organizations in advancing peacebuilding in post-[violent]¹¹
conflict situations, specifically Bosnia-Herzegovina and
Macedonia.

In chapter 4, "Peacebuilding and the Global War on Terror,"
we examine what preoccupied the US under former President
George W. Bush for the nearly eight years of his presidency,
not only at the expense of other pressing global issues but
in a manner that exacerbated them. One question is, in
what ways can the policies of, say the recently established
Group of 20 nations (G20), accompanied by "soft power"
US leadership under Barack Obama, benefit from peacebuilding theory and practice to build better relationships with
Muslims and others worldwide who have been alienated by
Western policies in general, and US policies in particular,
to the extent that they can justify launching terrorist
campaigns against the perceived source of their successive
frustrations?

Finally, in chapter 5, "The US and the Future of Peacebuilding," we address various forms of governance – with the EU as a model and the US a source of indispensible leadership – as possible sources of solution to components of the global problematique and their complex, interdependent relationships with political, ethnic, and other conflicts worldwide.

CHAPTER TWO

Complex Problem Solving in Violent Conflicts

Introduction

In the introductory chapter, we attempted to come to terms with the nature and need for peacebuilding as a comprehensive basis for addressing complex, interconnected global problems that also feature in the etiology of, or are otherwise impacted by, intractable, identity-based conflict systems, such as the Israeli–Palestinian conflict. This chapter builds on the introduction by identifying frameworks, typologies, and other constructs that can facilitate comprehensive analyses of complex conflict systems that may be causally or otherwise linked to those global problems. The premise of this discussion is that, in order to prevent civil war in many developing countries, for example, we may also have to deal with other global problems manifest in those countries, such as poverty (see Collier, 2007a). Once the elements and drivers of those conflicts have been identified, a number of third-party conflict-handling goals can then be pursued, for example:

- *prevention* of violent conflict "from scratch";
- *management* of an existing violent conflict to prevent its escalation within its original locus of origin or across it and other regions;
- *settlement* of the conflict by halting its violent manifestations, either through coercive third-party mediation and/ or through the deployment of military force;

- *resolution* of the conflict by dealing with the underlying, combustible factors that led to its violent expression; and/or
- *transformation* of the conflict by working with the survivors on their long-term relationships so that, the next time they have a problem, they do not have to "burn down the house," the neighborhood, and the commons in dealing with it. This may include the "post-[violent] conflict" creation of new mechanisms which, had they been in place earlier, may have led to the prevention of the violent conflict being addressed.

"How" a select conflict can be framed to facilitate analyses and recommendations for addressing it in various ways is dependent on the theories, models, hypotheses, concepts, and other constructs a researcher has available for profiling the conflict and the factors, including other global problems, that have led to and/or might be exacerbated by it.[1] Revisiting the four worlds' model (4WM) introduced in chapter 1, if a researcher's World 2 (mental world) lacks a concept corresponding to a certain conflict-relevant theme (e.g., "structural violence"), then, when analyzing the conflict, she or he will be unable to "see" that theme or the "reality" corresponding to it. Worse, not being able to see the "reality" corresponding to the invisible construct means that it will not be addressed in recommendations to achieve any of the five peacebuilding goals mentioned above. If the missing reality remains unaddressed, then the conflict intervention may "unintentionally" become a part more of the problem than of the solution.

Accordingly, to borrow from an earlier work:

> Our purpose in this chapter is to identify and discuss *typologies of conflict*. A typology facilitates analysis and a typology of conflict could facilitate resolving as well as analyzing conflicts. Arguably, the more distinct, or even overlapping the types of conflict the better, as one would then have different,

albeit interrelated insights into a given conflict situation. Such insights could enable an analyst and potential third-party intervener to see a conflict from various angles, thereby enhancing the likelihood of a more effective response. (Sandole, 2003, p. 39, emphasis in original)

These various angles, when applied to theory, comprise the "beams of light" mentioned by Collier (2007a, p. x). When those insights guide applied peacebuilding in the field, they constitute various "checklists" found to be essential in the effective performance of other complex tasks, such as surgery, architectural design and construction, investing, and piloting an aircraft (see Gawande, 2009). Given peacebuilding's less than stellar record, "checklists," comprising multiple theory-embedded typologies, are appropriate.

As indicated in chapter 1, peacebuilding has tended to be reactive, ad hoc, and minimalist. It has been applied primarily to "post-[violent] conflict" situations, where overt hostilities have ceased and some degree of negative peace has been established between previously warring parties, in Bosnia-Herzegovina, Kosovo, Northern Ireland, Cyprus, and South Africa, among others. There are a number of conceptual approaches for guiding the challenging work of third parties involved in facilitating dialogues between representatives of parties to such conflicts who, in many cases, still exist in an unstable relational state of narcissistic rage toward each other (see Kohut, 1971). Hence, the regrettable fact that thirty-one of thirty-nine armed conflicts that have occurred in the past ten years have been recurrences – i.e., their deep-rooted causes and conditions have not been effectively addressed (see Hewitt, 2010b; Hewitt et al., 2010, pp. 1, 3–4) – provides another example of the tendency toward a minimalist approach to peacebuilding.

Depending upon the skills and experience of third parties conducting an intervention, plus the willingness of conflicting parties to explore with them alternative orientations for framing and dealing with their situation, perhaps facilitated by appropriate checklists, conflicts may become less wedded to traditional, counterproductive, self-defeating approaches that lead to various self-made traps, and more responsive to positive collective approaches and outcomes.

The Prisoner's Dilemma and Tit-for-Tat

A useful introductory peacebuilding-relevant checklist is provided by a game-theoretic framing of conflict, such as the Prisoner's Dilemma (PD), which captures a confounding situation inherent in many conflict situations existing at multiple levels (Axelrod, 1984). According to Anatol Rapoport's (1964, p. 49) clear exposition of PD, this generic dilemma can be graphically expressed as shown in figure 2.1.

PD can be interpreted as involving a clash between *Realpolitik*-driven *individual rationality* (+10–10/–10+10) and

		Party II	
		C	D
	C	+5, +5	–10, +10
Party I			
	D	+10, –10	–5, –5

Figure 2.1 The prisoner's dilemma[2]

Idealpolitik-driven *collective rationality* (+5+5), with the counter-intuitive result being that individually rational choices, although seemingly successful in the short term, eventually lead to collective loss over time (–5–5).[3]

In the experimental literature, especially in psychology, where PD tends to be "played" once, the *Realpolitik* option is often dominant, which undoubtedly says something about "human nature" (see Sandole, 1999). In Robert Axelrod's (1984) "Evolution of Cooperation" project, however, PD was played iteratively, thereby allowing it to approximate the real world more closely. In this multi-play context, "tit-for-tat" emerged as the dominant strategy because:

1 it is *friendly* – i.e., one is never to be the first to defect (D) from a cooperative strategy (C);

2 it is *reciprocal* – i.e., a player always reciprocates the other's choice, even if it is a defection (D);

3 it is *forgiving* – i.e., after experiencing successive defections (D) by the opponent, a player can cooperate (C). This injects cognitive dissonance (Festinger, 1962) into the process, thereby generating an opportunity for the "defector" to pause, reflect, and perhaps change course, which could turn a vicious circle into a virtuous one;[4]

4 it is *clear* – i.e., after conditions (1)–(3) have been expressed by players for a period of time, tit-for-tat emerges as the dominant strategy.

Tit-for-tat appears to be a viable means for escaping from PD even in situations where there is no central authority and no assumption of altruism on the part of the participants, and where the participants are intent on defending their own interests, as is commonly the case in *Realpolitik*-framed contexts. What is essential, however, is that the players expect that their relationships will, in one form or another, continue over time – that there exists what Axelrod (1984) calls the "shadow of the future."

If tit-for-tat is not attempted, or if it is and it fails, as it did during the "live-and-let-live" trench warfare of World War I (see Axelrod, 1984, ch. 4), PD can shift "catastrophically" to the Game of Chicken.[5] "Chicken" represents a clash between *Realpolitik* prestige and *Idealpolitik* survival: +10–10/–10+10 "on steroids," with the nonzero-sum/"lose–lose" outcomes shifting from –5–5 to catastrophic collective loss. This is precisely what the global community faced during the Cold War, with its specter of thermonuclear mass annihilation.[6] "Mutually Assured Destruction" was also an example of the "security dilemma," where parties actually wind up being less secure after investing in what they believed to be conducive to enhanced security (Herz, 1950). Chicken, far more than PD, is compatible with the current security dilemma faced by the international community with regard to the self-fulfilling "clash of civilizations" discourse (Huntington, 1993, 1996; Sandole, 2005a, 2005b) and its specter of a long war of "catastrophic terrorism" (Hamburg, 2002; White, 2008), perhaps including terrorists' use of weapons of mass destruction (see Frantz and Collins, 2007).

PD can escalate to Chicken – as the Israeli–Palestinian conflict has shifted to embrace the "Global War on Terror" (GWOT)[7] as well as a potential nuclear confrontation between Israel and Iran (see Morris, 2008b) – not because of the original causes and conditions of a conflict leading to counterproductive violence (–5–5), but because of the dynamics of the conflict process itself. Here we can distinguish between conflict-as-startup-conditions and conflict-as-process. For many observers, what keeps a conflict alive are its underlying causes and conditions ("conflict-as-startup-conditions") if they remain unaddressed. Clearly, as long as these are still active, they continue to play a role in protracting the conflict. Less obvious, however, is that, beyond a certain point in the escalation in frequency and/or intensity of a given conflict, the process itself may become the primary driving force – i.e., beyond some critical point, "conflict-as-process" becomes a self-stimulating/self-perpetuating violent conflict process which overwhelms and overtakes "conflict-as-startup-conditions" (see Sandole, 1999, ch. 6).[8]

"Conflict-as-process" is the fire that diplomats and military forces attempt to prevent (preventive diplomacy), manage (peacekeeping), or settle (coercive peacemaking). "Negative peace" is their objective, either maintaining or restoring it, as is currently the case in many "conflict-habituated" areas throughout the world (Diamond, 1997). Conflict resolution (noncoercive peacemaking) and conflict transformation (peacebuilding) have, until recently, rarely been thought of or considered by policymakers. The avoidance or absence of these two approaches to achieving and maintaining "positive peace" is the crux of the research *and* the practical (political) problem with which this volume is concerned (see Sandole, 1999, ch. 1).

Given the tendency for conflicts to escalate because of quasi-deterministic processes fuelled by the prisoner's and security dilemmas, what other frameworks, typologies, or conceptual approaches, beyond tit-for-tat, might be helpful to facilitate conflict analysis and conflict resolution practice to assist parties to escape from these self-made traps and then to shift to maximalist peacebuilding?

The Three Levels of Conflict Reality

When conflicting parties persist in digging themselves deeper into the abyss of the joint prisoner's and security dilemmas, the self-stimulating/self-perpetuating violent conflict spiral becomes further exacerbated, with parties tending to overperceive and overreact to threat (see Holsti et al., 1968). In the event, the fragility of unstable zero-sum/"win–lose" outcomes is increased as are prospects for the PD/SD to escalate to the Game of Chicken, where collective rationality (+5+5) is completely trumped by individual rationality (+10–10/–10+10). At some critical point in this dynamic escalation, some variant of Zartman's (1989) concept of "ripeness" should become operational in which, perhaps through a third-party initiative, another checklist becomes available to the conflict-embedded parties, the "Three Levels of Conflict Reality" (Sandole, 2007a), where:

- Level 1 refers to *conflict-as-symptoms.* "Symptoms" are observable discrete events which can be perceived as scaled indices (frequencies, intensities) of select categories of conflict (e.g., ethnic conflict, genocide, terrorism) and characteristics of actors involved in conflict (e.g., "failed" state, low level of economic development, autocratic political system, unstable regional environment) (see Hewitt et al., 2008). As the stuff from which early warning systems are constructed and media reports fashioned, "symptoms" tend to be our "first line of defense." As such, they can easily be framed by concerned policymakers and others as indicators of political and/or research problems in need of prevention, management, solution, or, in general, some kind of control.
- Level 2 refers to *conflict-as-challenged-relationships* that lead to "symptoms" (*"conflict-as-process"*). "Relationships" captures the dynamic, fluid, real-life, "give-and-take" of parties' relationships during select periods of time when aspects of latent or manifest conflicts are developing.
- Level 3 refers to *conflict-as-deep-rooted-causes-and-conditions* (*"conflict-as-startup-conditions"*) underlying the "conflict-as-challenged-relationships." These are the "independent variables" (e.g., the antecedent/explanatory variables) which affect the behavior of the "dependent variables" (e.g., aspects of the conflicted relationship) of interest to researchers, policymakers, and practitioners.

Examples of Level 1, conflict-as-symptoms, include the terrorist attacks in New York City and Washington, DC, on 11 September 2001; Bali, Indonesia, on 12 October 2002; Madrid, Spain, on 11 March 2004; and London on 7 July 2005. These "symptoms" reflect some subjective sense of conflict-as-challenged-relationships between, on the one hand, Americans, Spaniards, Britons, and the Indonesian government and, on the other, Islamic fundamentalists who perceive the drivers of globalization as current manifestations of the "Crusaders" bent on marginalizing and destroying Islam (see Sandole, 2002c, 2004).

Conflict-as-deep-rooted-causes-and-conditions refers to the origins of the challenged relationships between the parties, including the Israelis and Palestinians, whose intractable conflict plays a pivotal role in driving Islamist terrorism locally, regionally, and globally. Although "deep-rooted causes and conditions" can be subjected to empirical analyses, they have tended not to be addressed by members of the concerned international community – a condition which has itself probably played a significant role in the overall causal mosaic of the violent expression of conflict.

The paradox of the three levels of conflict reality is that, for a variety of reasons – greatly amplified by the armed forces, security and police services, media, and entertainment industry – conflict-as-symptoms gets all the attention while conflict-as-deep-rooted-causes-and-conditions gets the least. Conflict-as-symptoms is the first line of defense, where the heat of the "fire" associated with challenged relationships is experienced, either directly or vicariously. This is also where those who bear the heat of battle in distant lands or in their own communities attempt initially to deal with the "fires." The problem is, because relevant parties are either cognitively and affectively overwhelmed by symptoms (see chapter 5 of this volume) or attracted to the "addictive" allure of battle that symptoms represent (see Hedges, 2002; Van Creveld, 1991, p. 164), few people other than conflict resolution practitioners deal with the challenged relationships, and fewer still, other than conflict researchers, deal with the underlying causes and conditions of the challenged relationships that give rise to the symptoms.

This preoccupation with conflict-as-symptoms is part of what drives the tendency to implement the minimalist form of peacebuilding in primarily post-[violent] conflict situations, thereby leaving unaddressed conflict-as-deep-rooted-causes-and-conditions with perhaps minimal attention given to conflict-as-challenged-relationships. A third party can intervene at the level of the latter and effectively "turn off," through coercive means, the "violent conflict-as-process" that drives the symptoms. However, by leaving in place the original "conflict-as-startup-conditions," interveners are basically ensuring that another eruption of the still-intact conflict origins is likely to take place sometime in the future. This is the fundamental flaw of the minimalist approach to peacebuilding!

Conflict analysts can indicate to conflicting parties, peacebuilding practitioners, and policymakers the likely implications of a sole focus on conflict-as-symptoms. Such superficiality can lead, for example, to the further development and maintenance of identities that exclude the "Other," which can reinforce vicious ($+10$–$10/$–10+10) cycles leading to lose–lose (-5–5) outcomes at the expense of potential virtuous ($+5$+5) cycles (see Deutsch, 1973). As a further plea for collective rationality, conflict analysts can also pressure the parties, policymakers, and practitioners to make a conscious effort to embrace the ignored levels of challenged relationships and deep-rooted causes and conditions, while continuing to hold on to symptoms as sources of early warning and conflict monitoring and causes for concern.

President Obama's "Three Legs of the Foreign Policy Stool"

Interestingly enough, even before his inauguration, President Barack Obama had started to move in this more comprehensive, holistic direction, articulating a foreign policy strategy in general, and for Afghanistan in particular, that includes the "three d's" (3Ds) or "legs of a stool" that correspond directly to the three levels of conflict reality: (1) defense to handle conflict-as-symptoms; (2) diplomacy to handle conflict-as-challenged-relationships; and (3) development to handle conflict-as-deep-rooted-causes-and-conditions (see Clinton, 2009). The 3Ds are a distillation of the wisdom inherent in General (Dr) David Petraeus's counter-insurgency strategy developed in Iraq to use negotiations and access to resources to re-empower disaffected Sunni Arabs who had lost their positions of power and privilege through the overthrow of Saddam Hussein's regime, and the subsequent disbanding of the Baathist Party and armed forces. The idea now is to do the same in Afghanistan by "relegitimating" the former Pashtun/Taliban enemy (see Sprinzak, 1991), encouraging them to work with the US-led NATO force in "nation-building" in Afghanistan, the International Security Assistance Force (ISAF). As General Petraeus has repeatedly said, this goal cannot be met solely at the level of symptoms by shooting or killing our way to victory (see FP, 2009).[9]

It is becoming clearer to the concerned international community that the foreign policy agenda of President Obama is increasingly embracing challenged relationships (through diplomacy) and the underlying, deep-rooted causes

and conditions of relational challenges (through development), as well as the symptoms to which relational challenges
give rise (through defense). This new, post-Bush American
leadership "by example" may be sufficient to encourage others
to follow the US lead in capturing the three levels of conflict
reality and, in the process, strengthen prospects for overall
peacebuilding efforts to shift from the minimalist to the maximalist mode.

Lederach's Leadership Pyramid

There are a number of other theory-embedded checklists that
can assist in this process – for example, the "leadership
pyramid" developed by John Paul Lederach, comprising levels
of society embedded in violent conflict within which certain
initiatives must be taken (Lederach, 1997, p. 39). This is
shown in figure 2.2.

   As one moves from the top level leadership to the grassroots,
those affected by conflict *and* peacebuilding processes increase
in number – hence, the "pyramid" metaphor. For Lederach, the
optimal level at which to intervene is the middle range (level 2):

> Important features of this level characterize the key actors
> within it. First, middle-level leaders are positioned so that
> they are likely to know and be known by the top-level leader-
> ship, yet they have significant connections to the broader
> context and constituency that the top leaders claim to repre-
> sent. In other words, they are connected to both the top and
> grassroots levels. They have contact with top-level leaders,
> but are not bound by the political calculations that govern
> every move and decision made at that level. Similarly, they
> vicariously know the context and experience of people living
> at the grassroots level, yet they are not encumbered by the
> survival demands facing many at this level.[10] (Lederach,
> 1997, pp. 41–2)

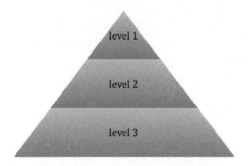

Types of actors

Approaches to building peace

Level 1: Top leadership
Military/political/religious
leaders with high visibility

Focuses on high-level negotiations
Emphasizes cease-fire led by highly
visible, single mediator

Level 2: Middle-range leadership
Leaders respected in sectors
Ethnic/religious leaders
Academics/intellectuals
Humanitarian leaders (NGOs)
Insider-partial teams

Problem-solving workshops
Training in conflict resolution
Peace commissions

Level 3: Grassroots leadership
Local leaders
Leaders of indigenous NGOs
Community developers
Local health officials
Refugee camp leaders

Local peace commissions
Grassroots training
Prejudice reduction
Psychosocial work in postwar
trauma

Figure 2.2 Actors and approaches to peacebuilding

Let's briefly examine applications of Lederach's three leadership levels to various conflicts to explore further their value in efforts to deal with challenged relationships and underlying causes and conditions.

Top leadership

At the top leadership level, there have certainly been high-level negotiations dealing with the intractable conflict between Palestinians and Israelis, such as the very visible mediation conducted by former US President Bill Clinton in July 2000. Camp David II, regrettably, collapsed into the second Intifada. Even more regrettably, there have been no major American initiatives since then, with the possible exception of the "Annapolis Process," launched by George W. Bush at the US Naval Academy in Annapolis, Maryland, in late November 2007 to achieve a peace agreement between Israelis and Palestinians before his presidency expired in January 2009. This process collapsed as well, in part because of the exponential poisoning of the Israeli–Palestinian relationship by the three-week Israeli assault on Gaza immediately before the inauguration of President Obama. Given the intimate connection between global Islamist terrorism and the Israeli–Palestinian conflict, and the likelihood that the new Israeli government led by Binyamin Netanyahu will be even less supportive of a positive peace process with Palestinians than its predecessor, there is clearly a need for further negotiations mediated by high-level persons. This undoubtedly accounts for one of President Obama's first decisions once in office: the appointment of former Senator George Mitchell as his personal envoy for the Middle East.[11]

Middle-range leadership

The "high-level negotiations" led by a "highly visible, single mediator" under Leadership Level 1, involving "military, political, religious leaders with high visibility," are "track 1" processes, where the players tend to be official, governmental actors whose objective is to strike some kind of deal with their opponent. By contrast, the "problem-solving workshops" conducted under Leadership Level 2 tend to be "track 2" (and beyond) processes, where the players are nongovernmental (but often former track 1) actors whose objective is, in the presence of trained, experienced facilitators, to share perceptions with one another about the conflict and how it might be dealt with.[12] Track 2+ can help pave the way for, or otherwise feed back into, track 1 processes, highlighting opportunities as well as challenges for cross-track communication, coordination, cooperation, and collaboration (Nan, 2003).[13]

In some conflict situations, as in Cyprus, ethnic and religious leaders might be trained in conflict resolution theories and skills *before* they are brought together in a track 2 problem-solving workshop. By the time they address their common conflict, therefore, they are able to speak the "same language," thereby enhancing efforts to "explore attitudes, values, wisdom, behaviors and interactive patterns; and . . . consider how [to] integrate learnings on these subjects and apply them to back home situations" (Diamond, 1997, p. 357; see also Reychler and Paffenholz, 2001, chs. 10.1–10.2).

Whether for training or problem-solving workshops, "insider-partial teams" might be involved as part of the training or facilitation staff. Their obvious value is that, as "insiders," they know the languages, cultures, parties, and issues – the "day-to-day lives" of the conflict participants – far better than the "outsider-impartials" (see Wehr and Lederach, 1991).

Peace commissions, including those conducted at the grassroots under Leadership Level 3, are attempts to repair broken relationships by bringing justice to a situation where human security has been severely compromised (see Reychler and Paffenholz, 2001, chs. 12.1–12.8). South Africans, who experienced a society-wide peacebuilding process (see Marks, 2000), had a Truth and Reconciliation Commission led by Bishop Desmond Tutu (TRC, 2003). After the atrocities committed at Srebrenica in Bosnia-Herzegovina in mid-July 1995, resulting in nearly 10,000 Muslim male adults and children being summarily executed solely because of their ethno-political identity, it is clear that Bosnia-Herzegovina is in great need of such a process as well. This may be one major reason why, fifteen years after the Dayton peace process brought negative peace to Bosnia, the ethno-politically driven situation there has barely progressed toward positive peace. Indeed, Bosnia remains a tense situation characterized by standing von Clausewitz ([1832] 1968) on his head, where "Politics is war by other means."[14]

Grassroots leadership

Grassroots training also tends to be done by track 2 personnel. Skills are imparted to conflict participants and others so that they can then deal with a variety of tasks necessary in the nation-(re)building process – e.g., conducting elections, establishing independent media, and implementing the rule of law and educational and economic reform. Training can also endeavor to reduce prejudice, often expressed as virulently ethnocentric discrimination against stereotypes of whole groups of people, leading in extreme cases to genocide (Sandole, 2002b). Prejudice can remain in the minds and behaviors of conflict parties and their successors for years – even centuries – after the termination of some hostile event, often mythologized to facilitate political manipulation and mobilization of "chosen traumas" (see Volkan, 1997). Prejudice reduction and "psychosocial work in postwar trauma" are especially significant for those suffering from vicarious and existential trauma, or post-traumatic stress disorder.

Dugan's "Nested Paradigm"

Maire Dugan's "nested paradigm" (Dugan, 1996; Lederach, 1997) is another peacebuilding-relevant checklist. It represents an innovative approach to expanding the scope of conflict analysis by embracing, in one simple diagram, relationships and causes as well as symptoms, plus a point of departure for third-party conflict-handling in terms of Lederach's three leadership categories. Imagine a series of successive semicircles, with "issue" at the bottom inside the smallest. Then, surrounding "issue," we have the next semicircle, for "relationship," followed by the next semicircle, for "subsystemic" environment, and then, finally, the most inclusive, macro-, semicircle of all, for "systemic" environment (see figure 2.3).

A quick spot-check of the nested paradigm as a conceptual basis for better framing, understanding, and dealing with, for example, the Israeli–Palestinian conflict provides a sense of its potential utility. First of all, a major issue in that intractable conflict is the locus of sovereignty over the commonly claimed land of the West Bank and Jerusalem. Secondly, one major source of exacerbation of the sensitivity of sovereignty as a major issue is the ongoing fractured Israeli–Palestinian relationship. The negative energy of this relationship is, in turn, further fueled by subsystemic and systemic as well as local

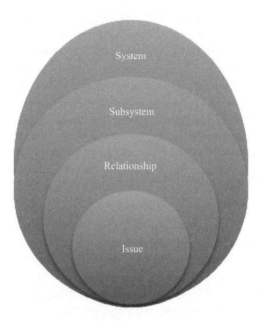

Figure 2.3 The nested paradigm

factors, such as, on the Israeli side, the continuing occupation, further annexation of Palestinian land, and recent assault on Gaza; on the Palestinian side, continuing rocket attacks and other acts of violence against Israelis; and, from others in the region and the international community as a whole, decision-making paralysis and acceptance of an unstable status quo. These factors are among the constituent elements of a tight, self-stimulating/self-perpetuating feedback loop in the Israeli–Palestinian relationship (Sandole, 1999) and a major security dilemma driving global Islamist terrorism.

The underlying premise of the nested paradigm is that, in this case, efforts to deal effectively with the jointly determined Israeli–Palestinian sovereignty issue and fractured relationship between the two parties must be located within the sub-systemic (the Middle East, the Iraq war, the Arab League, Iran) and systemic environmental domains (the US, EU, G20, UN, Organization of the Islamic Conference, Afghan war, and "global war on terrorism"). This suggests that the concerned international community needs a coordinated, regional, multi-track approach to deal with the three levels of conflict reality as well as all four spaces of the nested paradigm, simultaneously and/or in sequence, to capture the complexity of the problem (Sandole, 2002a, 1999; Diamond and McDonald, 1996). What this might look like may be preoccupying President Barack Obama and his Middle Eastern team, who will likely be influenced by, among others, Lederach's peacebuilding framework.

Lederach's Peacebuilding Framework

Adding to the diversity and typological richness of our discussion, Lederach (1997, ch. 6) has modified Dugan's nested paradigm as a basis for developing his integrated framework for peacebuilding:

Issue = Crisis intervention
Relationship = Preparation and training
Subsystemic environment = Design of social change
Systemic environment = Desired future

When steps are undertaken to manage the immediate crisis, interveners deal with the issue in contention at the level of symptoms (immediate action: 2–6 months). When they take steps to prevent the crisis from recurring, interveners deal with the challenged relationship that has given rise to the symptoms (short-range planning: 1–2 years). When they take steps to shift the crisis to a desired social change, they deal with transformation at the subsystemic level of causes and conditions (decade thinking: 5–10 years). When they deal with the deep-rooted causes and conditions of the crisis, interveners operate at the systemic level, as they continue to do when they subsequently contemplate desired social structures and relationships in the future (generational vision: 20+ years) (ibid.).[15]

Diamond and McDonald's Multi-Track Framework

Complementing Lederach's unique contribution of a temporal dimension to the overall peacebuilding enterprise is a radical upgrade to the spatial dimension by the development of a "multi-track" approach to designing and implementing interventions into complex conflicts and the problems that may impact those conflicts. As with many other concepts, the idea of different "tracks" has been absorbed so quickly into the peacebuilding lexicon that we often take it for granted that everyone knows what we mean by "multi-track" peacebuilding, with its implications for coordinated, sequenced, or simultaneous multi-actor/multi-sector interventions.

The development of the multi-track framework represents a high point in the maturation of peacebuilding-relevant checklists. It corresponds to the growth in international governmental and nongovernmental organizations since the end of World War II, which impacted the quality and quantity of sectors likely to become involved in peace operations, contributing to both the terminological/definitional and the coordination challenges involved in multi-actor interventions. By the 1980s, distinctions were being made in the CAR literature between official, governmental actors – states and international organizations – involved in international interventions ("track 1") and a growing number of unofficial, nongovernmental organizations ("track 2"), which did what the official actors could or at least did not do (see Davidson and Montville,

1981–2; McDonald and Bendahmane, 1987). The complexity of "track 2," corresponding to the complexity of multi-track intervention, eventually developed into a nine-track framework (see Diamond and McDonald, 1996).

- *Track 1, peacemaking through diplomacy,* remains the preserve of official, governmental activity at Lederach's top level of leadership. Examples are President Obama's fact-finding missions on the post-Gaza Israeli–Palestinian conflict, conducted by Senator George Mitchell, and on the Taliban insurgency in Afghanistan and Pakistan, conducted by Ambassador Richard Holbrooke.
- *Track 2, peacemaking through professional conflict resolution,* occurs at Lederach's grassroots and middle-range levels of leadership. Examples are the nongovernmental problem-solving exercises conducted by, among others, John Burton, Herbert Kelman, and Christopher Mitchell (see Mitchell and Banks, 1996; Ramsbotham et al., 2005, ch. 2; Fisher, 1997).
- *Track 3, peacemaking through commerce,* captures the growing tendency of business corporations to invest in conflict-embedded regions in ways that advance negative and positive peace (see Wenger and Möckli, 2003).
- *Track 4, peacemaking through personal involvement,* deals with the peace initiatives of private citizens, including former high-level, "eminent persons" such as former US President Jimmy Carter, South African President Nelson Mandela, and UN Secretary General Kofi Annan.
- *Track 5, peacemaking through learning,* deals with the research, training, and education conducted by a growing number of NGOs and universities operating at Lederach's middle-range and grassroots levels (see Alger, 2007).
- *Track 6, peacemaking through advocacy,* refers to the activism of NGOs, much of it at the grassroots level, that focuses on human rights violations of political prisoners, women, children, refugees, displaced persons, trafficked persons, and others (e.g., Amnesty International).

- *Track 7, peacemaking through faith in action*, deals with contributions to constructive conflict handling by religion and religious organizations often thought of as causing rather than mitigating violent conflict (see Gopin, 2000, 2002, 2004; Abu-Nimer, 2003).
- *Track 8, peacemaking through providing resources*, refers to the growing number of philanthropic organizations funding various components of peacebuilding processes (e.g., the Bill and Melinda Gates Foundation).
- *Track 9, peacemaking through information*, deals with the media as a primary basis for the communication of images, information, "real time" processes, and the like, with regard to conflict and conflict handling. It is often characterized, including in this volume, as fixed on the level of "conflict-as-symptoms," with a steadfast adherence to the imperative "If it bleeds, it leads," and there are a growing number of instances where – often through magazine programs on public television or radio in the US (e.g., PBS's *Frontline*) or comparable programs offered by the BBC and similar government-supported outlets in other countries – efforts are made to get beyond symptoms and into relationships and the deep-rooted reasons why they "go bad." Print media also get beyond symptoms with their reviews of books, with the *New York Review of Books* being an exemplar in this regard. Further, interventions into active, intractable conflict situations have actually occurred through the media – for example, the *Nightline* news programs presented by Ted Koppel of ABC News on apartheid in South Africa and the Israeli–Palestinian conflict (see Botes, 1997, 2003, 2004).

A role for civil society

One implication of the multi-track framework is that it alerts researchers, policymakers, and practitioners to the role that civil society can play in conflict and conflict handling. Civil society has developed, in large part, to ensure that state security and human security do not exist in a zero-sum relationship with one another. This is a direct response to the tendency of *Realpolitik* – the most prevalent political paradigm in human history – to advance state security at the expense of human security. Indeed, in many cases of ethno-political violence since the end of the Cold War, the state has been the source of oppression of minorities and, therefore, a major factor in the corresponding political violence. Accordingly, the role of civil society in peacebuilding – protection, monitoring, advocacy, socialization, social cohesion, facilitation, service delivery, and, in general, governance of post-[violent] conflict societies, such as those in the Western Balkans – has received increasing attention (see Paffenholz, 2009b, 2010; Benedek, 2006).

The value of civil society in rebuilding war-torn societies is that its inclusion in the design and implementation of interventions guarantees that some degree of attention is paid to fractured relationships and the underlying causes and conditions of why relationships regress into self-stimulating/self-perpetuating violent conflict systems. This more comprehensive framing of conflict, inclusive of all three levels of conflict reality (corresponding to President Obama's 3Ds), is a requisite for moving beyond fragile minimalist into sustainable maximalist peacebuilding.[16]

Clearly, once we start to visualize combining Lederach's leadership triangle with his integrated peacebuilding model, Dugan's nested paradigm, and Diamond and McDonald's multi-track framework, with its implications for civil society involvement, Susan Allen Nan's (2003) emphasis on the need for more effective communication, coordination, cooperation, and collaboration becomes of paramount importance if peacebuilding is ever to succeed in shifting beyond its current minimalist preoccupation with symptoms. Increasing the likelihood that this shift in trajectory will occur is a final construct in our typological survey – a comprehensive framework in terms of which all the elements of our discussion in this chapter can be integrated to facilitate the design *and* implementation of coherent peacebuilding interventions into complex, identity-based conflicts.

The Three-Pillar Framework (3PF)

I developed the last of our select checklists, the three-pillar framework (3PF), initially as a basis for integrating into a coherent whole all the information I discovered on conflict analysis and resolution from years of teaching from a vast multidisciplinary literature. Eventually, I also realized the value of the 3PF for identifying elements of this literature that could be useful in "mapping" any particular conflict as a basis for responding to it in an effective manner (see Sandole, 1998a, 1998b, 1999, ch. 6; 2003, 2007a, ch. 2).

The 3PF rests on the fundamental premise that, in order to do something (pillar 3) about any conflict (pillar 1), we have to know what makes the conflict "tick" (pillar 2). Accordingly, pillar 1 deals with conflict elements – parties, issues, objectives, means, conflict-handling orientations, and conflict environment. Pillar 2 deals with conflict causes and conditions – the factors that drive the conflict under pillar 1, emanating from the individual, societal, international, and global/ecological levels. Finally, pillar 3 deals with third-party interventions, including, first of all, third-party objectives – violent conflict prevention, management, settlement, resolution, and/or transformation (discussed in chapter 1). Pillar 3 also deals with third-party means for achieving select objectives: confrontational and/or collaborative approaches, negative peace and/or positive peace orientations, and track 1 and/or multi-track actors and processes (see table 2.1).

Table 2.1 Three-pillar comprehensive mapping of conflict and conflict resolution (3PF)		
Pillar 2:	**Pillar 1:**	**Pillar 3:**
Conflict causes and conditions	**Conflict elements**	**Conflict intervention**
Individual	Parties	*Third-party objectives*
Societal	Issues	[Violent] Conflict prevention
International	Objectives	Conflict management
Global/ecological	Means	Conflict settlement
	Conflict-handling orientations	Conflict resolution
	Conflict environment	Conflict transformation
		Third-party means for achieving goals
		Confrontational and/or collaborative means
		Negative peace and/or positive peace orientations
		Track 1 and/or multi-track actors and processes

Pillar 1: Conflict elements

The first issue to address under Pillar 1 is at what level of intensity a select conflict is occurring. Is it *latent* – a conflict that should be occurring but is not yet in the consciousness of one or more of the parties (Deutsch, 1973)? If manifest, is it being expressed nonviolently or violently? In the former case, a conflict analyst can categorize the conflict as a manifest conflict process (MCP) – a situation where two or more parties, or their representatives, pursue their perceptions of mutually incompatible goals through means designed to undermine the decision-making efficacy of one another (Sandole, 1999). If it is violent, the conflict can be labeled as an aggressive manifest conflict process (AMCP) – a situation where two or more actors, or their representatives, pursue their perceptions of mutually incompatible goals by damaging and destroying high-value cultural symbols and infrastructure (e.g., churches, mosques, synagogues, national libraries; on 9/11, the World Trade Center and Pentagon) and/or by injuring and destroying each other (ibid.).

Clearly, at this stage, the analyst has an opportunity to be proactive: if the select conflict is latent, and has been revealed by one or more early warning systems to be developing, then the analyst can alert appropriate "first responders" to implement "early action" to prevent the incipient conflict from escalating into an AMCP.

Usually, however, for reasons already cited (also see Lund, 1996, 2009), the concerned international community tends not to be proactive but, instead, reactive, as it responds to *fait accompli* "houses *already* on fire"!

In any case, no matter where a select conflict falls on a gradient of manifest intensity, there are parties to be identified, who are waging conflict over particular issues in order to achieve certain goals by using certain means, which may or may not reflect the parties' preferred conflict-handling orientation and, in particular, conflict settings.

Parties

"Parties" can be neatly subdivided into "substance" and "structure." Under "substance," we can address whether the parties involved in a select conflict are representing themselves, as is likely in interpersonal disputes (e.g., a divorce mediation), or are being represented by "others" (e.g., lawyers, diplomats). Whether the parties are self- or other-represented, they may be individuals (e.g., members of a family in dispute), groups (e.g., various ethnic, religious, racial, and/or class

groups laying claim to the same disputed territory), organizations (e.g., labor and management disputing over workers'
health plans), societies (e.g., states disputing over territory),
or regions (e.g., territorially based alliance or regime systems
disputing over scarce energy resources) (Sandole, 2003). If
the parties are other-represented, the representatives may be
"insider-partials," "outsider-impartials," or some combination
of the two (Wehr and Lederach, 1991).

"Structure" under parties opens up multiple conceptual
possibilities, especially with regard to the intra-party level of
analysis – e.g., intra-personal, intra-group, intra-organiza-
tional, and the like. Quite often, when we think about conflict
between parties, we tend to overlook the conflicts within each
of them. This is especially true with regard to the intra-personal level, where conflicts between different motives (e.g.,
approach-avoidance), different parts of the same role (e.g., the
wife and mother responsibilities of the married woman), or
different roles (e.g., married woman vs. working woman) may
be playing themselves out.[17] This is also the level where traumatic memories – "chosen traumas" (Volkan, 1997) – are
located: the domain of trauma-healing workshops.

One interesting phenomenon occurring at the intra-personal level is the process of "transference," where a certain
image of an actor, associated with an experience "mentally
recorded" at an earlier point in time, is "transferred" to the
same or another (in some way similar) actor at a later point
in time. The process usually applies to psychiatric clients
transferring their early feelings about their parents or any
other authority figure onto their psychotherapists. But transference can also occur for members of identity groups, who
transfer historical memories and images onto groups with
which they are locked in current conflict. One example is the
impact of the Armenian–Turkish conflict over the issue of the
1915 genocide against Armenians on the current conflict

between Armenia and "Turkic" Azerbaijan over the status of Nagorno-Karabakh, the Armenian enclave in Azerbaijan. As one indicator of the operation of transference in this case, Armenians tend to refer to the Azerbaijanis as "Turks," who are completing the mission they first undertook in 1915 (see Sandole, 2002b, 2009b).

At the inter-actor level, "structure" tends to be about power balances or imbalances, symmetries or asymmetries (e.g., power asymmetry between a husband and a wife, a minority "out-group" and a majority "in-group"). When such asymmetries exist, we speak initially of "structural violence" (Galtung, 1969). This is a condition where members of certain national, ethnic, racial, religious, class, gender, professional, regional, and other "minority" groups are denied access to political, social, economic, educational, security, and other resources typically presided over and enjoyed by the mainstream dominant in-groups. This exclusion typically occurs not because of what members of the minority group have done, but because of who they are! When "structural violence" is celebrated in the mainstream culture through media and entertainment stereotyping, then it has shifted to "cultural violence" (Galtung, 1996). One response to structural and cultural violence on the part of the minority is "direct violence" (Galtung, 1969, 1996), including terrorism. This, in turn, is usually matched by counter-violence conducted as police operations or counter-terrorism by the dominant in-group, which tends to control government. The outcome of this "bite" and "counter-bite" process is often an escalating conflict spiral with implications for spillover elsewhere.

Issues

"Issues" are what parties are in conflict about. Often, the issue in contention is territory and who controls it – hence, the conflicts over Jerusalem, Kosovo, Nagorno-Karabakh, South Ossetia, Abkhazia, or elsewhere, including urban and organizational landscapes. However, whether for states, ethnic groups, gangs, or occupants of certain roles, "territory" seems to be not only one among others, but the dominant driver of conflict, including violent conflict. Indeed, for John Vasquez, "concerns over territory, not power, have been the underlying and fundamental source of conflict that ends in war" (1993, p. 124). Vasquez also argues that territoriality is "deeply ingrained and is part of humanity's collective genetic inheritance," not in a "hard-wired" but in a "soft-wired" way, to include "a proclivity to react with violence over the issue of territory" (ibid., pp. 139–40). For example, with regard to the Russian–Georgian war of August 2008:

> The larger dilemma facing the [Bush] administration is how to show Russia that it made a serious mistake in invading Georgia, without making Moscow feel even more isolated and aggressive. In the view of administration officials, the new Russia has one foot in the 21st century and a growing stake in the global marketplace. But Prime Minister Vladimir Putin, who has been driving Russia's policy toward Georgia, is seen by Washington as having his other foot in the 19th century – with an outmoded "great power" mystique about Russia's interests *in which he sees control of physical space as the key to security and stability.* (Ignatius, 2008, emphasis added).

However otherwise framed, a conflict over territory is a prime example of "realistic conflict." Lewis Coser (1956), in further developing the sociological theory of Georg Simmel (1955) on the "functions of social conflict," defines realistic conflict as a conflict that is really about something. In realistic conflicts, parties employ means that they define as instrumental to obtaining certain ends – scarce territory, status, or other resources. If they discover that alternative means are available to those they originally selected, they might change these while remaining fixed on the same objectives (Coser, 1956, pp. 48–55). By contrast, a "nonrealistic conflict" is "only" about letting off steam. In nonrealistic conflict, the very act of aggression is expressive, itself the objective, while the objects of violence (e.g., members of certain minority groups) may vary. Indeed, whereas in realistic conflicts the means are of secondary importance and can vary from violent to nonviolent, in nonrealistic conflicts they are of primary importance: "In such cases, there is less likely to be a weighing of peaceful against aggressive means, since it is precisely in the aggressive means and not the result that satisfaction is sought" (ibid., p. 51).

Complexity arises or is reinforced when the violence associated with a realistic territorial dispute unleashes nonrealistic affective energy which must be directed somewhere, either externally or internally: "Realistic conflict situations may be accompanied, especially where there are no adequate provisions for the carrying out of the struggle, by unrealistic sentiments which are deflected from their source. In concrete social reality an admixture of both 'pure' types will be found" (ibid., p. 53).

Even when the realistic issue is resolved to the parties' satisfaction, the nonrealistic affect may remain because the parties have been addressing the wrong issue. In such "displaced conflicts" (Deutsch, 1973, p. 13), the parties dwell on a manifest conflict instead of a more significant underlying conflict: "The manifest conflict will usually express the underlying conflict in a symbolic or idiomatic form; the indirect form is a 'safer' way of talking about conflicts that seem too volatile and dangerous to deal with directly" – e.g., having a "quarrel over household bills" instead of addressing "an unexpressed conflict over sexual relations" (ibid.). Residual nonrealistic sentiments can also be displaced, through transference, onto future targets, with no one, especially the victims of subsequent aggression, being the wiser.

Just as a realistic conflict might generate nonrealistic affect, which "may reinforce realistic contentions" (Deutsch, 1973, p. 55), nonrealistic affect might generate realistic conflict. This can lead to what Deutsch calls "misattributed conflict" or what I call the "oldest hypothesis [maxim] in the study [practice] of politics": "when the natives are restless, find an enemy – even invent one if necessary – and then threaten or actually go to war"! As Deutsch puts it, a conflict may start out as false – with no "objective" basis – "but elicit new motives and attitudes that transform it into a true conflict" (ibid., p. 14, emphasis added).[18]

Objectives

Parties wage conflict over certain issues in order to achieve one of two generic objectives: to maintain a status quo (a change-IN-the system/"stability" goal, achieved via "balancing" or "hegemony") or to change the status quo (a change-OF-the system/"revolutionary" goal).[19] The clearest example of the potency of these contradictory objectives is the clash between self-determination and territorial integrity that has been a primary driver and characteristic of the "new warfare" occurring within states since the end of the Cold War (see Van Creveld, 1991; Kaldor, 2006). Hence, Kosovar Albanians have demanded self-determination while Serbia insists on retaining Kosovo as part of its territory; Abkhaz and South Ossetians want self-determination while Georgia wants to retain both Abkhazia and South Ossetia as part of its territory; Armenians in Nagorno-Karabakh want self-determination while Azerbaijan wants to retain Nagorno-Karabakh as part of its territory. In each of these cases, war has occurred. To make matters worse, the contentious issue of territory in each of these cases has drawn in other actors. The US and much of the EU, for example, have supported Kosovo's declaration of independence from Serbia, but condemned the Russian-supported secessionist aspirations of the Abkhaz and South Ossetians from Georgia.

The zero-sum framing and double-standard application of the territoriality issue played a major role in generating a confrontational stand-off between Russia and its former Cold War adversaries following the Russian–Georgian war over South Ossetia in August–September 2008. It clearly needs to be addressed, lest the emerging peacebuilding agenda of the twenty-first century becomes overwhelmed by an exceedingly complex, resurrected East–West ("mutually assured destruction") as well as North–South ("clash of civilizations") conflict overlay.

Means

The "means" used by parties to wage conflicts over certain issues in order either to maintain or to change some definition of the status quo can be either nonviolent (MCP) or violent (AMCP). Anatol Rapoport (1960) provides the following basis for enhancing this framing of means:

> 1 *fights* (AMCPs), where opponents frame each other as "enemies" whom they attempt to destroy;
> 2 *games* (MCPs), where opponents attempt to outwit one another; and
> 3 *debates* (MCPs), where opponents attempt to persuade each other and/or a third party.

The violent conflicts worldwide addressed earlier are clearly examples of "fights," accompanied by some element of "games" (intelligence gathering) and declarations about the value of "debates," but often with little corresponding reality:

witness the initial resistance of the Russians in August–September 2008 to comply with successive agreements, negotiated with French President Nicholas Sarkozy acting on behalf of the EU, to withdraw from Georgia to their pre-war positions (see Barber, 2008).

The traditional *Realpolitik* paradigm often influences policymakers to frame "fights" as being in their best "interests." However, beyond some critical point in the continuation and/or escalation of violence, when conflicts become self-stimulating/self-perpetrating with "lives of their own," fights tend to become mutually costly, as indicated in our discussion earlier of the prisoner's dilemma (–5–5), and security dilemma.

This again highlights the issue of "collective rationality" (+5+5) as the optimal orientation toward security based on positive peace, which seems to be so difficult for parties locked in conflict spirals to steer toward. Hence, the need for competent, experienced third parties to help the conflicting parties radically to change course, including, among other objectives, attending to fractured relationships and both their underlying causes and conditions and their symptoms.

Preferred conflict-handling orientations

Whether third parties can succeed in helping to extricate conflicting parties from counterproductive, self-defeating conflict spirals may depend, in no small measure, on the conflicting parties' "preferred conflict-handling orientations," which may or may not be reflected in the manifest "means" employed for expressing their conflict. Generally, conflict-handling orientations can be thought of as being either cooperative (collaborative), with constructive outcomes (+5+5), or competitive (confrontational) (+10–10/–10+10), with destructive outcomes

(–5–5) (Deutsch, 1973). Thomas (1975) has expanded on this gradient as follows:

1 *Avoidance*: When a conflict party prefers, for cultural, religious or personal reasons, to deny the existence of a conflict and, therefore, ignores it.

2 *Accommodation*: When the "bully" in a developing conflict process stays "in the face" of an avoiding opponent, the avoider may decide to cut his or her losses and simply "give in" to get the bully off their back.

3 *Confrontation*: Needless to say, some bullies, like blackmailers, come back for more, which may frustrate the original avoider to the point of fighting back.

4 *Compromise*: When the prisoner's dilemma (–5–5) results in successive security dilemmas, "hurting stalemates" (Zartman, 1989), and likely or actual escalation to the game of chicken, a third party may be called upon to help the conflicting parties to "split the difference" – a traditional option in diplomacy.

5 *Collaborative problem solving*: When conflicting as well as third parties realize that "splitting the difference" may not lead to durable, sustainable outcomes, they may try creatively to "think outside the box" (of *Realpolitik*) and develop alternative ways for achieving and maintaining positive-sum/"win–win" outcomes (+5+5).

A third party team might discover that one or more parties to the violent conflict they have been called upon to assist in handling would prefer to employ nonlethal means. The third party determines that the party concerned prefers not just to achieve a compromise, but to work toward an integrative agreement (Pruitt, 1987) through a collaborative process in which a mutually satisfying agreement (+5+5) could emerge. It would be far easier to shift the conflict from a fight to a debate in this case than if the party's underlying preferences were for more confrontation and escalation (+10–10/–10+10).

Conflict environment ("space")

Whatever a third-party team decides to do with regard to a particular conflict may depend a great deal on the nature of the "space" within which the conflict is occurring. "Conflict environments" can be framed in a variety of ways, some of which overlap with Pillar 2 (conflict causes and conditions). These include environmental, historical, cultural, economic, political, and institutional environments which, even if they are not among the original or direct causes of the conflict (Pillar 2), may still serve to make its violent expression more likely. Hence, for Thomas Homer-Dixon (1999, 2008), environmental scarcity, or "resource stress," does not cause conflict directly but, through complex interaction with other factors, could exacerbate existing tensions, leading to violent conflicts over territory. Similarly, Hewitt, Wilkenfeld, and Gurr (2008) include in their "Peace and Conflict Instability Ledger" the extent to which any state is located within a context of "neighborhood war," where: "The presence of an armed conflict in a neighboring state (internal or interstate) increases the risk of state instability. The contagion effects of regional armed conflict can heighten the risk of state instability, especially when ethnic or other communal groups span across borders" (ibid., p. 19).

Anatol Rapoport (1974, p. 175) presents an interesting basis for characterizing conflict environment by analyzing whether – or to what extent – a conflict environment is endogenous or exogenous. If endogenous, the conflict space incorporates "mechanisms for maintaining a steady state," including means "for controlling or resolving conflict between . . . subsystems." If exogenous, no such means exist.

Clearly, maximalist peacebuilding aims to "endogenize" the conflict environment as much as possible by creating mechanisms to deal with potential (proactive) or actual (reactive) deep-rooted causes and conditions (Pillar 2). By contrast, minimalist peacebuilding aims for a less durable state of affairs by avoiding underlying causes and conditions. Hence, the urgency of Pillar 2, which addresses the third and least well-attended level of conflict reality.

Pillar 2: Conflict causes and conditions ("drivers")

Once analysts select a conflict in need of scholarly or policy attention and identify the parties, issues, objectives, means, preferred conflict-handling orientations, and conflict environment, they *should* then address the conflict's underlying causes and conditions. Otherwise, efforts by conflict-handling third parties are not likely to get beyond fragile, minimalist peacebuilding, which, again, is the prevailing mode in contemporary interventions into complex conflict situations (Call and Cousens, 2008; Call, 2007).

Conflict drivers may have their origins at the individual, societal, international, and/or global/ecological levels of explanation (Waltz, 1959; North, 1990). This is quite a multidisciplinary mosaic of causal complexity, given that the individual level comprises at least biology, philosophy, physiology, psychiatry, psychology, and theology; the societal level, at least anthropology, economics, history, political science, and sociology; the international level, international relations; and the global/ecological level, climatology, ecology, geography, and geology. This complexity is rendered especially acute by the proposition that complex conflicts, even at the interpersonal level, can be impacted by factors from all four levels of explanation, while the majority of conflict researchers and interveners have been schooled in only one discipline at one of the four levels.

Accordingly, to avoid becoming or remaining more a part of the problem than of the solution, conflict/conflict-resolution theorists, researchers, and practitioners schooled in one discipline – which is still the norm (see Sandole, 2007a, ch. 2; Alger, 2007; Galtung, 2008) – must somehow become proficient in multiple disciplines in order to encompass the wide array of perspectives necessary to capture Pillar 2 in all of its multidisciplinarity. One relatively simple method for achieving this otherwise daunting goal is to ensure that the "third party" is a multidisciplinary team.

Once the drivers of any conflict have been identified, the conflict-handling third parties under Pillar 3 are ready to design and market an appropriate intervention or series of successive interventions, ensuring that the causal complexity is matched not only by the intervention design but also by the modalities involved in its implementation.

Pillar 3: Conflict (third-party) intervention

In chapter 1, we addressed the question of how peacebuilders could respond to a conflict situation by using the metaphor of a "burning house," common to diplomats and other governmental practitioners. Our responses to the question captured the first part of Pillar 3, dealing with "third-party objectives": (a) [violent] conflict prevention, (b) conflict management, (c) conflict settlement, (d) conflict resolution, and (e) conflict transformation. As that discussion indicated, peacebuilders could aim to achieve any one of these five objectives or a sequenced combination of them. We will now explore these options in further detail, plus the various means for achieving them.

Third-party objectives

If third-party interveners elect to be "proactive," they could attempt to prevent a house from catching on fire, especially when an early warning system (EWS) indicates that such is likely to be the case. The sole example of the United Nations undertaking a preventive mission is the UN Preventive Deployment Force. UNPREDEP successfully prevented the genocidal implosion of the former Yugoslavia from spilling over from Bosnia-Herzegovina into Macedonia (see Sokalski, 2003; Williams, 2000).[20] Regrettably, the proactive choice is not the norm, as [violent] conflict prevention (preventive diplomacy) is rarely undertaken (see Lund, 1996, 2009). The concerned international community usually waits for the house to be set alight through intra-state conflict dynamics and only then "reactively" responds to prevent the fire from spreading (conflict management = peacekeeping). This was the goal of the UN Protection Force (UNPROFOR) during the collapse of the former Yugoslavia.

Efforts to prevent a fire from spreading often fail, as occurred during UNPROFOR's mission in Bosnia-Herzegovina – tragically symbolized by the genocidal Serb assault on the Bosnian Muslim enclave and UN "protected area" of Srebrenica from 12 to 18 July 1995 (see Honig and Both, 1996; Rohde, 1997). When the fire spreads, third-party interveners may then decide to suppress it – the "conflict-as-symptoms" – through assertive negotiation and/or military force, as the Dayton peace process and NATO forces did successfully after the Srebrenica massacre (see Bildt, 1998; Holbrooke, 1998). Traditionally, following successful conflict settlement (coercive peacemaking), official state (track 1) interveners tend to consider their job done and leave the maintenance of negative peace in the hands of an appropriate international or regional organization such as NATO, which led the Implementation Force (IFOR) and Stabilization Force (SFOR) until November 2004 and then handed over peacekeeping duties to the European Union, with its EUFOR "Althea."

As the international community acquired further experience with peace missions following the end of the Cold War, it became increasingly clear to diplomats, military planners, and others that the goal of international interventions had to be more than merely putting out the fire. They became convinced that there was a need for conflict resolution (noncoercive peacemaking), whereby interveners identified and dealt with the underlying "combustible" causes and conditions of the fire so that it would not be rekindled. This led conceptually to conflict transformation (peacebuilding) and the idea that the interveners, together with the survivors of the fire, should work on the survivors' future relationships so that, the next time they had a problem, they would not have to burn down the house, the neighborhood, and the larger commons. As mentioned earlier, this effort could entail establishing and implementing new mechanisms that, had they been in place earlier, might have prevented the original fire from occurring.

The dominant example of effective conflict resolution (noncoercive peacemaking), coupled with conflict transformation (peacebuilding), is the European Union (EU) – the closest entity on the planet to Immanuel Kant's ([1795] 1983) "perpetual peace" (*ewiger Frieden*) system. We will discuss the EU as a model for regional/global governance and peacebuilding in chapter 3.

Third-party means for achieving objectives

The very same diplomats and others who realized the need to go beyond conflict settlement (coercive peacemaking) also realized the need for new approaches, orientations, and actors. Traditionally, track 1 actors, representing states and international governmental organizations (IGOs), utilized confrontational approaches to achieve and maintain negative peace – which is as far as conflict settlement (coercive peacemaking) takes us. Since conflict settlement (coercive peacemaking), like minimalist peacebuilding, does not address Pillar 2's underlying causes and conditions, the result is rarely self-sustaining. Hence, thoughtful practitioners and observers advocated a need for "multi-track" actors and processes to use collaborative approaches to achieve and maintain positive peace.[21]

Instead of generating a clash between the traditional security paradigm of track 1 actors using confrontational approaches to achieve and maintain negative peace, and an alternative security paradigm of multi-track actors using collaborative approaches to achieve and maintain positive peace, the issue is to embrace both systems in a new postmodern security paradigm, where both confrontational and collaborative approaches, in appropriate sequence, are required to deal with situations involving, for example, genocide (see Dallaire, 2004; Evans, 2008). The point is to have a Pillar 3 design that captures the complexity of Pillars 1 and 2 (see Sandole, 1999): "Given the complexity of much contemporary conflict, attempts at conflict resolution have to be equally comprehensive" (Ramsbotham et al., 2005, p. 104).

Conclusion

In this chapter, we have addressed a number of theory-embedded checklists that could be useful in designing and implementing more effective peacebuilding interventions into actual or potential complex conflict situations – as, for example, the fifty to sixty failing states containing the "bottom billion" of impoverished humanity (Collier, 2007a; Ghani and Lockhart, 2008).

We began with the prisoner's dilemma (PD) and tit-for-tat responses to it, followed by the three levels of conflict reality (which correspond to the three legs of President Obama's foreign policy "stool"), Lederach's leadership pyramid, Dugan's nested paradigm, Lederach's peacebuilding frame-work, Diamond and McDonald's multi-track framework, with its implications for civil society, and, finally, my comprehen-sive three-pillar framework (3PF). One remaining task is to combine these constructs in some fashion to maximize syn-ergistically their collective utility for the peacebuilding researcher and practitioner. So, which of the various frame-works or checklists discussed is sufficiently comprehensive to incorporate all of the others? Both impressionistically and after further thought, the best candidate seems to be the three pillar framework (3PF). Although lacking in the potential for capturing the nonlinearity inherent in complex systems pos-sessed by, for instance, Dugan's nested paradigm, its compre-hensive breadth makes up for its tilt toward simplistic linearity. Hence, table 2.2, which could fit on a plastic laminated card for use in the field, seems to do the job.

Attempting to integrate these various frameworks into a comprehensive checklist – an "enhanced" 3PF – has the value, in one diagram, of alerting conflict analysts and third-party practitioners to a host of potentially significant aspects of a complex conflict situation that might require attention if an intervention is to transcend the minimalist and move appre-ciably toward the maximalist level:

> the utility . . . of types of conflict [is that the] more types – the more angles or perspectives we have on conflict – the more likely it is that we are capturing the whole beast and not just any one part of the proverbial elephant as defined by any of the three blind men (or women). The problem with the

Table 2.2 An *enhanced* three-pillar comprehensive mapping of conflict and conflict resolution (3PF)

Pillar 2:	Pillar 1:	Pillar 3:
Conflict causes and conditions	Conflict elements	Conflict intervention
Conflict- as-underlying causes	Parties	*Third-party objectives*
Individual (*World 2*)	Issues	[Violent] Conflict prevention
Societal (*World 3*)	Objectives	Conflict management
International (*World 3*)	Means	Conflict settlement
Global/Ecological (*World 1*)	Conflict-handling orientations	Conflict resolution
	Conflict environment	Conflict transformation
Leadership level 1 = System (societal)		*Third-party means for achieving goals*
Leadership level 2 = Subsystem (community)		Confrontational and/or collaborative means
Conflict-as-process = Relationship		Negative and/or positive peace orientations
		Track 1 and/or *multi-track* (*track 2–9*) actors and processes
Leadership level 3 = Issue (individual) =		
Conflict-as-symptoms = Prisoner's dilemma = +10–10/–10+10		
Security dilemma = –5–5		
Complexity:		
"Everything is connected to everything else" (Waldrop, 1992) = *the Law of unintended consequences.*		

fragmentation of knowledge associated with the traditional disciplines and our academic degrees is that we tend to have only one of those perspectives at a time. (Sandole, 2003, p. 52)

Much of the integration occurs within the conflict environment(s) of Pillar 1, where the usually static 3PF assumes a dynamic character, especially with regard to complexity. Complexity captures the "edge of chaos" of Complexity Theory (see Waldrop, 1992), where slight shifts in existing trajectories of events might lead to catastrophic "tipping points" and trend reversals (e.g., from +5+5 to –5–5 and vice versa) – for instance, from a narcissistic rage- or apathy-driven entropy to a compassion-driven empathy in human affairs (see Ramadan, 2010; Rifkin, 2009; Gladwell, 2002; Thom, 1989; Gleick, 1988). This is where we encounter the "fluid battlefield" comprising conflict-as-symptoms, where von Clausewitz's ([1832] 1968) "fog of war," both literally and metaphorically, obscures a clear assessment of facts on the ground at any point in time – a situation rendered even more complex by the fact that many people seem to be attracted, often intoxicatingly, to the "action" in the dynamic conflict space (see Van Creveld, 1991; Hedges, 2002).[22]

Given these and other challenges of the peacebuilding project, the value of this discussion is that it has revealed a number of conceptual tools – checklists – for organizing information and guiding thinking and action on the design and implementation of peacebuilding that pay attention both to challenged relationships and their underlying causes and conditions and to symptoms. As part of this continuing effort to optimize prospects for shifting from minimalist to maximalist peacebuilding, in the next chapter we review the record of interventions to explore to what extent they reflect or deviate from the analytical diversity and richness implicit in these constructs. We also examine two particular "models" for how peacebuilders might proceed in the future.

CHAPTER THREE

Improving the Record

Introduction

As indicated in the conclusion to chapter 2, the utility of the comprehensive checklist, the "enhanced" three-pillar framework (3PF), is that it provides a holistic construct approaching an ideal type for assessing (a) what has been done and (b) what still needs to be done with regard to peacebuilding in the twenty-first century.

We have already mentioned the conceptual distinction between minimalist and maximalist peacebuilding (Call and Cousens, 2008), and that the minimalist mode, or something between it and the maximalist mode, dominates in the peacebuilding field. The enhanced 3PF provides an additional basis for determining what still needs to be done for researchers, policymakers, and practitioners to pay attention to conflicted relationships and their underlying causes, conditions, and symptoms, which typically direct most of the perceptual and behavioral traffic:

> Assuming that actors have the *political will* – the determination, even in the face of initial resistance from constituents and opposition parties – to do what it takes to act effectively at the right time, this is the point where an integrated set of conflict typologies [e.g., the "enhanced" 3PF] could be useful in facilitating a *proactive* instead of a *reactive* response. To use a metaphor well known to diplomats, some appropriate typologies could help to prevent a "house from catching on fire." (Sandole, 2003, p. 41)

The Record on Peacebuilding

Even a cursory assessment of the record on peacebuilding indicates that it has not been too effective and, indeed, may have actually made matters worse in some cases (see Anderson, 1999). In addition to the relative absence of effective communication, coordination, cooperation, and collaboration (Nan, 2003) among multi-sectoral actors within a multi-track framework (Diamond and McDonald, 1996), there are a number of other possible challenges impeding conflict resolution/peacebuilding that account for the positive peace-deficit. First of all, as already noted, post-[violent] conflict peacebuilding tends to be minimalist, aiming primarily to achieve and maintain negative peace. Maximalist efforts, on the other hand, which are aimed at securing positive peace by addressing deep-rooted causes of violent conflicts (conflict reality level 3/Pillar 2), are viewed by some as an "ideal standard for a social good" that is "too blunt to differentiate between modest progress and outright failure and therefore unhelpful for practitioners" (Call and Cousens, 2008, p. 7). This may help to explain why, despite the decline in the symptoms of conflict – i.e., "the total number and intensity of wars . . . globally . . . by roughly half since the very early 1990s" (ibid., p. 5; Hewitt et al., 2008) – there is, as already indicated: "a troubling rate of recurrence[, including] war recurrence[, that] also accounts for a good portion of the world's 'new' wars. Thus, seven of the nine armed conflicts that broke out in 2005 represented renewed fighting between previous foes" (Call and Cousens, 2008, p. 7).

Other factors that may account for negative peace being prioritized at the expense of positive peace within the overall peacebuilding project are an absence of operational coherence between sustainable development, economic growth, and social justice, such that they do not lead to and reinforce one another in practice as they are supposed to in theory (Victor, 2006). This problem area correlates with an absence of integration between (a) development and (b) conflict resolution/ peacebuilding researchers and practitioners, plus an absence of efforts to translate research-based insights into appropriate policy (Paffenholz, 2009a; Paffenholz and Reychler, 2007; Carpenter, 2008; UN/PBSO, 2008). These deficits have helped to prioritize the simplistic, "one-size-fits-all" liberal peace paradigm which, despite protestations to the contrary, fails to privilege local actors, identities, cultures, and conflict/ conflict resolution knowledge (ethnoconflict theories) and processes (ethnoconflict praxes).[1]

These and other problems (Call and Cousens, 2008, pp. 11–19), including the growing complexity of peacebuilding and Western bias in the expanding literature (UN/PBSO, 2008), have helped to tilt peacebuilding toward single-issue efforts, especially by funder-dependent NGOs (Murray, 2009), thereby reinforcing the overall tendency to leave unaddressed the complex, interconnected causes and conditions of violent conflict. This primary deficit has been exacerbated by the low regard with which governments hold NGOs (Sokalski, 2003, p. 195), a negative orientation which has spilled over to governmental agencies and international organizations also involved in development work. In his recommendations for what needs to be done to address the appalling poverty of the "bottom billion" – a major driver of conflict and terrorism worldwide – Paul Collier combines this phenomenon and other factors in his observation that:

> Traditionally, development has been assigned to aid agencies, which are low in almost every government's pecking order. The U.S. Department of Defense is not going to take advice from that country's Agency for International Development. The British Department of Trade and Industry is not going to listen to the Department for International

Development. To make development policy coherent will require what is termed a "whole-of-government" approach.[2] To get this degree of coordination requires heads of government to focus on the problem. And because success depends on more than just what the [US] or any other nation does on its own, it will require joint action across major governments. (Collier, 2007a, pp. 12–13)

These and other deficits are embedded within, and enhanced by, an international humanitarian system – the first line of defense in international intervention – that is fragmented and dysfunctional, if not broken. In response to the growing complexity of the "new wars" (see Kaldor, 2006) and the interventions they require or invite, the number of humanitarian organizations has soared. With each characterized by an autonomy bordering on "ferocious independence," effective coordination among them is counter-intuitive: "With no central power of the purse and no wherewithal to ensure compliance . . . cohesive action in [such] an atomized system is the exception rather than the rule" (Weiss, 2007, p. 147). Overall, the situation resembles a Kuhnean crisis, with its "proliferation of competing alternatives, the willingness to try anything, the expression of explicit discontent [and] the recourse to philosophy and to debate over fundamentals" (Kuhn, 1970, p. 91). After twenty years of weighty challenges, members of the international humanitarian community are re-examining who they are, what they do, and how they do it.

These deficits in coordination, status, self-image, and confidence among agents of peacebuilding allow conflicts to persist across generations and centuries, often in latent form, and sometimes involving full-blown hostilities (e.g., in Bosnia-Herzegovina).[3] To illustrate some of these daunting challenges further, let's examine a compelling collection of case studies assembled by Call (2007) that deal with the hybridization of two of the many dimensions ("single issues") of peacebuilding – justice and security sector reform (JSSR) in war-ravaged societies in Latin America and the Caribbean, Africa, the Balkans, and elsewhere. The contributors, with intimate knowledge of their select cases, were asked to respond to a core thematic question, followed by two sets of other questions. Call's ultimate objective was to distill common (nomothetic) patterns from the various (ideographic) case studies that could form the basis for recommendations to policymakers in need of sound advice in future peacebuilding planning and implementation.

The central thematic question addressed by each contributor was, "Can societies emerging from armed conflict create systems of justice and security that ensure basic rights, apply the law effectively and impartially, and enjoy popular support?" (Call, 2007, pp. 6, 375). This core theme was then subdivided into a set of three other questions (ibid., pp. 17–18):

1 To what extent is constructing justice and security even possible in war-ravaged societies?
2 What role do international actors play in transitions?
3 What linkages exist between different aspects of justice, policy, and law reform?

The contributors considered a number of other questions as well, among them: (a) Do present and former victims perceive new justice and security systems as legitimate? (b) How successful have tribal, local, or religious systems of justice and conflict resolution been? (c) Can efforts to combat postwar crime and build respect for citizens' rights be implemented at the same time? And (d) Do security and justice reforms result in "losers"? If so, can their loss be alleviated? (ibid., p. 18).

Call's comprehensive introductory chapter sets the tone, followed by contributions on attempted JSSR in some of the most complex peacebuilding projects of the post-Cold War era, in El Salvador, Haiti, Guatemala, South Africa, Rwanda, Bosnia-Herzegovina, Kosovo, and East Timor. In addition, there is a significant contribution on the role of gender in JSSR. In his concluding chapter, in which he employed the three sets of questions as an overarching framework, Call identified commonalities generated by the eight case studies. The record of lessons learned and of best practices that Call distills is rather mixed, indicating that the answer to his core thematic question is "yes, but":

"Perhaps *the most salient empirical finding of this volume is the near-universal emergence of new forms of insecurity in the wake of war. . . .* Wars end, but violence in a society does not. Instead, the formal end of war transforms the nature of a society's violence" (2007, p. 377, emphasis added).[4] The increase in social violence is acutely apparent to females:

> in Central America, Haiti, and Bosnia, women's groups reported that peace coincided with an increase in domestic violence, as demobilized soldiers returned home with limited job opportunities. (Ibid., pp. 381–2)
>
> . . . family violence increased at the end of many wars; peace brought violence from the battlefield into the home. Domestic violence was aggravated [not just] by the lack of jobs for demilitarized soldiers, [but] by socialization to violence, and by resentment at the opportunities and the (usually obligatory) mobility women experienced during wartime. (Ibid., p. 392; see also Leatherman and Griffin, 2009)

In addition to filling gaps in the peacebuilding literature (e.g., combining justice and security reform), this collection of studies of JSSR in postwar societies achieves one of Call's goals of providing insight for policymakers who may want to do better the next time they attempt to "put Humpty Dumpty back together again" (or, more challengingly, construct him from scratch). Call and his fellow contributors make it compellingly clear that this will not happen unless the *local* is privileged and addressed:

> one of the most striking outcomes of this volume is the absence, and difficulty, of citizen participation in military, police, or judicial reform processes after conflicts. Neither everyday citizens nor civil society organizations figure prominently in these accounts of justice and security sector reform. Postwar JSSR efforts are generally state initiated or externally directed, top-down reforms to state institutions that have marginalized citizen input. Two salient points [that emerged] are that the end of war does not end violence and that *formal institutional changes have generally failed to transform the daily practices of justice and security in postconflict societies.* (Call, 2007, pp. 401–2, emphasis added)

This, of course, has been the continuing challenge of the "liberal peace project" (see Richmond, 2005). Despite the best of intentions, it still seems to be primarily a neo-imperialistic enterprise. Until Max Weber's outsider-driven "explanation" (*erklären*) is matched by insider-driven "understanding" (*verstehen*) – and the single-issue focus is replaced by a multi-issue frame (Murray, 2009) – the mixed record found by Call and his colleagues will continue to characterize peacebuilding in the postmodern world. This is a consequence of the focus on minimalist peacebuilding, to the detriment of all concerned. Given the increasingly discernible operation of the "law of unintended consequences," this can only result in further undermining the legitimacy of the local and the human security imperative for the international community to comply with the responsibility to protect (R2P) (Evans, 2008; Weiss, 2007, ch. 4).[5]

There are always exceptions to the rule, however, which are just as illustrative, if not more so than the statistical norm, of what has been done. Let's examine, for example, noteworthy efforts by the United Nations and the European Union that reveal further insights into how the concerned international community can pursue peacebuilding in the future, *and* in a more effective manner than it has done thus far.

A United Nations Exemplar

For many observers, especially conservative American critics, the United Nations is a bloated bureaucracy that is totally ineffectual and, worse, provides a podium for enemies of the West to vent their venomous wrath (e.g., Venezuelan President Hugo Chávez's rant at the General Assembly in September 2006 about President George W. Bush being the "devil"; CNN, 2006). For less ideologically, less emotionally challenged critics, the UN is "merely" in desperate need of reform. On either end of the affective spectrum, there is a desperate disconnect between what this global actor should be doing and perceptions of what it actually is or is not doing worldwide to generate and maintain peace and stability.

In the final chapter, we will address the UN's new peacebuilding architecture, established in 2005, as one means of responding to these images and corresponding challenges (UN/PBSO, 2008). For now, we will address one of the "world's best-kept secrets," the United Nations Preventive Deployment Force (UNPREDEP), the UN's first-ever preventive deployment mission, which took place in the Yugoslav successor state of Macedonia.

Immediately following publication of then UN Secretary-General Boutros Boutros-Ghali's *An Agenda for Peace* (1992), which outlined "peacekeeping," "peacemaking," and "peacebuilding," as well as "preventive diplomacy," as forms of intervention relevant to the post-Cold War era, the UN dispatched UNPREDEP to Macedonia in late 1992. The deployment, based upon paragraphs 28 to 32 of *An Agenda for Peace*, was a response to an invitation by then Macedonian President

Kiro Gligorov. UNPREDEP's mission was to prevent (1) aggression from any of Macedonia's neighbors; (2) genocidal warfare in neighboring Bosnia-Herzegovina from spilling over into Macedonia; and (3) local tensions between ethnic Macedonians and ethnic Albanians from erupting into open warfare.

"Preventive diplomacy," for UNPREDEP, was linked to peacebuilding and its emphasis on addressing root causes as the optimal approach to preventing violence. It is, therefore, an example of "*pre*-[violent] conflict peacebuilding." According to Henryk Sokalski, who led UNPREDEP for much of its existence during the years 1995 to 1998:

> We adopted a *proactive* approach to conflict prevention that we felt would be more effective than a *reactive* one. We also thought that dealing with the *underlying causes of conflict* was preferable to addressing their destructive postconflict outcomes. Many of the factors in Macedonia's crisis had *very, very deep roots*, and addressing them would call for perseverance, astute methods and strategies, financial support, and educational programs. (Sokalski, 2003, pp. 103–4, emphasis added)

UNPREDEP's unusually flexible mandate, allowing preventive action to be embedded within a peacebuilding frame, comprised "three pillars," corresponding to the "three levels of conflict reality" (and President Obama's 3Ds) outlined in chapter 2:

1 *troop deployment*: traditional peacekeeping and coercive peacemaking (to deal with conflict as symptoms);
2 *good offices and political action*: noncoercive peacemaking (to deal with conflict as relationships); and
3 *the human dimension*: peacebuilding and conflict transformation (to deal with conflict as underlying, deep-rooted causes and conditions).[6]

Sokalski (1999) captures the generic peacebuilding richness of the mission with his and his colleagues' recognition that, for intervention in Macedonia to be effective, it had to deal with the root causes of *potential* conflict, which they attempted even though they lacked appropriate funding. They also recognized that "Poverty or intolerance or both are the most common root causes of conflict in the world today." Given that increasingly more crises, requiring some form of preventive intervention, tend to generate socio-economic consequences, they decided that there was a need for "a complementary and coherent balance between the tools used to resolve conflict-prone emergencies." Thus, UNPREDEP dealt with a complex situation by designing and implementing "a multi-track and multi-functional" intervention that meant involving complementary relations among the various national, regional, and international actors on the assumption that no one actor or procedure could do it all alone.

UNPREDEP's profile

Six dimensions comprise UNPREDEP's record:

1 UNPREDEP demonstrated that, "under appropriate circumstances," violent conflict prevention – long-term peacebuilding – can succeed. One telling reason for this success is that UNPREDEP nurtured partnerships among, and integrated the "distinct and overlapping" contributions of, the OSCE, NATO, the European Union, the Council of Europe, numerous organizations and agencies of the United Nations system, and the NGO community into a suitable peace operation (Sokalski, 2003, p. 216).

2 It indicated that an intervention to prevent violent conflict could facilitate the development of "newly independent or newly stable states," in large part by facilitating dialogue among ethnic Macedonians and Albanians, in the process

providing a forum that had not previously existed in Macedonia (ibid., p. 217).

3 It was able to contain the tensions existing between the polarized ethnic Macedonian and Albanian communities – no mean feat, given the combustible nature of their relations which erupted into open hostilities two years after UNPREDEP's abrupt termination.[7]

4 It indicated that a multidimensional and integrated approach to prevention was not only feasible but also effective: "The comprehensive three-pillar formula for action (troop deployment, good offices, and the human dimension) proved to be a forerunner of the precepts for peace-keeping missions that the international community embarked upon on the threshold of the twenty-first century. In that regard, UNPREDEP was *a unique laboratory of prevention*" [e.g., "soft peacekeeping"] (ibid., p. 218, emphasis added).

5 It revealed that violent conflict prevention can be cost-effective, with implications for other international interventions. While its annual costs came to US$55 million, an intermediate war of some two years' duration could have cost $15 billion, with a larger conflict between Macedonia and several other countries costing as much as $144 billion: "Hardly anything else can better illustrate the maxim that prevention is better – and indeed cheaper – than cure" (ibid., p. 218).

6 By providing a "blueprint for early noncoercive prevention," UNPREDEP set into motion a dynamic toward further development "of preventive concepts and their application" (ibid., p. 219).

UNPREDEP's lessons

Among the "lessons learned" from UNPREDEP, a significant factor underlying its success – that preventive action can make a difference – was that UNPREDEP "privileged the local." Whenever appropriate, it used its good offices to work together with Macedonia's governing officials, demonstrating that the UN presence was designed to further, rather than hamper, self-reliance, peace, and stability. The objective was not to teach imperialistically but to share lessons learned from elsewhere, in the process searching for and identifying points of convergence among parties to potential conflict and bringing them closer together. "We treated our hosts as partners, not as supplicants. Impartiality was the name of our game, and it determined the degree of our credibility" (Sokalski, 2003, pp. 104–5).

Privileging the local includes public relations to inform local as well as elite audiences (domestic and international) appropriately about the mission and all of its activities (Sokalski, 2003, pp. 164–9). Without transparent information and educational campaigns about, among other issues, human rights, electoral processes, the rule of law, and the accountability of all involved in the mission, especially the military peacekeepers, local acceptance of, participation in, and *ownership* of the process would likely be impaired. Part of privileging the local is that, whenever peacekeeping troops are deployed, as they were in UNPREDEP, it is essential that they are well behaved, "befitting the dignity of a disciplined, caring, considerate, mature, respected and trusted soldier"; that they show respect toward the locals' land, culture, traditions, customs, and practices; that they treat the locals with respect, courtesy, and consideration; and that they affirm the human rights of all (ibid., pp. 119–20).[8]

Part of this respect toward the locals is that peacekeeping troops should not sexually, physically, or psychologically abuse or exploit locals (or international staff), particularly women and children (Sokalski, 2003, p. 120). This overlaps with Sokalski's observation that "The empowerment of women figured prominently in UNPREDEP's human dimension outreach" (ibid., p. 163). For two successive years, UNPREDEP, together with local NGOs and elect government agencies, organized on 8 March the anniversary of International Women's Day. The 1997 celebration occurred at the same time as an inter-ethnic symposium organized by UNPREDEP on "Gender Equality: Fact or Fiction," which "reviewed women's position in Macedonian society regarding political participation, health, employment, law, social status, and mass media" (ibid.). Subsequently, UNPREDEP, together with Macedonian organizations, celebrated International Women's Day at the national level.

Locals, in contrast to governmental elites, clearly include youth. Leaders of political youth organizations, ethnic Albanian and Macedonian alike, were far more receptive than their elders to joint cooperative ventures. They proved to be both excellent and imaginative partners and saw their past, present, and future as citizens of Macedonia. Indeed, in fifteen monthly working discussions with a total of forty-six youth leaders, no intermediaries were required (Sokalski, 2003, pp. 142–4).[9]

Youth organizations were most active in UNPREDEP's work with NGOs, which relates to the value of partnerships. Partnerships with other international organizations and NGOs "are precisely what a preventive operation must seek in order to consolidate its accomplishments on behalf of peace and stability; the wider the scope of the mission's work, the more international partners it will need" (Sokalski, 2003, p. 173). Once established, partnerships need to be carefully coordinated in an *integrated approach to human security*, in which the efforts of the various actors must be *complementary*.[10] Just among the UN and other international organizations (e.g., the OSCE and its high commissioner on national minorities; see ibid., pp. 187–92),[11] there was a need: "to enhance their cooperation for conflict prevention [and] collaboration, including regular consultations, better flows of information, exchanges of liaison officers, extended working-level visits between headquarters, and similar measures as determined on a case-by-case basis" (ibid., p. 174).

In significant contrast to past experience, which had left a good deal of prejudice toward NGOs among different political actors (Sokalski, 2003, p. 195), such NGOs as the Open Society Institute–Macedonia, Search for Common Ground, the Friedrich Ebert Foundation, the National Democratic Institute, the Catholic Relief Services, the International Research and Exchanges Board (IREX), the Institute of Sustainable Communities, and the International Red Cross were already in Macedonia doing good work when UNPREDEP arrived. They had "monitored the first general and presidential elections, launched projects to tackle national political and ethnic cleavages, and started conflict resolution training and the establishment of national NGOs" (ibid., p. 196; also pp. 197–202).

The objective of UNPREDEP's partnerships was to replace the prevailing culture of reaction with a culture of prevention, in the process establishing a basis for "an organic link between conflict prevention *and* peacebuilding" (Sokalski, 2003, p. 174, emphasis added). In this regard, another lesson was that successful peacebuilding can occur only if efforts toward it are consistent and reflect a "continuum of action." For UNPREDEP this was a challenge, given that the international community had underestimated the need for "peacebuilding initiatives in preventive action," plus failed to organize a donor's conference to support further development projects in the country (ibid., p. 161).[12]

Hence the need for appropriate funding. Had Macedonia received appropriate international assistance, the resulting growing economy could have undermined a good deal of the inter-ethnic tension. Instead, whenever its socio-economic problems were ignored, Macedonia's political tensions were reinforced. Sokalski and his colleagues learned, therefore, that a peacebuilding mission cannot be fully effective if it is denied funding for humanitarian and developmental projects, as UNPREDEP was.[13]

Embedding UNPREDEP's supportive, complementary partnerships within Lederach's (1997) "leadership pyramid" (see this volume, chapter 2), it is clear that:

> Conflict prevention is a *top-to-bottom* and *bottom-to-top process*. Unless we understand this axiom in both word and deed, the chances for real success are pretty slim. Exercises in ethnic or political rapprochement start at the top with the [UN], and NGOs initiate the crucial corresponding action at the bottom; individual governments and regional organizations normally add their projects and actions to fill the space in between. (Sokalski, 2003, p. 202, emphasis added)

It is also clear that, without such partnerships in both pre- and post-[violent] conflict prevention, the efforts of the UN and others will tend to diminish. Such complex operations, however, require a good deal of the head of mission's time, as "there are many programs, people, and organizations to *coordinate* [where] the *careful timing* and *sequencing of events* can mean everything to the mission's success" (ibid., emphasis added).

Such efforts in Macedonia were guided by an approach that was both multi-track and multifunctional, in which national, regional, and international initiatives were complementary. Reflective of the complexity inherent in UNPREDEP's mission, major issues and partnerships were characterized by interdependence and reciprocity. A distinction was also made between the "pre-conflict peacekeeping" practiced by UNPREDEP and the more conventional pre- or post-conflict troop deployment of the UN.

Complexity, multi-level actors, coordination, timing and sequence, interdependence, and complementarity all argue for still another lesson – the need for a regional approach. This resulted from the way in which the international community had approached the Kosovo crisis of 1999 – i.e., in terms of endemic ethno-national conflict and hatred instead "of its own remediable policy failures" (Sokalski, 2003, pp. 226–7). Under the circumstances, it was difficult to imagine that Macedonia would not be affected by the precipitous removal of UNPREDEP, leaving the country extremely vulnerable. According to Sokalski, should the West lose interest or a concerted action plan fail to materialize, the region would remain "weak, unstable, and a persistent security concern." Similar concerns were expressed by Carl Bildt, former UN special envoy for the Balkans and EU High Representative for Bosnia-Herzegovina under the Dayton Peace Accords: "If we approach Kosovo in isolation, we will never succeed. *Any solution will have to take in the region as a whole. Our approach to Kosovo should be a consequence of our approach to the region as a whole – not the other way round*" (ibid., pp. 226–7, emphasis added).

Perhaps the most critical lesson learned from UNPREDEP, "the first major example of noncoercive prevention in UN history, [was] that the premature withdrawal of an operation can prove harmful to its very purpose" (Sokalski, 2003, p. 219). The abrupt termination of UNPREDEP on 1 March 1999, shortly before NATO launched its 78-day bombing campaign against Serbia for its ethnic cleansing of Albanians in Kosovo, on Macedonia's border, helped set into motion a dynamic that propelled ethnic Albanians and Macedonians toward open warfare.

Sokalski frames this development appropriately in "counter factual" terms, stating that, in spring 2001, a former colleague in Skopje, Kannan Rajarathinam, sent him a brief e-mail message, indicating that "The problem with preventive peace-keeping is that peace has to be breached for it to be vindicated – in retrospect" (2003, p. 239). Two years following the winding up of UNPREDEP, armed conflict broke out in Macedonia between ethnic Albanians and the Macedonian government. Although too late, preventive peacekeeping had been vindicated and the core lesson of UNPREDEP was reinforced: prevention is indeed less costly and less disruptive than cure.

The European Union Exemplar

While the United Nations has had only one experience in violent conflict prevention as a form of peacebuilding – pre-[violent] conflict peacebuilding – the European Union's *raison d'être* has been all about peacebuilding, not just among its current twenty-seven members, but also among others in its "neighborhood" and worldwide.

Earlier I indicated that the EU is the exemplar par excellence, anywhere on the planet, of Immanuel Kant's classic concept of "perpetual peace." This may appear to be an extraordinary assertion, given that, for many, the EU is an unwieldy bureaucratic nightmare that generates more yawns than positive affect. Consider, for example, that turnout for elections of members of the European Parliament has been on a steady decline since 1979 (see Leonard, 2005, p. 97) in contrast, say, to the number of Europeans watching World Cup football (soccer) on television.

As with many phenomena, the reality of the EU is complex: it may be tedious, but everyone wants in. Simply put, the EU is transformational (Leonard, 2005), turning "national interest" – as framed by the historically and cross-culturally dominant *Realpolitik* paradigm – on its head. Using the developmental momentum generated by the Marshall Plan to rebuild Europe after World War II, the EU grew out of the European Coal and Steel Community, formed by the initial six members in 1952. The ECSC was a response to the prevailing security paradigm that had led to the war and the Holocaust, finally and resolutely shutting down the system that had spawned the horror: "First, the obsolescence of war [see Mueller, 1989] is not a global phenomenon but a European one; second the disappearance of war after 1945 created both a dramatically new international system within Europe and a new kind of European state" (Sheehan, 2008, p. xvii).

> This system provided the incubator within which the states of Western Europe were gradually *transformed*. They became *civilian states*, states that retained the capacity to make war with one another but lost all interest in doing so. The result was an eclipse of violence in both meanings of the word: violence declined in importance and it was concealed from view by something else – that is, by the states' need to encourage *economic growth, provide social welfare, and guarantee personal security for its citizens*. The eclipse of violence happened gradually. It was a slow, silent revolution, hidden in plain sight, but it was nonetheless a revolution as dramatic as any other in European history. (Ibid., p. xx, emphasis added)

By transcending the Westphalian state, inviting candidates for membership to surrender voluntarily some of their sovereignty to the European Commission, European Council, and European Parliament, the EU allows national interest to become collective (regional and global) interest and, in the process, to generate +5+5 instead of the +10–10/–10+10 choices and –5–5 outcomes associated with successive prisoner's and security dilemmas.

The EU is both cause and effect: it reproduces and expands itself by holding out the prospect of voluntary membership to others who wish to enjoy the manifold benefits of a growing, robust commons: "The EU's 'gravitational pull' has proved to be the ultimate *conflict prevention strategy*" (EU, 2008, p. 6, emphasis added).

The tacit "theory-in-use" of the EU, articulated by, among others, Jean Monnet (see Leonard, 2005, chs. 1–2), is that peace and prosperity can be a positive-sum (+5+5) collective good enjoyed by all and not just a few, at least within the parameters of agreed membership. As already implied, the ultimate objective of founders such as Monnet was to provide Europeans with means other than war for achieving their goals, including further development and security, by reframing the nature of their interaction (see Anastasiou, 2007). But, to realize these benefits, candidates for membership must comply with political and economic criteria established in June 1999 by the Copenhagen European Council:

> Membership criteria require that the candidate country must have achieved stability of institutions guaranteeing democracy, the rule of law, human rights, and the respect for and protection of minorities; the existence of a functioning market economy as well as the capacity to cope with competitive pressure and market forces within the Union; [and] the ability to take on the obligations of membership including adherence to the aims of political, economic and monetary union. (European Council, 1993, para. 7[A][iii])

In addition, members must bring their national laws into conformity with the body of EU law known as the *acquis communautaire* (i.e., 80,000 pages of EU legislation in thirty-one volumes) (see Leonard, 2005, pp. 42, 45).

Since the end of the Cold War, the "EU-as-Kantian peace experiment" has expanded from fifteen to twenty-seven members, absorbing states from the former Soviet empire in Eastern and Central Europe (the Czech Republic, Hungary, Poland, and Slovakia), the former Soviet Union (Estonia,

Latvia, and Lithuania) and the former Yugoslavia (Slovenia, with Croatia to follow).

There have, however, been challenges along the way. Although membership conditionality, the EU's tacit theory-in-use, is by far the most powerful conflict-resolution mechanism available, it has not always been effective (Çelik and Rumelili, 2006, p. 207). Membership conditionality was not, for example, sufficient to prepare all of Cyprus for entry into the Union. Only the Greek-Cypriot part was successful on 1 May 2004, causing an uproar in EU circles concerned with enlargement. The then commissioner for enlargement, Günter Verheugen, was especially upset because he had been led to expect a Greek-Cypriot approval of former UN Secretary General Kofi Annan's plan for reconciliation and, therefore, joint entry into the Union with Turkish-Cypriots (Anastasiou, 2007; Eralp and Beriker, 2005).

Another example of the EU's less-than-stellar success is Bosnia-Herzegovina. In contrast to Macedonia, this war-ravaged Yugoslav successor state continues to be mired in virulent ethnocentrism and ethno-political paralysis (Sandole, 2002b). Indeed, in Bosnia, von Clausewitz's dictum that "War is politics by other means" has been turned completely upside down, into "Politics is war by other means," suggesting that "a new outbreak of violence remains a possibility" (McMahon and Western, 2009; Mrkic, 2009; Whitlock, 2009b).

In addition, the bureaucracy in Bosnia is so bloated that, in a country divided between two "entities" – the Muslim-Croat Federation and the Bosnian Serb Republic – there are, for example, three ministries at the national level for education – one for the Bosniak Muslims, one for the Croats, and one for the Serbs. In the Muslim-Croat Federation alone, there are sixty government ministers, eleven health funds, and eleven employment agencies. Further, according to the World

Bank, it takes sixty days to start a company in Bosnia, compared with five days in Hungary or nine days in Afghanistan (Bilefsky, 2009). All this renders EU efforts to negotiate with a "coherent" national voice nearly impossible (Eralp, 2009). As the BBC's Allan Little put it during a recent return to the country:

> The entities, not the Bosnian state, have real executive power. *The Bosnian state barely functions.* It is incapable of carrying out the reforms that Bosnia desperately needs. And so as Croatia and Serbia continue their respective journeys to the European mainstream – to EU and possibly Nato membership – *Bosnia, still broken, still paralysed, is being left behind, and is in danger of sinking further into corruption, poverty and organized crime.* (2008, emphasis added)

Despite these challenges, the EU is expanding, with some commentators envisioning a future Union of fifty members (Leonard, 2005, ch. 8), perhaps eventually including even Morocco, Israel, and Russia. In addition, the EU is a model for regional governance elsewhere and, arguably, for global governance as well, with China, among others, adopting its template (see Söderbaum and Stålgren, 2009; Leonard, 2005, chs. 9–10).

Somewhere between the EU as enlargement and the EU as model are the recent efforts by Turkey to further the introduction of EU norms and values into the South Caucasus region, site of the Russian–Georgian war over South Ossetia in August 2008. On 6 September 2008, Turkish President Abdullah Gül visited Yerevan, Armenia, in response to an invitation from Armenian President Serzh Sargsyan, ostensibly to watch the World Cup playoff match between their two national teams (Turkey won: 2–0). This was the first trip by a Turkish leader to Armenia since the 1930s.

The temporal context of the visit heightened the urgency to understand the meaning of this historic meeting. One framing of the sequence of events begins on the eve of the spectacular opening ceremony of the Beijing Olympics, when Georgia – a neighbor of both Armenia and Turkey – launched a military assault on South Ossetia, one of its two breakaway regions (the other is Abkhazia). This was followed by Russia's swift retributive attack on and occupation of Georgia, for committing aggression against Russian "peacekeepers" and "citizens" in South Ossetia.[14] One result of this multi-level conflict was a renewed fear worldwide of a resurrected East–West confrontational stand-off, replete with nuclear-tipped "mutually assured destruction" (see Fukuyama, 2008; Ignatius, 2008). Gül's visit to Armenia occurred approximately one month after the onset of these hostilities. The spatial setting added to the drama: Armenia has been in "frozen conflict" with "Turkic" Azerbaijan over Nagorno-Karabakh, the Armenian enclave in Azerbaijan, which, since a ceasefire was agreed to in May 1994, has been in a state of negative peace framed locally as "neither peace nor war."[15]

Adding to this challenge is Armenia's historical conflict with Turkey over the meaning of atrocities committed against Armenians during the final days of the Ottoman empire, which has impacted Armenia's conflict with Azerbaijan over Nagorno-Karabakh (see Sandole, 2009b). Accordingly, Armenians and others have been wondering what the implications of Gül's visit to Yerevan might be: Opening the Armenian-Turkish border? Establishing lucrative trade relations? Working collaboratively toward common security in the tumultuous Caucasus region? Resolving the Armenian–Azerbaijani conflict over Nagorno-Karabakh? Establishing an oil pipeline from Georgia through Armenia into Turkey? Finally laying to rest the Armenian–Turkish conflict over the

1915 genocide issue? Making the region more attractive to foreign direct investment? *All of the above?*

To explore answers to these and other questions, one must examine the foreign policy objectives of the Armenian and Turkish governments. Turkish Prime Minister Recep Tayyip Erdogan has made great strides in taking his country into the European Union, including improving Turkey's human rights record. Turkey has also evolved into a credible mediator between Israel and Syria over the Golan Heights. Nevertheless, Erdogan's government is sufficiently "Islamist" to have incurred a direct assault on its legitimacy by Turkey's secular establishment, which nearly succeeded in toppling the government through constitutional means. Turkey also claims that the 1915 genocide never happened, although it does admit that thousands of Armenians *as well as* Turks were killed in civil war. In this regard, Turkey aggressively lobbies Western governments not to accede to the Armenian diaspora's demands to recognize the genocide (see Sandole, 2009b).[16]

The Armenian government of Serzh Sargsyan, elected in the tumultuous presidential elections of February 2008, does not want to forget the genocide issue, which is kept alive primarily by the more prosperous and populous diaspora than by Armenian citizens themselves. On the other hand, Sargsyan wants to improve relations with Turkey (Sargsyan and Baghdasaryan, 2008). Indeed, in April 2009, Sargsyan told the *Financial Times* that, for him, the improvement of relations with Turkey was the "greatest achievement of his presidency" (Strauss et al., 2009).

So, what is the verdict? Given Erdogan's and Gül's post-Russian/Georgian war development of the Caucasus Stability and Cooperation Platform – to comprise Turkey, Armenia, Azerbaijan, Georgia, and Russia – it seems likely that the region could be on the precipice of a radical shift toward collaborative peace, prosperity, security, and stability, with clear implications for resolution of the Armenian–Turkish, Armenian–Azerbaijani, and Georgian–South Ossetian/ Abkhaz/Russian conflicts.[17] Much depends on what happens between Armenia, Turkey and others, including Barack Obama and his Russian counterparts.[18]

The probability that this sanguine view is valid has been strengthened by subsequent developments. For example, building upon its European Neighbourhood Policy, the EU has proposed the "Eastern Partnership" – to comprise Armenia, Azerbaijan, Georgia, Ukraine, Moldova, and Belarus – as its "boldest outreach to ex-Communist nations since the EU expanded in 2004 and 2007 to embrace the Baltics and all the former Warsaw Pact nations of Eastern Europe" (Castle, 2008). In addition, immediately before Barack Obama was sworn in as president, Recep Erdogan traveled to Brussels in order to revive Turkey's bid for EU membership, which had been held up as a result of tensions over Cyprus, political inertia within Turkey, and waning enthusiasm for enlargement among EU members. Further, shortly after Obama's inauguration and meetings with Turkish and Armenian leaders in Istanbul, on 22 April 2009, the two countries announced that they had agreed on a "comprehensive framework for the normalization of their bilateral relations," with implications for addressing, among other issues, their disputes over the 1915 massacres and Nagorno-Karabakh. By the end of August 2009, following several months of mediation by the Swiss and persuasion by the US, Turkey and Armenia agreed to start six weeks of internal political consultations as a prelude to establishing diplomatic ties and reopening their borders. Clearly, reconciliation was in the air.

Against this increasingly favorable background, continuation of "football diplomacy" between Armenia and Turkey can only help to strengthen prospects for this admittedly idealistic vision of regional integration *and* peacebuilding in the South

Caucasus region to become reality, as "ping-pong diplomacy" did nearly forty years ago when it helped to restore US–Chinese relations (see PPD, 2006). In this spirit, although the Armenian and Turkish teams were no longer in the running for the World Cup, President Sargsyan visited Bursa, Turkey, for a return match on 14 October 2009, just days after Turkey and Armenia signed bilateral protocols in Zurich for the establishment of diplomatic relations between the two countries (again, Turkey won: 2–0). As of this writing, the primary obstacle to further progress on the Turkish–Armenian front is the "frozen conflict" between Armenia and Azerbaijan (see AP, 2010; Freizer, 2009; Economist, 2009, p. 56). Nevertheless, a "peace momentum" has been generated, largely by civil society, that seems destined to overcome even this intractable challenge, producing thus far results that are surprising to even the most entrenched skeptics of any significant developments occurring outside the *Realpolitik* box:

> Tens of . . . thousands of Armenians vacation on Turkey's Riviera each summer, while up to 40,000 Armenian passport holders are now employed in Istanbul. For a decade, civil society organizations have been setting up a wide range of Turkish-Armenian joint events amongst artists, photographers, youth, journalists, intellectuals, business persons . . . The very day of the Bursa match, twenty of the most prominent Turkish and Armenian journalists met in a nearby hotel to discuss how they could further support reconciliation.
>
> These projects achieve varying success, but each has broadened public support for the recent diplomatic progress. In parallel Turkish thinking about the Armenian genocide question has opened up remarkably. Last December [2008] some 30,000 Turks signed an on-line letter apologizing for what happened in 1915. (Freizer, 2009)

Conclusion

The EU has traveled far and wide with a tacit "theory-in-use" based primarily on membership conditionality. One can imagine what might be possible if the EU's traditional processes of expanding its influence as a Kantian peace system were complemented in Bosnia-Herzegovina by the addition of explicit peacemaking and peacebuilding components similar to the second pillar (good offices and political action) and third pillar (human dimension) of the under-resourced, abruptly terminated UNPREDEP mission in Macedonia.

Indeed, given the remarkable structural convergence – i.e., triangulation (Brewer and Hunter, 2006) – between (1) the three pillars of UNPREDEP, (2) the three levels of conflict reality, (3) Lederach's peacebuilding framework, and (4) the three legs of Barack Obama's "stool" of foreign policy (his 3Ds), it seems clear that, for any intervention in Bosnia-Herzegovina or anywhere else to be successful, relationships and what causes them to become destructive, as well as their symptoms, must be dealt with. It is also clear that the results of peacebuilding would likely be more positive for all concerned if the international community committed itself, at the outset, to various degrees of long-term peacebuilding (e.g., "Marshall Plan"-type) interventions of ten to twenty years' duration.[19]

Accordingly, the EU presence in Bosnia-Herzegovina should be complemented by something like UNPREDEP, with its three pillars of troop deployment (conflict-as-symptoms), good offices and political action (conflict-as-relationships), and the human dimension (conflict-as-underlying-causes-and-conditions). The EU already has a peacekeeping mission in Bosnia-Herzegovina, EUFOR "Althea," which replaced NATO's SFOR on 2 December

2004, in effect extending the international peacekeeping presence in the country. The EU – and certainly some of its members, e.g., Sweden (Eralp, 2009) – has a presence in Bosnia in terms of good offices and the human dimension as well. What may be lacking is an appropriate integrative framework, ensuring, for example, that all "preventive action [strives to deal with] issues by implementing effective development activities through what some experts term . . . a *'conflict prevention lens'* " (Sokalski, 2003, p. 175, emphasis added; see also Paffenholz, 2009a).

On the assumption that there may be other examples of UNPREDEP's lessons being ignored in Bosnia, it would be useful for EU and other architects of post-Cold War peace and security in Europe to revisit those insights in search of further potential policy options for the continuing intervention in Bosnia and missions elsewhere.

UNPREDEP's lessons correspond remarkably well to the findings on "lessons learned" from peacebuilding efforts in general compiled by the Working Group on Lessons Learned of the United Nation's Peacebuilding Commission (UN/PBC, 2008, p. 1). This added value builds on the remarkable overlap between UNPREDEP's three pillars, the three levels of conflict reality, Lederach's peacebuilding framework, and Obama's 3Ds. According to the working group's comprehensive assessment:

> One consistent conclusion that emerged from comparative experiences is that each post-conflict country is unique: there are no "one-size fits-all" models in peacebuilding. There are, however, *useful lessons and common principles for effective peacebuilding that have relevance across different contexts* which include the following:
>
> • Adopting a *holistic and strategic approach*
> • Promoting *national ownership*

- Strengthening *national capacities*
- Providing *sustained engagement*
- Achieving *effective coordination*
- Fostering *mutual accountability*
- Ensuring *prioritization and sequencing*
- Integrating a *gender perspective*
- Encouraging a *regional approach.*

(Ibid.: emphasis added)

Given the enhanced, triangulated value of UNPREDEP as an experiment and model for peacebuilding – each of whose lessons in Macedonia corresponds to those generated by the UN/PBC assessment of peacebuilding in general – integrating this "ad hoc" model with the more "*a priori*" EU would clearly constitute a reinforced basis for improving the chances of the latter to prepare *all* countries of the Western Balkans, including Bosnia-Herzegovina and Kosovo, for successful entry into the Union and, in the process, preempt state failure in the region.[20]

In chapter 4, we address the continuing challenges of peacebuilding in "failed/failing" states that have given, or are likely to give, rise to terrorism. In this case – exacerbated by the worst global financial and economic crises since the Great Depression – the need (but regrettably not the demand) is great for well-funded, regional, integrated, coordinated, multi-issue, interdependent, sequenced, transparent, and conflict prevention-oriented processes. Such processes, to be successful, must empower local women, children, youth and men within a comprehensive framework (e.g., the enhanced 3PF) that would encourage analysts, policymakers, and practitioners to address conflicted relationships and their underlying causes and conditions, as well as symptoms.

In the fifth and final chapter, we address the linkage between complex problem solving and global governance. This includes a crucial role for the United States, essential for future peacebuilding to reflect the triangulated UNPREDEP/ UNPBC lessons learned, enhance the prospects for maximalist ("transformative") interventions to trump minimalist ("technical") interventions, and to close "the painful gap between rhetoric and action in peacebuilding" (Schmelzle and Fischer, 2009, p. 6).

CHAPTER FOUR

Peacebuilding and the "Global War on Terror"

Introduction

Shifting one's attention from the Balkans to the "Global War on Terror" as a source of remaining challenges for peacebuilding is itself a challenge. It represents movement from the relative simplicity of focusing on, and attempting to "manage," a specific region, to the complexity of multiple regions worldwide comprising states that are "utterly incapable of sustaining [themselves as members] of the international community (LaFree et al., 2008, p. 39). For Collier (2007a) there are approximately fifty failed states, while for Ghani and Lockhart (2008) the number may be as high as sixty. Considering that both estimates were made before the onset of the worst global financial and economic crisis since the Great Depression, it is safe to assume that more states have joined, or will join, the list. In this regard, the current (sixth) annual Failed States Index, compiled by the Fund for Peace and *Foreign Policy*, lists sixty of the 177 states it ranked as being among the "most vulnerable" (FP, 2010). Whatever the number, LaFree et al. (2008, p. 54) find a strong correlation between state failure and terrorism, although the presumed linkage may be less clear than has been assumed since 9/11.

The "failed state" category is a conceptual repository of multiple variables, each significant in its own right (e.g., poverty, governmental ineptitude, corruption, unemployment, domestic violence, vulnerability to conflict spillover from neighboring countries), but, when examined together, make for an environment robustly conducive to terrorism: anarchy breeds more anarchy. When we consider the catastrophic shift in the European order wrought by just one terrorist with a pistol on 28 June 1914, followed by the shift in the global order caused by nineteen young men with box cutters on 11 September 2001, the thought of multiple sources of state failure and possible terrorism beyond Iraq, Afghanistan, and Pakistan to scores more, where the rogue use of WMD is becoming ever more likely, makes terrorism a worthy candidate for analysis *and* response through a comprehensive peacebuilding lens.

Terrorism is a bottom-up rendition of globalization that brings the threat of violence to all of us in our daily lives. It is more personal and "intimate" than many other threats to our individual and collective security. Any one person can do it *and*, most importantly, can be impacted by it. Perhaps not surprisingly, we tend to invest a lot more, conceptually and materially, in countering terrorism than we do in dealing with other aspects of the global problematique embedded in World 1 (e.g., water stress) and World 3 (e.g., North–South structural inequities), in part because it is easier and something that we can actually do (and, politically, be "seen" to be doing). According to some, this is precisely what the war in Afghanistan is about and why we must remain there (Lloyd, 2009). But terrorism remains a major challenge for peacebuilding because, in many cases, it represents its failure: peacebuilding either not attempted or peacebuilding that has not adequately addressed the underlying causes and conditions of conflicts and other complex global problems that have worsened. Indeed, increased terrorism in Europe and elsewhere could emerge as one of the consequences of failed peacebuilding in the Balkans!

This chapter argues that, by the time a person becomes a "terrorist," he or she will have undertaken a journey involving a number of experiences that have to be taken into account by those concerned with preventing future acts of terrorism: a major goal worldwide in the post-9/11 world. Despite contrary statements by some world leaders, preventive efforts include negotiating or, more generally, talking with the terrorists themselves to dissuade them from using violence to achieve their goals. The chapter examines a number of insights from conflict analysis and resolution on violent conflict initiation and termination. It concludes with recommendations on how to make peacebuilding a more successful enterprise with regard to nipping terrorism in the bud – clearly a bold aspiration – in particular how to initiate and maintain negotiations or dialogues with those who would do us harm.

Terrorism: An Epiphenomenon of Deep-Rooted Conflict

In order to prevent terrorism, whether of the contingent or absolutist variety (Zartman, 2005),[1] it is essential to deal effectively with the deep-rooted origins of political violence, of which terrorism may be a manifestation or a symptom. Interestingly, this proposition is more widely accepted in the developing than in the developed world. For example, in discussions generated in March 2005 by the plans of former UN Secretary General Kofi Annan for UN reform, the Algerian ambassador to the UN said, "You should not deal with terrorism without addressing its root causes, and its root cause is occupation" (cited in Srulevitch, 2005). In order to stop an ongoing terrorist campaign (e.g., in Paris, Algiers, or Baghdad) or to prevent acts of terrorism from the outset, therefore, a third-party intervener intent on initiating negotiations with terrorists would have to do much more than merely "manage" or "settle" conflicts that have led to terrorism. The third party would have to take steps to "resolve" and/or "transform" such conflicts. This requires a paradigm shift (Kuhn, 1970) from the traditional "counter-terrorist" response, which tends to deal only with symptoms (see Sandole, 2007a, ch. 2).

Mapping Conflicts that Lead to Terrorism

A major premise of this chapter is that the prevention of terrorism can benefit from the multidisciplinary field of conflict analysis and resolution (CAR). Implicit in our discussion in chapter 2 is the proposition that CAR offers a number of concepts that can assist in revealing the nature of the journey from grievance to conflict to terrorism. The first of these is cognitive dissonance, which, according to Leon Festinger (1962), refers to a disconnect between a preferred state of affairs (e.g., not living under occupation) and an actual state of affairs (e.g., living under occupation). Dissonance so defined establishes pathways to other concepts that capture the experience of disconnection: a variably painful gap, perhaps colored by "narcissistic rage" (Kohut, 1971), which those who are affected may attempt to close by violent means, including by acts of terrorism.

One concept associated with "dissonance" is structural violence (Galtung, 1969): a situation whereby members of a certain ethnic, racial, religious, national, socio-economic class, regional, gender, or other "minority group" are denied equal access to political, social, economic, and other resources typically enjoyed and presided over by the dominant "in-group," not because of what members of the minority group have done, but because of who they are – i.e., because of their (often) involuntary membership in those minority identity groups.[2]

Structural violence is a form of power – including resource-access – asymmetry, which may or may not be obvious to those affected by it as well as those who benefit from it. However, when structural violence shifts to cultural violence (Galtung, 1996) – i.e., when the asymmetry is "celebrated" in the popular culture through the media, entertainment industry, political representation, and the like – then the structural violence is likely to be perceived (felt) by those who are among its victims.

Two concepts capture perceived structural violence. One is rank disequilibrium (Galtung, 1964), a form of status inconsistency which occurs when a person scores high on one or some indicators of socio-economic measurement (e.g., education) but low on many others (income, class, profession, health, security, wealth, etc.). The second is relative deprivation (Gurr, 1970), where a person's "value expectancies" (VE) exceed his or her "value capabilities" (VC). Value expectancies are the goods and resources to which one feels entitled, in contrast to value capabilities, which, following a "reality check," are the goods and resources one feels one is likely to obtain and hold on to. When the distance between value expectancies (preferred state of affairs) and value capabilities (actual state of affairs) reaches a critical point, which may differ from person to person, the affected person may attempt to mobilize other members of his or her identity group to close it by violent means (including by acts of terrorism).

Whether or not the gap between the preferred and the actual has reached a critical threshold will likely depend on the outcome of the frustration-aggression cycle (Dollard et al., 1939). "Frustration" occurs when one is blocked from achieving a certain goal at a certain point in time. According to the theory's original formulation (ibid.), whether or not this blockage leads to aggression depends on the interplay of four factors:

1 the *importance* of the blocked goal (e.g., ending military occupation);
2 the *intensity* of the blockage (e.g., use of disproportionate force, imprisonment, targeted assassinations, home demolitions, harassment at checkpoints);
3 the *frequency* of the blockage (e.g., daily, and over many years);
4 the *anticipation of punishment* for responding aggressively to the perceived source of the blockage (e.g., the occupying military forces, the political authority that has deployed them, and their ethnic/religious kin and other supporters worldwide).

At this point in the potential journey from grievance to terrorism, depending upon the nature of the social policy that has been implemented to deal with minority group concerns, the frustrated person may or may not respond – and, if so, violently – to the perceived source of the frustration. If the policy reflects an enlightened, humanistic (*Idealpolitik*) orientation, political authorities will seek to manage, if not reduce and eliminate, the sources of frustration for members of the minority group. If, however, policy reflects the paradigm which has prevailed throughout recorded history, at least since Thucydides' chronicling of the Peloponnesian War (431–404 BC) – when, in 416 BC, Athenian negotiators proclaimed to their Melian counterparts that "The strong do what they can and the weak suffer what they must" (1951, p. 331) – then political authorities will likely seek to reinforce the anticipation of punishment through coercive (*Realpolitik*) means. In the event, they will exacerbate the original frustration–aggression dynamic, in effect, a ticking time bomb.

Here it is useful to be cognizant of Ehud Sprinzak's (1991) observation that groups that eventually engage in terrorism start out nonviolently to try to get their voices (and grievances) heard. It is only when they fail repeatedly, because of their delegitimation by dominant in-groups, that they decide to use violence to "blast their way" into the in-group members' conscious minds. Hence, as Kevin Spacey's serial murderer character poignantly declares in the film *Seven*, "If you want people to listen to you, you can't just tap them on the shoulder; you have to hit them with a sledge-hammer."

When that attack occurs, the frustrated actor's long-term violated needs for identity, recognition, and security (Burton, 1979, 1990, 1997) may finally start to be fulfilled, on account of the affirming, empowering nature of the act and its results. Among terrorism's consequences can be unprecedented media attention and analysis; overreaction by the dominant group, which is continually justified by reference to the act; a clear sense that the act has effectively paralyzed the dominant group's decision-making apparatus; and an increase in the academic, media, and publication worlds' focus on the act and its perpetrators, trying to answer the enigmatic question "Why do they hate us?"

If, at some point, the government of the dominant group communicates, through a back channel (Pruitt, 2006), a willingness to negotiate with the minority group concerned (or vice versa), one challenge then is to explore acceptable ways for dealing resolutely with the grievances that constitute the underlying sources of the minority group's terrorist response to their perceived victimhood.

Unless the grievances are adequately addressed (e.g., finally ending the occupation), members of the minority group who have experienced the affirmation and empowerment provided by the acts and results of political violence are likely to continue resorting to terrorism in response to the dominant group's continued maintenance of the structurally violent status quo through physically and psychologically violent means.

The challenge here, once again, is that saying that something *should* happen (i.e., grievances must be addressed) is not the same as making it happen. The overall journey from (a) unheard grievances to (b) frustration-based rage, (c) acts of terrorism, (d) negotiations, (e) getting voices heard, and (f) having underlying grievances addressed to the satisfaction of all concerned is not straight-forward. Political philosophers of all persuasions, from *Realpolitik* to Marxist (Sandole, 1999, pp. 110–13), claim that political power is rarely, if ever, surrendered (or even "shared") voluntarily, which is precisely the perception of what must be done when grievances are addressed and dealt with to the satisfaction of those whose voices have not been heard and, worse, often suppressed.

There is a need, therefore, for theoretical guidance which can fill in the gaps above between (d) and (f) to complement that which has already been provided, offering some sense of direction for the journey from (a) to (c). We turn now to appropriate insights from the multidisciplinary field of conflict analysis and resolution (CAR), all of which are identifiable – explicitly or implicitly – within the context of the comprehensive checklist, the enhanced three-pillar framework (3PF) discussed in chapter 2.

Conflict Resolution Theory and Terrorism

Shortly after the catastrophic attacks of 11 September 2001, the Institute for Conflict Analysis and Resolution (ICAR) at George Mason University – located not far from one of the targets of the attacks, the Pentagon – convened a meeting of its faculty to discuss what could be done in response to what seemed to be a new form of terrorism: in contrast to earlier forms, the attackers were now, for religious or other reasons, prepared to give up their own lives in the infliction of death and destruction on "soft targets" in the US and elsewhere (Sandole, 2004).

Some of my colleagues declared there was nothing that we could do. Clearly, we could not deal with the obvious (tactical) "law-and-order" issues of protecting passengers on airliners and at airports, retrofitting impenetrable cockpit doors on airliners, tracking down other terrorists who might conduct future attacks (by "burning them out of their caves"), and the like.

What we could do, however, was enhance our understanding of the motivation for such attacks and our capability as a field to recommend long-term as well as shorter-term responses to the "new" terrorism. One immediate consequence was that I established the Working Group on War, Violence, and Terrorism at ICAR to provide an institutional basis for faculty, students, and others to come together to generate responses to the question of what we as a field could do to understand and respond better to post-9/11 terrorism.[3]

Serendipity in the development of triangulated (enhanced) theory

The quest to examine the field of conflict analysis and resolution to distill insights relevant to preventing terrorism received a boost when, some six months following 9/11, a reflective conference on what we know (and don't know) as a field took place during 21–3 March 2002, at John Jay College in New York City (Sandole, 2006a). At the meetings conflict resolution pioneer Morton Deutsch (2003) provided an overview of developments in the field during the previous fifty years. He highlighted nine questions that the field addresses, overlapping many themes generated during other presentations and discussions at the meetings.

1 What are the conditions that give rise to a destructive or constructive process of conflict resolution?

Related themes: absence or presence of proactive problem-solving mechanisms; negative vs. positive perceptions (e.g., presence or absence of stereotypes); fractured vs. fulfilling relationships; absence or presence of effective communication processes; dominance of *Realpolitik* vs. *Idealpolitik* (or a mix of) paradigms; presence or absence of relative deprivation and frustration-based anger.

2 What circumstances, strategies, and tactics allow one party to do better than others?

Related themes: training; education; socio-economic class.

3 What determines the nature of agreements that the parties are able to reach?

Related themes: training; education; socio-economic class; timing.

4 How can third parties be used to prevent conflicts from becoming destructive?

Related themes: training; education; timing; use of dialogue processes to facilitate communication, listening, building of trust, shifting from *Realpolitik* to *Idealpolitik* perspectives (or at least to a more comprehensive paradigm which includes elements of both), empowerment, improved relationships, and pursuit of justice.

5 How can people be educated to manage their conflicts more constructively?

Related themes: sensitivity to costs associated with adhering solely to a *Realpolitik* paradigm; modeling of constructive behavior by others; training; university undergraduate and graduate programs.

6 When and how should third parties intervene in a protracted conflict?

Related theme: timing: intervening proactively "before the house burns down."

7 Why/how do ethnic, religious, and other identity conflicts frequently take on a protracted, destructive character?

    Related themes: socio-economic class and other identity group-based disparities, relative deprivation and frustration-based anger.

8 How applicable to other cultural contexts are theories and processes developed in the US and Western Europe?

    Related themes: generic processes (e.g., Robert Axelrod's [1984] "tit-for-tat"; Vamik Volkan's [1997] "chosen trauma" and "time collapse").

9 How do we overcome oppressive power?

    Related themes: judicious use of *Realpolitik*-based force when conditions warrant, but only as part of a more comprehensive strategy that allows for the subsequent pursuit of *Idealpolitik*-based justice for all concerned in any particular relational system (see Sandole, 1999, ch. 7; 2007a, ch. 3).

In his concluding remarks, Professor Deutsch commented that we don't have enough knowledge to deal with the problems we will face in the future (e.g., among other elements of the global problematique, water shortages; related themes: knowledge deficit; the "ingenuity gap" (Homer-Dixon, 2000)).

Given the nine questions addressed by Professor Deutsch, plus what research methodologists refer to as "triangulation" – i.e., convergent or similar findings on a common area generated by different methods (see Brewer and Hunter, 2006) – it seemed clear that the John Jay conference had produced an "exquisite synergy" that was conducive to the further development and refinement of theory. This was especially true for conflict handling by the parties and third-party conflict management, resolution, and transformation, with implications for understanding and dealing with terrorism (Sandole, 2007a, ch. 2) – all grist for the mill of comprehensive peacebuilding.

Refined conflict resolution theory

This refined theory involves, for domestic and international conflicts, the following steps that disputants and third parties can take when exploring alternatives to violence, thereby enhancing the prospects for peacebuilding not to fail:

1 Establishing, further developing, and maintaining proactive mechanisms at all levels: in effect, responding to Jean-Jacques Rousseau's claim that "wars [and violent conflicts at other levels, including their terrorist manifestations] occur because there is nothing to prevent them" (cited in Waltz, 1959, p. 232).
2 Initiating, in the short term and at other points in time, training and dialogue processes to facilitate communication, trust- and credibility-building, the surfacing of all voices, the development of empathy, the surfacing of negative perceptions (stereotypes), a shifting from *Realpolitik* to *Idealpolitik* perspectives (or at least to a more comprehensive paradigm that includes elements of both), and eventually reconciliation.
3 Initiating, in the middle to long term, processes to manage and reduce disparities between socio-economic, ethnic, religious, and other identity groups within and between states, in order to manage and reduce relative deprivation and frustration-based anger and violent conflict; ultimately improving and further developing long-term relationships by achieving and maintaining significant degrees of social justice for all concerned in any particular relational system.
4 As part of these short-, middle-, and long-term processes, developing and maintaining carefully monitored and coordinated coalitions across class, ethnic, racial, religious, organizational, national, regional, and other identity lines to ensure that everything functions as intended – and, if not, to make the appropriate tactical adjustments or strategic shifts.

Generic drivers of violent conflict

This refined theory implies generic elements that contribute to the etiology of violent conflict across levels and types, among them the suicide bombings carried out by four British-born Muslims in London on 7 July 2005; a plan, approximately one year later, to blow up, with liquid explosives, at least seven American and Canadian airliners departing Heathrow Airport in London for the US; and approximately two years after the London Transport attacks, during the summer of 2007, the efforts of a number of foreign-born Muslim physicians to conduct terrorist attacks in London and Glasgow.[4] These generic elements include:

1 an absence of proactive problem-solving mechanisms (e.g., effective training, communication, monitoring, and early warning processes);
2 a dominance of male gender (and patriarchy);
3 a dominance of *Realpolitik* thinking and behavior;
4 negative perceptions (stereotypes);
5 fractured relationships;
6 class and other identity group-based disparities (absence of justice);
7 an absence of constructive empowerment options (perceived or actual) for those experiencing disparities and injustice; and, consequently,
8 felt relative deprivation and frustration-based anger, including narcissistic rage (Kohut, 1971; Hudson et al., 1999, pp. 31–2).

Conflict between North (West) and South (Islam)

While, clearly, not all Muslims are terrorists and not all instances of the "new" terrorism are carried out only by Muslims (see Bloom, 2005; Pape, 2005), the Muslim connection in 9/11 and subsequent attacks makes it appropriate, if not essential, to examine the relationship between "Western civilization" (the North) and the "Islamic world" (the South) in terms of the generic drivers of violent conflict.

1 There is an absence of effective problem-solving mechanisms to deal with North–South issues, although some might feel that the UN, World Bank, IMF, and World Trade Organization (WTO) already fulfill this need. However, given the massive protests that confront meetings of these international organizations (including, in Bali, Indonesia, during the UN Climate Change Conference of 3–15 December 2007, designed to find a successor to the Kyoto Protocol), it is clear, certainly from many of those protesting, that improvements are possible in this area. For example, there are few positive relationship-building (peacebuilding) mechanisms to deal with Islamic–Western "civilizational" or Israeli–Palestinian concerns.[5] This palpable deficit has likely contributed, to some extent, to hijacked, passenger-filled airliners careening into skyscrapers and Palestinian teenagers blowing themselves up in order to get their voices heard.

2 The dominance of male gender and patriarchy is significant to the extent that most acts of violence worldwide are committed by males aged fifteen to twenty-nine. This is a demographic group that is increasing in the South (see Hudson et al., 1999, p. 81; Kaplan, 2001; Barash, 2002). For example, all nineteen of those who hijacked the four aircraft on 11 September 2001 were male, as are most (but not all) Palestinian suicide bombers. One of the 9/11 hijackers, Mohammed Atta, was apparently not "male enough" in the eyes of his father (Lerner, 2002; Kimmel, 2002). This may have contributed to his participation in what for him and others was undoubtedly an act of intensely "masculine" violence, sacrifice, and heroism.

3 The dominance of virulent, perhaps even vulgar *Realpolitik* thinking and behavior is as clear in the actions of the hijackers of 11 September 2001 as it was in the post-9/11 actions of the Bush administration. It is also clear in Palestinian suicide bombings and Israeli responses. At various levels of conflict, we are witnessing the security dilemma: confrontational, lethal, "bite-and-counterbite" behaviors where, at the end of the day, everyone is worse off than they were before. At some critical point in time, conflict-as-process overwhelms and overtakes conflict-as-startup-conditions, where it does not matter "who threw the first punch," because the process itself, more than the initial causes, then drives the conflict. The conflict has become self-stimulating and self-perpetuating (see Sandole, 1999, 2005b). Hence, *Realpolitik* and its various correlates make war (and, by implication, terrorism) *more*, rather than less, likely (Vasquez, 1993).

4 There are clearly negative stereotypes at work in the relationships between North and South, "Western civilization" and Islamic civilization, Israelis and Palestinians. "Racial profiling," for example, has taken on new meaning in post-9/11 America, where hate crimes and detentions without trial have been recorded, or are feared, at new levels (see Pierre, 2002). Profiling has also been occurring in normally liberal, humanistic Western European countries, where far-right, anti-immigrant politicians have scored impressive electoral gains (see Applebaum, 2002). In the Russian Federation, perhaps, in part, on account of the devastating conflict in Chechnya, white supremacist groups have attacked anyone of "dark" complexion – among others, Chechen, Azerbaijani, and Tajik Muslims, Jews, Indians, Africans, and even fellow Christians (Armenians) (see Baker, 2002). This phenomenon has spread to Britain in the wake of the London bombings, where, among other examples of "profiling," British police

killed a Brazilian man mistakenly suspected of being a suicide bomber (see Frankel and Jones, 2005).

Not only has the "Global War on Terror" (GWOT) replaced (or at least complemented) the post-Cold War unipolar system with a new bipolar system – terrorists vs. the rest of us – it has also created a new binary ethnic/religious/racial system – Arabs vs. non-Arabs, Muslims vs. non-Muslims – which enhances the more traditional economic divide between "have-nots" and "haves," and, indeed, fulfillment of the ultimate trap: the self-fulfilling realization of a "clash of civilizations" (Huntington, 1993, 1996; Baxter, 2004).

5 It is clear, therefore, that fractured relationships exist between the North and the South, Muslims and non-Muslims, Arabs and non-Arabs, Israelis and Palestinians. Indeed, in one variant of the Muslim–non-Muslim relationship, Pakistan and India have threatened to go to war over Kashmir in a way that includes use of nuclear weapons:

> Although the current South Asian crisis seems to have ebbed, the underlying dynamic remains. The next flare-up will be even more dangerous if the region's nuclear confrontation develops in the same direction as the U.S.–Russian standoff – with nuclear missiles on alert, aimed at each other and ready to launch on warning. (Mian et al., 2002)

6 Profound, identity group-based economic and other disparities, and an overall lack of justice, characterize the fractured relationships between North and South, non-Muslims and Muslims, non-Arabs and Arabs, Israelis and Palestinians. Indeed, as was reported thirty years ago by the first Brandt Commission Report (see Brandt 1980a), "one fourth of the world's population (the North) has four-fifths of the world's income, while three-fourths of the world's population (the South) has one fifth of the world's income" (cited in Sandole, 1999, p. 126).

In the North, the average person can expect to live for more than seventy years; he or she will rarely be hungry, and will be educated at least up to secondary level. In the countries of the South the great majority of people have a life expectancy of closer to fifty years; in the poorest countries one out of every four children dies before the age of five; one fifth or more of all the people in the South suffer from hunger and malnutrition; fifty percent have no chance to become literate. (Brandt, 1980a, p. 32; cited in Sandole, 1999, pp. 126–7)

Willy Brandt (1980b, p. 7), former Chancellor of (West) Germany, basically concluded that these objective conditions of structural violence on a grand scale constituted the "great social challenge of our time. [Hence,] the two decades ahead of us may be fateful for mankind" (cited in Sandole, 1999, p. 127). It seems that, with 9/11, global warming, nuclear proliferation, and the worst financial and economic crisis since the Great Depression, we have clearly reached that point.

7 Most importantly, there is the relative absence of viable, "peaceful" alternatives to violent responses to ongoing humiliation, degradation, and structural, cultural, and physical violence (see Galtung, 1969, 1996). This mechanism deficit may be the single most powerful explanation for and predictor of terrorism. Who ensures that the "occupied" Palestinian voice gets heard – the Americans, the Israelis, the Arab League, the Organization of the Islamic Conference, the Palestinian Authority or the Hamas suicide bomber? As Mao Tse-tung (1961) said years ago, "Political power grows from the barrel of a gun." Sad, but true, especially within the context of the dominant political paradigm, *Realpolitik*, against the background of globalization, where events are communicated instantly via the Internet.

Finally, given the interactive accumulation of the above factors:

8 Perceived (felt) structural violence (relative deprivation, rank disequilibrium), frustration, and anger – including narcissistic rage (Kohut, 1971; Hudson et al., 1999, pp. 31–2) – contribute further to the tendency for "Violence [to be] the expression of impotence grown unbearable."[6] Such impotence, Jeanne Knutson tells us, reflects the absence of alternatives to the hopeless, hapless, helpless situation in which terrorists often find themselves and other members of their identity groups:

> Using Erikson's theory of identity formation, particularly his concept of negative identity . . . Knutson (1981) suggested that the political terrorist consciously assumes a *negative identity*. . . . In Knutson's view, terrorists engage in terrorism as a result of feelings of *rage* and *helplessness* over the *lack of alternatives*. Her political science-oriented viewpoint seems to coincide with the *frustration-aggression* hypothesis.
>
> Knutson (1984) . . . carried out an extensive international research project on the psychology of political terrorism. The basic premise of terrorists whom she evaluated in depth was "that their violent acts stem from feelings of *rage* and *hopelessness* engendered by the belief that *society permits no other access* to information-dissemination and policy-formation processes." (Hudson et al., 1999, pp. 30, 34–5, emphasis added; see also Galtung, 1964; and Sprinzak, 1991)

Accordingly, the above eight (triangulated) factors in the North (Western)–South (Islamic) relationship make terrorism more rather than less likely. One goal of starting negotiations with terrorists, therefore, would be to address (and eventually undermine) the causal efficacy of each of these factors in order to prevent this negative trajectory from actually occurring.

Thinking Outside the Box

What, then, can we in the CAR field claim that we know about how to start and maintain effective negotiations with potential or actual perpetrators of terrorism – and/or their recruiters, trainers, parents, and fellow-travelers – that might lead to a shift in attitude, strategy, behavior, and outcome? In other words, what knowledge does the CAR field possess to make +5+5 more salient and compelling than +10–10/–10+10?

This question represents a daunting challenge because the empowerment afforded by terrorism may have become nearly "hard-wired" for some.[7] In the aftermath of 9/11, many Muslims and others became convinced that the world had definitely changed – an unprecedented consequence of "asymmetric warfare."[8] There can be little doubt, therefore, that 9/11 represents the "poster child" of collective efforts by Muslims worldwide to defend the *Umma* against the continuing efforts of "the Crusader" to marginalize and, eventually, destroy Islam.

Many in the West are petrified, even paralyzed, by Islam, Arabs, and anything associated with them, viewing Islamic terror as an existential threat to Western civilization greater than anything experienced at least since World War II – for example, ". . . we have become so frightened of terrorism since Sept. 11, 2001, that we have begun doing the terrorists' job for them by undermining the legal framework of our democracy" (Ignatius, 2007).

> [Here is just] what Osama bin Laden has been hoping for. In a video-taped message in 2004, bin Laden explained his strategy with astonishing frankness. He termed it "provoke and bait": "All we have to do is send two mujahedin . . . [and] raise a piece of cloth on which is written

'al Qaeda' in order to make the generals race there, to cause America to suffer human, economic and political losses." His point has been well understood by ragtag terror groups across the world. With no apparent communication, collaboration or further guidance from bin Laden, small outfits from Southeast Asia to North Africa to Europe now announce that they are part of al Qaeda, and so inflate their importance, bring global attention to their causes and – of course – get America to come racing out to fight them. (Zakaria, 2007, p. 25)

Worse, for many, the threat of Islamic terrorism is developing right in their (*our*) own backyards (Bawer, 2006; Phillips, 2006; Sageman, 2008; Caldwell, 2009). According to suspects' comments in six alleged "martyrdom" tapes played for jurors during a trial in London of eight British Muslims for "allegedly plotting" to blow up at least seven American and Canadian transatlantic airliners in August 2006: "Sheik Osama has warned you many times to leave our lands or you will be destroyed, and now the time has come for you to be destroyed. . . . Stop meddling in our affairs. . . . Otherwise, expect floods of martyr operations . . . we will take our revenge [and leave] your people's body parts decorating the streets" (Sullivan, 2008).

The astonishing "asymmetrical" success of 9/11 has apparently encouraged al Qaeda to obtain weapons of mass destruction for use against the United States, in part to bring about another world-shifting impact, but clearly beyond the "shock and awe" of 9/11:

As early as 1993, Osama bin Laden offered $1.5 million to buy uranium for a nuclear device, according to testimony presented in federal court in February 2001. When the al Qaeda leader was asked in 1998 if he had nuclear or chemical weapons, he responded: "Acquiring weapons for the defense of Muslims is a religious duty. If I have indeed acquired these weapons, then I thank God for enabling me to do so." . . .

Al Qaeda proclaimed a religious rationale to justify the WMD attacks it was planning. In June 2002, a Kuwaiti-born cleric named Suleiman Abu Ghaith posted a statement on the Internet saying that "Al Qaeda has the right to kill 4 million Americans" in retaliation for U.S. attacks against Muslims. And in May 2003, at the same time Saudi operatives of al Qaeda were trying to buy three Russian nuclear bombs, a cleric named Nasir al-Fahid issued a fatwa titled *"A Treatise on the Legal Status of Using Weapons of Mass Destruction Against Infidels."* Interrogations of al Qaeda operatives confirmed that the planning was serious. Al Qaeda didn't yet have the materials for a WMD attack, but it wanted them. (Ignatius, 2007, emphasis added; see also Tenet, 2007, ch. 14).

Implicit here is another challenge for third parties wishing to launch negotiations, even with the less negotiation-susceptible total absolutist terrorists (Zartman, 2005). In addition to the potency of the meaning of the image of oneself as a martyr bent on a mission selflessly to defend the global Muslim community (Frankl, 1959; Hedges, 2002), there is the image of the act being sanctioned by the Almighty. This must make most, if not all, absolutist terrorists totally impervious to being "reasoned with" and eager to join the jihad against "the Crusader." According to one of the British Muslims on trial for allegedly plotting to blow up airliners over the Atlantic during August 2006: "This is revenge for the actions of the U.S.A. in the Muslim lands and their accomplices, such as the British and the Jews. . . . This is a warning to the nonbelievers that if they do not leave our lands, there are many more like us. . . . *We are doing this in order to gain the pleasure of our Lord, and Allah loves us to die and kill in his path"* (Sullivan, 2008; emphasis added).[9]

There is apparently no shortage of young people willing to blow themselves up in order to rid their lands of the occupier. In an interview with the BBC about problems encountered in getting people to become suicide bombers, Taliban spokesman Zabiyullah Mujahed said: "A lot of people are coming to our suicide bombing centre to volunteer. We have a problem with making sure they attack the right targets, avoiding killing civilians. It takes time to train them properly" (BBC, 2007).

With such persons as "subject matter," how can confidence be built with them so that "post-conflict" peacebuilding in this case is more likely to be successful? How can, for example, negotiations be started and maintained with them, especially to dissuade them from selecting the nuclear option, when that has been accorded legitimacy, religious and otherwise?

Toward a "Theory" of Negotiating with Terrorists

One approach to dissuading potential or actual terrorists from committing acts of "catastrophic terrorism" (Hamburg, 2002) would be to plant a contrary idea in their minds. As Rapoport tells us, "what men think or say about human conflict . . . has a great bearing on the nature of human conflict and *its consequences*" (1974, p. 7, emphasis added). Potential or actual terrorists, therefore, would have to become aware of the strategic possibility of viable alternatives to terrorist violence in the pursuit of their goals, before considering and attempting to employ them. However, the journey from awareness to acting on such alternatives is fraught with many challenges.

One possible way to short-circuit this complex process would be to generate cognitive dissonance (Festinger, 1962) – perhaps through creative reality-testing – in the minds of terrorists, resulting in their realization that, far from defending and advancing the interests of the *Umma*, their acts of terrorism would likely be self-defeating and counterproductive. Ideally, the "acute psychological distress" (Kuhn, 1970, pp. 62–4, 112) generated by the dissonance would be resolved by the terrorists coming to the conclusion that terrorism is futile – that they would be, in effect, killing not only innocent others but themselves and, worse, "for nothing"!

To complement efforts to negotiate with terrorists to avoid or cease committing acts of political violence, dominant global players, especially the US, must be convinced that the time has come finally and resolutely to deal with the deep-rooted causes of the frustration that has led to the "narcissistic rage" that terrorists now express violently. Otherwise, their numbers could well expand indefinitely.

There were some positive signs in this regard late in the Bush administration. For example, the "Annapolis Process," launched by the president at the US Naval Academy on 27 November 2007 to commit his administration to securing a two-state solution to the Israeli–Palestinian conflict, was complemented by the efforts of British Prime Minister Tony Blair acting on behalf of the UN, the EU, and the Russian Federation, as well as the US (the "Quartet"), to facilitate Palestinian economic development. Together, Bush and Blair's efforts could have provided the policy setting within which definitive resolution of the Israeli–Palestinian conflict – a pivotal source of anti-Western terrorism – could take place.

Regrettably, this did not occur, although then US Secretary of State Condoleezza Rice could be credited for generating cognitive dissonance for Israelis as well as Palestinians:

> [Dr] Rice . . . warned Israel . . . that its plan to build 300 houses on land captured in the 1967 war risked undermining fresh attempts to forge peace with the Palestinians.
>
> Delivering *what for the Bush administration [was] rare criticism of Israel* over its settlements policy, Ms. Rice said she had told [Israeli Prime Minister] Ehud Olmert's government

it must concentrate on building confidence with the Palestinians in the aftermath of the recent Annapolis conference. (Blitz and Buck, 2007, emphasis added; also see Witte, 2008)

Dr Rice's next steps should have included developing further the perception that the US had finally decided to become "even-handed" in its perhaps "too-little, too-late" efforts to deal with the Israeli–Palestinian conflict. The underlying assumption here is that friends of Israel should try to coax them out of the traditional, *Realpolitik*-driven +10–10/–10+10 option that tends to result in successive, reinforced security dilemmas (–5–5) and, instead, move them toward the *Idealpolitik*-driven (+5+5) option. Given the forty years of US bias solely in favor of Israel (for very understandable reasons), this is clearly no easy feat. However, building on President Bush's "Annapolis Peace Process" – which went very badly indeed (Economist, 2008b; Witte, 2008) –Bush's successor, Barack Obama, is clearly moving in the direction of ensuring a strategic shift toward inclusivity of all the parties – something which, given our discussion in chapter 3, we also need in the Balkans.[10]

For any of this to succeed, however, any awareness of the futility of terrorist violence on the part of terrorists must be complemented by recognition of a "terrorism equivalent" of William James's (1910) moral equivalent of war. The moral virtues and benefits of (asymmetrical) warfare – heroism, selflessness, bravery, discipline, group cohesion, excitement – must become emotionally attached to collective efforts to achieve less lethal, but nevertheless survival-relevant objectives, such as the superordinate goals (Sherif, 1967) or "killer-issues" of global ecological degradation and climate change. Terrorists must be encouraged to ask themselves the question "What is the point of blowing up oneself and others to create a new order if, in fact, the planetary infrastructure for sustaining that order is being progressively eroded and, in some cases, undermined by the terrorists themselves?" They must be persuaded that what might make tactical sense a few days, weeks, months, or even years after an assault on the sensibilities of Americans, Britons, Filipinos, Indonesians, Israelis, Spaniards, and/or others may come back later on to haunt, confound, and confuse the perpetrators themselves.[11]

Former British Prime Minister Gordon Brown made a small step in this direction, as the UN Climate Change Conference in Bali was winding up in December 2007, by reaching out to the Taliban in Afghanistan (much like US forces had done with Sunni insurgents and Shiite militias in Iraq; see, e.g., Dehghanpisheh et al., 2008). He recommended that they consider achieving their goals by laying down their arms and joining Afghanistan's political process, indicating that "they had a legitimate role to play" (FT, 2007).

Since Gordon Brown's initial comments, "talking with the enemy" has taken on new urgency in Afghanistan, with Afghan President Hamid Karzai actively pursuing negotiations with the Taliban, mediated by Pakistan and Saudi Arabia, two countries that recognized the Taliban government in pre-9/11 Afghanistan: "Besides working on ways to reconcile with the Taliban's top leaders, the Afghan government is finalizing a plan to coax low- and mid-level insurgent fighters off the battlefield" (Riechmann, 2010). In preparation for a "peace jirga" with community leaders and tribal elders planned for late April or May 2010, President Karzai met on 22 March 2010 with a five-member delegation from Hezb-i-Islami, led by former mujaheddin Gulbuddin Hekmatyar, a warlord and a prime minister in the 1990s, and designated by the US as a terrorist. Hekmatyar is also one of the three top leaders of the Afghan insurgency. The fact that this meeting took place is an indication of Karzai's seriousness in pursuing reconciliation. Indeed, unless these talks produce an endgame to halt the war, there is no possible way that President Obama can start, as planned, to withdraw US forces from Afghanistan by July 2011 (see Rashid, 2010).[12]

We can distill from the foregoing the skeletal structure of a political strategy for negotiating (or otherwise communicating) with terrorists, where potential third parties can:

1 open up and pursue channels of communication with terrorists or those likely to become terrorists, if necessary through secret "back-channel" means (see Pruitt, 2006);

2 use "creative reality-testing" to encourage terrorists to experience dissonance ("acute psychological distress") through the facilitated experience of a disconnect between (a) sacrificing the lives of themselves, their fellows, and others and (b) the realization that those sacrifices may amount to nothing;

3 facilitate the development of the awareness that terrorists could achieve their goals through less lethal means associated with issues that transcend narrow, zero-sum concerns with negative-sum ("lose–lose") consequences; and, most importantly,

4 encourage traditional great power defenders of the status quo, especially the US, to shift aspects of their policies in order to complement efforts to persuade those bent on terrorism from committing senseless acts of political violence.

Building upon Hans Toch's (1966) innovative concept of the peer interview, it might be helpful if the third party attempting to open up communications with terrorists was someone who looked like them, sounded like them, spoke their languages, and was a member of the same religion – and even of the same radical organizations (e.g., Muslim Brotherhood). Such an approach has been undertaken as part of fairly successful "deradicalization" efforts in Indonesia (Economist, 2007a), Egypt (Economist, 2007b), Pakistan

(Brulliard, 2010), and Saudi Arabia, Iraq, Britain, and the Netherlands (Stern, 2010).

One innovative recommendation in this regard comes from Ashley Bommer, a member of the US mission to the United Nations during the Clinton administration, with regard to Pakistan, "the center of world terrorism":

> The heart of the Taliban and al-Qaeda insurgency is in Balochistan [with 77 tribes], the Northwest Frontier Province and the tribal belt along Pakistan's border with Afghanistan known as the Durand Line [with 60 tribes]. . . .
>
> Pakistan cannot tackle the insurgents alone. *These harsh mountainous areas have never been controlled or conquered by military forces.* Aerial bombing raids by the Pakistani military to fight the insurgency only alienate the populace as civilians are killed and villages destroyed [also see Pruitt, 2006].

An effective counterterrorism strategy requires a global ground response to forge a *cooperative relationship* with the tribes that harbor the insurgents [including Osama bin Laden and his deputy Ayman al-Zawahiri] and the Frontier Corps responsible for border security. *We need to offer them more than the insurgency is offering* (Bommer, 2008, emphasis added).

Bommer's plan is to empower the oppressed people in the border areas to be allies against the insurgents. This would be done by establishing a "Global Tribal Fund" to raise money from around the world and direct money into a three-pronged strategy, consisting of:

1 Tribal Scouts: a coalition of locally recruited [Pashtun and Balochi] tribesmen and tribeswomen who would begin to contact and *negotiate* with the tribes in the border areas. . . .
2 Tribal Life Support: This would include provision of water, roads, transportation, health care, education, employment opportunities and security to live and work. . . .
3 Tribal Security Training, for the Frontier Corps – the paramilitary force consisting of close to 85,000 *locally*

> *recruited tribesmen who know the language, the tribes and the culture and are the logical security forces.* (Ibid., emphasis added)

Bommer concludes that "the need is urgent," making a powerful case for the "peer" approach to "negotiating with terrorists" – and, indeed, for long-term peacebuilding (see Lederach, 1997):

> Unless we help the local population, [al-Qaeda and the Taliban] will continue to erode the stability of both Pakistan and Afghanistan, *no matter how many forces and military measures we use.*
>
> To defeat extremism, we need a global response – an *independent public and private partnership* aimed at improving the lives of the people of the region. *We need native, on-the-ground, face-to-face negotiations.* We need to switch our ideology from winning the war to winning the border. (Bommer, 2008, emphasis added)[13]

President Barack Obama and his secretary of state Hilary Rodham Clinton seem, with their "3Ds approach" (version of the three levels of conflict reality) – defense, diplomacy, development – to have heard Bommer's call! Nevertheless, as of this writing, the emphasis of the Obama administration seems to be more on the first D at the expense of the second and third. According to Fareed Zakaria:

> The focus [in Afghanistan] must shift from nation building to *deal making*. The central problem in Afghanistan is that the Pashtuns, who make up 45 percent of the population and almost 100 percent of the Taliban, *do not feel empowered.* We need to start talking to them, whether they are nominally Taliban or not. *Buying, renting, or bribing Pashtun tribes* should become the centerpiece of America's stabilization strategy, as it was Britain's when it ruled Afghanistan. (Zakaria, 2009, emphasis added)

Conclusion

Given that traditional efforts at counter-terrorism tend further to radicalize the identity groups among which terrorists develop and which they represent (Pruitt, 2006), it is essential to start talking with them, perhaps first secretly but then openly, through people who look like them and speak their languages. Such talks can also occur directly or through an intermediary, such as the role played by Turkey in Israel's negotiations with Syria, by Egypt in Israel's negotiations with Hamas, by Germany in Israel's negotiations with Hezbollah, and by Saudi Arabia and Pakistan in Afghanistan's negotiations with the Taliban.

Once negotiations are underway, according to Jonathan Powell (2008), chief of staff for former British Prime Minister Tony Blair during ten years of negotiations leading to the Good Friday Agreement for Northern Ireland, steps should be taken to keep talks going. If terrorist groups do put their weapons aside, it is imperative to keep them talking, which necessitates constant attention and engagement. Israel clearly agreed, given its long-lasting negotiations with Hamas using Egypt as a go-between. These led to a six-month ceasefire agreement (Bekker and Saleh, 2008) which, regrettably, collapsed with Israel's assault on Gaza in January 2009. By contrast, former George W. Bush seemed to disagree, even when addressing Israel's parliament:

> When he spoke to [the Knesset] on May 15th, Bush blasted those who sought "the false comfort of appeasement" by negotiating with terrorists and radicals in the Middle East. Barack Obama assumed the barb was aimed at him. He in turn accused Mr. Bush and John McCain, the Republican candidate, of "hypocrisy and fear mongering".
>
> Mr. Obama had it right. Speaking to the enemy is an ordinary part of diplomacy and does not on its own amount

to appeasement. . . . Strange, then, that the very Mr. Bush who admonished the appeasers from Israel's parliament has allowed Americans to negotiate with [North Korea] for years. If these talks ever make Kim Jong-Il give up his nukes, nobody in his right mind will hold Mr. Bush's decision to talk against him. And if it is fine to speak to North Korea, why rule out talking, as Mr. Obama says he would, to Iran? As it happens, American diplomats already talk to their Iranian counterparts, though only about Iraq. (Economist, 2008a)

Clearly, Mr Bush was disingenuous in this case – another example of the "rhetoric–reality" disconnect that characterized his presidency (see Sandole, 2006b). Perhaps his successor will be more assertive in establishing dialogues with those who would do us harm, by building positive relationships (Lederach, 1997; Saunders, 2005) through dialogue and other means, realizing that the only alternative is to "burn them out of their caves" and, self-fulfillingly, to watch the numbers of enraged, empowered terrorists grow exponentially.

The problem may already be with us, as revealed by former CIA case officer Marc Sageman in his warning about the new generation of Islamist terrorist:

> The old guard [of al-Qaeda, "huddled in the Afghan–Pakistani border area"] is still dangerous and still plotting spectacular attacks. But it is the new wave that more urgently requires our attention. This cohort is composed of *homegrown* young wannabes who dream of glory and adventure, who yearn to belong to a heroic vanguard and to root their lives in a greater sense of *meaning* [Frankl, 1959]. Inspired by tales of past heroism, they hope to emulate their predecessors, even though, for the most part, they can no longer link up with al-Qaeda Central in the Pakistani badlands. *Their potential numbers are so great that they must now be*

seen as the main terrorist threat to the West. (Sageman, 2008, emphasis added)

For Sageman, the "process of radicalization," by which fairly ordinary youth "come to be so attracted to political violence . . . consists of four prongs, which need not occur in sequence":

1 having a sense of moral outrage;
2 seeing this anger as part of a "war on Islam" (e.g., Western occupation of Muslim lands; see Pape, 2005);
3 believing that this view is consistent with one's everyday grievances (e.g., unemployment and discrimination in host country); and
4 mobilizing through networks.

These elements of radicalization into terrorist violence are consistent with comments made in the "martyrdom tapes" by the eight British Muslim men on trial in London for allegedly plotting to blow up airliners over the Atlantic in August 2006 (see Sullivan, 2008).[14] These characteristics also fit young French Muslims, who "grew up and work in suburbs that became emblematic of the *frustration* among second- and third-generation immigrant youths that led to three weeks of riots in France in [October-November] 2005" (Bennhold, 2008, emphasis added).

While Mr Bush may have felt that talking with (potential) terrorists and radicals is a "foolish delusion," equivalent only to efforts to appease Hitler before the start of World War II, his State Department fortunately thought otherwise:

[a] small but growing [number] of influential Muslims in Europe [have] been invited to the United States on 21-day trips organized by the State Department as part of its International Visitor Leadership Program. The longstanding program, which seeks to introduce future leaders from

around the world to the United States, has become part of
an American effort [after 9/11] to reach out to Europe's
Muslims, especially the disaffected young people who
American officials fear could fall prey to jihadist talk. (IHT,
2008)

It is imperative, however, to ensure that such "consciousness-
raising" is embedded within a strategy of long-term structural
and cultural as well as more short- and medium-term personal and relational change (Lederach, 1997, ch. 6). Hence,
with regard to Afghanistan, "which requires an end to violence, followed by stability and development, in order for its
sense of nationhood to be developed:" . . . "Proper US strategy toward the country should be a mixture of nation-building, stability operations, long-term humanitarian and
economic development, precision-based counter-terrorism
strikes, political negotiations with the Taliban – plus counter-
insurgency to put down the Taliban" (Moselle, 2010).

Nothing much will have been achieved if young French
Muslims return to Clichy-sous-Bois and other French suburbs
from their leadership visits to the United States and they
continue to be subjected to neglect, discrimination, unemployment, frustration, and rage. French President Nicolas
Sarkozy, himself a veteran of the leadership visits to the
United States (Bennhold, 2008), served as interior minister
during the 2005 riots and, arguably, given his volatile rhetoric
and policies at the time, played a role in those disturbances.
He clearly has his work cut out.

So does the first occupant of the White House in the post-
Bush era, especially with regard to climate change, stressed
resources, WMD proliferation, state failure, and other elements of the global problematique in addition to global terrorism. This necessitates the US playing a leading role in
global governance to facilitate the effective tackling of these
and other complex, often interconnected global problems.

This is precisely what President Sarkozy indicated at Columbia University in New York City on 29 March 2010 with regard to the global financial and economic crisis: "The world needs an open America, a generous America, an America that shows the way, an America that listens." And it is to global governance and the US role in it that we now turn.

CHAPTER FIVE

The US and the Future of Peacebuilding

Introduction

Our journey in this volume began in chapter 1 with a discussion of the global problematique, comprising complex problems that defy the efforts of any one actor, even the world's surviving superpower, to solve on its own. Such problems, increasing in ferocity and interdependent consequences, appear to exacerbate political, ethnic, and other conflicts typically dealt with, at least conceptually, by conflict analysis and resolution (CAR) researchers and academics, as well as by policymakers, who tend to ignore the impact on these conflicts of other elements of the global problematique. We identified peacebuilding in its various framings – reactive vs. proactive, ad hoc vs. comprehensive, minimalist vs. maximalist – as an overarching approach for dealing usefully with these conflicts and the complex global problems that help to sustain them and which, in turn, are sustained by the conflicts (e.g., poverty–conflict–poverty).

In chapter 2, we identified a number of frameworks, "checklists," that could be useful in pursuing a peacebuilding approach to dealing with these conflicts and their complex interdependent relationships with various global problems: the prisoner's dilemma, tit-for-tat, the three levels of conflict reality, Lederach's leadership pyramid, Dugan's "nested paradigm," Lederach's peacebuilding framework, the three-pillar framework (3PF), and, finally, as an amalgam of the other frameworks, a comprehensive checklist, the enhanced 3PF.

We examined peacebuilding's record in chapter 3, noting the "goodness of fit" between it and what a comprehensive frame such as the enhanced 3PF would lead us to expect. The record is rather mixed, involving an absence of conceptual and operational integration and coherence, an absence of coordination and of a regional orientation in implementation, the predominance of donor-driven parochial, single issue foci, and a major assumption, implicit in the liberal paradigm, of a "single size fits all" approach to peacebuilding, not to mention a negative view of IGOs and NGOs involved in development. In addition, complementing these and other shortcomings is an institutional preference for a minimalist approach to peacebuilding which leaves unaddressed the deep-rooted, underlying causes and conditions of conflicts. Finally, exacerbating these and other deficits is a broken, dysfunctional international humanitarian system. We concluded chapter 3 by examining the United Nations' first-ever (and only) violent conflict prevention mission, UNPREDEP, in Macedonia and the European Union's overall efforts to realize Immanuel Kant's "perpetual peace" in Europe and worldwide in the post-World War II, post-Cold War, and post-9/11 worlds.

Concluding chapter 3 in this way allowed us to examine the efforts of the UN and the EU against the background of "lessons learned" compiled by the UN's new peacebuilding architecture – specifically, the Peacebuilding Commission (PBC). While the European Union has been the greatest accomplishment, the dominant exemplar, of peacebuilding in the last sixty years, the Israeli–Palestinian conflict has been the greatest failure, driving terrorism locally, regionally, and worldwide. Indeed, according to al Qaeda founder and funder Osama bin Laden, this conflict played a pivotal role not only in al Qaeda's creation but in the 11 September 2001 attacks on New York City and Washington, DC. Accordingly, in chapter 4, we examined the continuing challenges for peacebuilding of global terrorism, revealing, through application of the 3PF, a major lesson: the potency of continuing dialogue even with "our enemies"!

We will now, in this concluding chapter, attempt to "connect the dots" exposed by our discussion in the previous four chapters, especially with regard to the global governance necessary to deal with the complex transnational problems driving ethnic, political, and other conflicts which, in turn, help to sustain the underlying problems.

The US as the World's Indispensable Nation

In the conclusion to his comprehensive review of violent conflict prevention, or "pre-conflict peacebuilding," Michael Lund – in many ways the primary shaper of the concept and praxis of violent conflict prevention – maintains that the prospects for preventive action can be enhanced if three conditions are met: (1) consolidate what is known; (2) focus the consolidated knowledge on emerging (i.e., latent) conflicts; and (3) conduct more basic research, especially on the conditions under which certain combinations and sequences of preventive tools are more likely to be successful for certain stages of conflicts (Lund, 2009, pp. 307–8).

Lund himself has played a major role in consolidating knowledge about pre-conflict peacebuilding (violent conflict prevention). Generalizing these criteria to post-conflict peacebuilding, Charles Call and Elizabeth Cousens (2008) have made a significant input toward clarifying what is known. In addition, Neclâ Tschirgi (2004) and her colleagues at the newly established Peacebuilding Support Office (UN/PBSO, 2008) of the United Nations Peacebuilding

Commission (UN/PBC, 2008) have made impressive contributions.

Insights implicit in what is known could be further explored via research programs and, in some cases, tested as hypotheses. Such exploration/testing could also occur in the field when, at some point(s) after implementation of interventions, evaluation of mission effectiveness could take place.[1] In either case, "evidence-based practice" (EBP) – an idea associated with the behavioral health and social service fields (Ray, 2008) as well as peacebuilding (UN/PBSO, 2008, p. 2) – would be the objective.

It is precisely EBP that policymakers should want to use in responding to either emerging conflicts or post-[violent] conflict situations. Although Lund (2009, p. 307) mentions the UN, the EU, regional organizations such as the OSCE, governments, and NGOs, as well as the US, he clearly has a prominent role in mind for the United States, which both Bill Clinton and Madeleine Albright have famously referred to as "the indispensable nation" (Albright, 2008, p. 20).

If not the "new Rome," then what might "indispensable" mean in this context? In his now classic work on *Preventing Violent Conflicts*, published during President Clinton's second term, Lund tells us:

> If the idea of a multilateral, stratified regime of preventive diplomacy is to become a reality, it must be championed by an actor or actors of global stature, able both to advocate the adoption of such a plan and to actively support it at the local, regional, and global levels. For several reasons, the [US] is not necessarily the only, but clearly one of the best candidates to undertake this role. In the first place, the [US] has the world's most extensive foreign policy bureaucracy and information-gathering apparatus, thus affording it unparalleled opportunities to become involved in or supportive of preventive diplomacy. . . . [In effect,] the [US] remains the

> one actor on the world stage that can marshal the political will to provide leadership and resources on the widest range of issues. (1996, pp. 195–6)

Similarly, in her *Memo to the President Elect*, before the election of Barack Obama, Secretary Albright acknowledges:

> Although [the US] has much in common with others, it has no current competitor in power and reach. This creates opportunities but also temptations. For better or worse, American actions serve as an example. If we attempt to put ourselves outside the law, we invite others to do the same. That is when our moral bearings are lost and the foundation of our leadership becomes suspect. I have always believed America is an exceptional country, but that is because we have led in creating standards that work for everyone, not because we are an exception to the rules. (2008, p. 21)

For Secretary Albright, therefore, the eight years of the Bush administration, which some commentators have characterized as the worst presidency in American history (see Sandole, 2006c),[2] did not undermine America's pre-eminent position in violent conflict prevention (pre-conflict peacebuilding) in terms of which Lund framed it earlier. What can we say about the first post-Bush occupant of the Oval Office, Barack Obama, that might agree with, or detract from, the sanguine Lund/Albright view of the prominent role of the US in peacebuilding?

The Election of Barack Obama

When Americans went to the polls on Tuesday, 4 November 2008, they launched a revolution in American society:

> 1 they elected a black man, Barack Obama, in a country that is still coming to terms with its racist past;

2 Obama's disconnect with his predecessor in the White House, George W. Bush, could not be starker; and

3 Obama's promise for emerging from the abyss of the Bush presidency is palpable on a worldwide scale.

Race in America

Volumes could be, and have been, written about race in America, beginning with the genocidal conquests of indigenous peoples by the Spanish Conquistadors and other Europeans in South and North America, followed by the ubiquitous African slave trade, including in the Caribbean. African Americans – the identity group with which most Americans and others worldwide associate President Obama – have been slaves, servants, and segregated second-class (non)citizens in a quasi-apartheid social system, subjected to lynching and other egregious violations of their basic humanity (see Myrdal, 1962; Alexander, 2010). Against this background, Barack Obama emerged as the 44th president of the United States: truly a revolutionary development!

Obama's departure from Bush

Volumes could also address this theme, and will continue to do so for years to come (see Sandole, 2006c). The presidency of George W. Bush was characterized by aggressive unilateralism, resulting in a "war of choice" in Iraq whose only beneficiaries seem to be Halliburton, Black Water USA/World, oil companies, and, of course, Iran (see Haass, 2009). The Iraq war, predicated upon dubious premises, has killed more than 4,000 Americans and wounded more than 30,000 others, who have returned home in some cases to substandard medical treatment. The war has also killed, wounded, and displaced tens of thousands of Iraqis. According to the CIA and other intelligence agencies, the war has become a PR coup for al Qaeda and a magnet for many Muslim males worldwide, radicalizing them to participate in the jihad against "the Crusader." In the process, they have been "tested under fire," learning how to kill Americans and other "infidels" and "apostates," before returning home prepared to continue their "holy war," whether in Peshawar, Mumbai, Amman, Cairo, Gaza, Mindanao, Pattani, Bali, London, Madrid, Amsterdam, Brussels, Moscow, Brooklyn, or Jersey City. Abu Ghraib, Guantánamo Bay, "extraordinary rendition," violations of Americans' and others' civil rights (including due process), incompetence, and total failure on multiple domestic (e.g., Hurricane Katrina) and international (e.g., the war in Afghanistan) fronts have also come to characterize the Bush administration. Further, Bush's "Hobbesian state-of-nature" political/economic philosophy is disturbingly compatible with the current global financial and economic crisis – the most catastrophic since the Crash of 1929 (see Sandole, 2005b, 2006c).

These national and global developments helped set the stage for Barack Obama's presidency. He is a black man whose middle name is Hussein. His mother was a white Christian from Kansas, his father a Muslim from Kenya. He lived as a child in Indonesia and Hawaii. For these and other reasons – for example, his community organizing work in Chicago (Obama, [1995] 2004) – Obama offers hope to millions domestically and worldwide for bringing together people from a wide variety of backgrounds to work on constructive change toward open and accountable government, enhanced human and civil rights, and a return of America to its historical and cherished role as a founding architect of liberal democracy, plus a renewal of America's mission in assuming a leadership role in galvanizing others to help solve complex global problems.

Obama's promise

President Obama's overall promise to "change America and the world" derives from his multiracial, multicultural, and multi-religious background, his ascent from an economically strained (but loving) childhood to the heights of Harvard Law School and editorship of the *Harvard Law Review*, and his experience as a community organizer on the South Side of Chicago, assisting the survival of some of America's "Wretched of the Earth" (Fanon, 1968). As a consequence, he possesses an uncanny capability to see the world in terms of multiple perspectives, including those captured in Samuel Huntington's (1993, 1996) "clash of civilizations."

Being able to see the world empathically as others do, including those against whom Bush had been perceived to be at war, enables Obama to be the "global community organizer," bringing people together from a wide variety of perspectives and, through dialogue, arriving at consensus on how things can and should be done. In this way, he is clearly an agent of the "empathic civilization" (see Rifkin, 2009).

Obama's global problem-solving agenda

President Obama is in agreement with, among others, the Brookings Institution's Managing Global Insecurity project that "Global problems require global solutions!" (MGI, 2008a). Subsumed under this radical shift from the policies of President Bush is the belief that "National interest has become global interest, and global interest is national interest!" As Obama has said, "We are all in this together!" This implies inclusivity of voices, especially those who have never been heard, who tend to be marginalized, disrespected, oppressed, and even killed – a major component of the genesis of terrorism. The recent expansion of the G7/8 to the G20 in mobilizing global efforts to counter the current financial and economic crisis reflects this recognition of a "new realism."

Implied here is a need for global *governance* (not government), where representatives of states, international governmental organizations, nongovernmental organizations, indigenous peoples, religion, the business world, media, and others come together to listen to each other respectfully as they brainstorm solutions to complex global problems.

Implicit here is also the necessity to change traditional mindsets, to undergo a "paradigmatic shift," or develop a capacity to "think outside the box" (Kuhn, 1970). One of President Obama's distinguishing characteristics is a motivation and capacity to help shift people away from zero-sum (+10−10/−10+10) *Realpolitik*, and its accompanying "security dilemmas" (−5−5), and toward a more positive-sum (+5+5), global problem-solving world view.

In addition, Obama believes that there is still a need for American leadership in the world, not as the hegemon – the "new Rome" – characteristic of George W. Bush's neoconservative America, especially during his first term, but as a leader "by example" and source of resources in joint efforts to tackle pressing global issues (e.g., by providing airlift capacity to EU peace operations in Africa).

Obama's foreign policy goals

In July 2008, then presidential candidate Obama (2008) delivered his first foreign policy speech at the Ronald Reagan Building in Washington, DC, indicating that, as president of the United States, he would focus on five primary issues:

1 ending the war in Iraq responsibly;
2 dealing more effectively with al Qaeda and the Taliban in Afghanistan and Pakistan;
3 preventing weapons of mass destruction from falling into the hands of terrorists;
4 breaking America's dependence on foreign (e.g., Middle Eastern) oil and, in the process, undermining the escalating trajectory toward global warming;
5 forging regional and global partnerships to deal with other pressing issues (e.g., the Israeli–Palestinian conflict).

Each of these goals has a bearing on security elsewhere in the world. For instance, ending the war in Iraq would deprive the theatre of operations in Asia – the regional setting for the new rising powers of India and China (Mahbubani, 2008; Zakaria, 2008) – of its allure to global jihadists. By dealing effectively with al Qaeda and the Taliban in Afghanistan and Pakistan – clearly, no mean feat! – President Obama would be closing down sources of inspiration, recruitment, and training for jihadists, including those who might be drawn from, and then return to, countries in Asia. By preventing WMD from falling into the hands of terrorists through underground networks such as those established by the "Father of the Islamic Bomb," Dr Abdul Qadeer Khan of Pakistan,[3] Obama would be reducing the likelihood that, for example, a nuclear device might be used against an American city – an operation for which a Saudi Wahhabist cleric has given permission to Osama bin Laden to conduct (Frantz and Collins, 2007, pp. xi–xii, 263–5; Linzer, 2004) – or any other city. Breaking America's dependence on Middle Eastern (especially Saudi) oil would reduce the level of indirect support for Saudi jihadists such as Osama bin Laden and terror operations in, among others, Asia (e.g., Mumbai). And dealing effectively and resolutely with the Israeli–Palestinian conflict – the primary driver of global terrorism – should bring about a reduction in the worldwide frequency and intensity of terrorism.

In an article entitled "Renewing American Leadership" in the journal *Foreign Affairs*, then presidential candidate Obama wrote:

> as we strengthen NATO, we must build new alliances and partnerships in other vital regions. As China rises and Japan and South Korea assert themselves, I will work to forge a *more effective framework in Asia* that goes beyond bilateral agreements, occasional summits, and ad hoc agreements, such as the six-party talks on North Korea. We need *an inclusive infrastructure with the countries of East Asia* that can promote stability and prosperity and help confront transnational threats from terrorist cells in the Philippines to Avian flu in Indonesia. I will encourage China to play a responsible role as a growing power – to help lead in addressing the *common problems of the twenty-first century*. We will compete with China in some areas and cooperate in others. *Our essential challenge is to build a relationship that broadens cooperation while strengthening our ability to compete.* (2007, p. 12, emphasis added)

Exactly one year later, when he articulated his five foreign policy objectives, he said: "It's time to strengthen *our partnership* with Japan, South Korea, Australia and the world's largest democracy – India – to create a stable and prosperous Asia. It's time to engage China on *common interests like climate change,* even as we continue to encourage their shift to a more open and market-based society" (Obama, 2008, emphasis added).

Clearly, what the president has in mind is working with the countries of East Asia to develop new infrastructure to deal with the problems of the region. Such infrastructure could be based upon existing institutions and mechanisms, such as the Association of South East Asian Nations (ASEAN),

ASEAN + 3 (China, Japan, and South Korea), the ASEAN Regional Forum (which includes, among others, Russia, the US, and the EU), and/or the Six Party Talks on North Korea, which is the preference of former Australian Prime Minister Kevin Rudd (see ABC, 2008). As implied in the Brookings Institution's Managing Global Insecurity project, the European Union could provide a model of global governance to help upgrade these institutions and mechanisms.

Realizing US Foreign Policy Goals through Enhanced Global Governance and Problem Solving

For example, at the conference at which the Managing Global Insecurity project's *Plan for Action* (MGI, 2008a) was presented, Brookings president Strobe Talbott said:

> The European Union is the most impressive, accomplished, and promising experiment in transnational governance on the planet today, and that has been immensely good for the half billion or so people of Europe. It has taken a huge swath of real estate, which is as bloodied as any on the planet historically, a region of the world where there was a major war every generation from the 17th century on up to the E-day, and turned it into a zone of peace. No mean accomplishment. (MGI, 2008b, p. 63)

Following Talbott's remarks, Javier Solana, then the EU's High Representative for the Common Foreign and Security Policy, commented:

> I think the European Union is the best example today of how [we] can begin to resolve [the] contradiction [between the global and the local]. . . . Therefore, the [EU] is a model which is good for us, and I think it will be good for others, and that's why other parts of the world are beginning to

[understand] the European Union as a model [e.g., ASEAN].
(Ibid., p. 68)

However, at a time when the European Union, like states
and other actors in the global system, is under assault by the
worst economic and financial crisis since the Great Depression,
framing the EU in this positive light may be, at best, idealistic
and, at worst, disingenuous, especially since the EU, like
others, is tilting, more and more, toward dangerous, lose–lose
(−5−5) protectionism:

> Jose Manuel Barroso, the president of the European
> Commission, says this resurgence of economic nationalism
> is not a "specifically European" problem. He is right.
> Protectionism is on the rise everywhere from Washington to
> Delhi.
>   Yet if Europe, with its deep experience of shared interests,
> cannot resist the pressures, how can it expect others to
> uphold open markets? (Stephens, 2009). The stress on the
> EU is certainly real: "The risk now is that, as the recession
> deepens, popular disturbances become self-sustaining: that
> a defensive move here fans the embers of nationalism there;
> that the single market unravels. The newer democracies of
> the Union in eastern and central Europe are particularly
> vulnerable." (Ibid.).

Germany's former foreign minister Joschka Fischer has gone
further, arguing that not only is Europe "at the beginning of
a huge world crisis that will put [it] under extreme pressure
and strain," but "that the fallout from the economic crisis will
undermine, if not destroy, the extraordinary achievement of
EU enlargement that brought eastern and western Europe
together. [The crisis] could also threaten the single market"
(cited in Quentin Peel, 2009).

Despite these risks in the short- to middle-term, however
– which are remarkably similar to the failure of the Socialist

Second International to prevent World War I (see Waltz, 1959, ch. 5) – the EU remains a viable model for regional governance elsewhere and, ultimately, for global governance as well, because of its impressive status as the only viable candidate anywhere for Kant's "perpetual peace" system. This singular uniqueness of the EU explains its relationship to the Managing Global Insecurity project, where, among other things, Javier Solana is an MGI advisory group member. According to Solana:

> The aim of the MGI project is ambitious and urgent: to launch a new reform effort for the global security system in 2009 . . . for the global system is in serious trouble. *It is simply not capable of solving the challenges of today.* You all know the list: terrorism, nuclear proliferation, climate change, pandemics, failing states . . . *None can be solved by a single government alone.* (MGI, 2008a, p. 5, emphasis added)

This is also the view of US Secretary of State Hillary Rodham Clinton, who represents the official foreign policy voice of President Obama's approach to global problem solving. During her first trip abroad as secretary of state, which, in recognition of recent shifts in economic power from West to East, was to Asia, Clinton remarked that the purpose of her trip was to create networks of partners in order to deal with the problems that no nation, even the US, can deal with alone.

The European Commission's John McClintock (2008; Corner, 2008) attributes this global problem-solving deficit to the absence of appropriate global governance based on the "shared sovereignty" principle exemplified by the European Union. Interestingly, the MGI project talks about "responsible sovereignty," which appears to be on a continuum leading eventually to shared responsibility:

> The MGI Project's consultations have informed and validated the view that a new era of international cooperation

should be built on the principle of *responsible sovereignty*: the idea that states must take responsibility for the external effects of their domestic actions – that sovereignty entails obligations and duties towards other sovereign states as well as to one's own citizens. To protect national security, even to protect sovereignty, states must negotiate rules and norms to guide actions that reverberate beyond national boundaries. Responsible sovereignty also implies a positive interest on the part of powerful states to provide weaker states with the capacity to exercise their sovereignty responsibly – a *responsibility to build*. (MGI, 2008a, p. 10, emphasis in original)

Among the current contenders for global governance, in addition to a radically reformed United Nations, are the "League of Democracies" (Kagan, 2008); "Concert of Democracies" (Slaughter and Ikenberry, 2008); "Union of Unions" (Leonard, 2005), and "Global Union of Democracies" (McClintock, 2008; Corner, 2008). In its consultations with concerned, relevant individuals in Africa, Asia, Europe, Latin America, and the Middle East, the MGI project found few supporters for either the "League of Democracies," championed by Senator John McCain during the 2008 presidential campaign, or the "Concert of Democracies." Among other problems, these

would alienate China, whose cooperation is essential for progress across other areas of shared interest, such as climate change, terrorism and nonproliferation. Instead of building on international convergence, MGI interlocutors in China said such a concept could form the basis for a second Cold War. Policymakers in India argued that such a club would heighten, not reduce, international security by creating divisions rather than unifying nations, while officials from other key states allied with the [US] privately underscored that such an institution would be counter-productive, especially by isolating China. (MGI, 2008a, p. 25)[4]

Indeed, as then Senator Obama indicated earlier, one of his major foreign policy objectives would be to forge a constructive partnership with China to deal with complex global problems, such as those outlined in chapter 1, but especially global warming and, more recently, the global economic recession. This "strategic dialogue," which was on the agenda for further articulation by President Obama and Chinese President Hu Jintao at the G20 summit in London in April 2009, was launched during Hillary Clinton's trip to China in late February 2009. Although she upset human rights activists for failing to emphasize the need for China significantly to upgrade its compliance with international human rights norms – as she had when she was First Lady – Clinton said that "human rights concerns can't interfere with pressing China for greater cooperation on the economic front, the environment and the impasse over North Korea's nuclear program" (Kessler, 2009).

Since China has recently eclipsed the US as the world's largest emitter of harmful gases, Secretary Clinton is reflecting not only the foreign policy positions of President Obama, but his pragmatism as well. Clearly, given that policymakers around the globe have less than ten years to reverse the problem of global warming, lest "species extinction" become a viable option, working with China on this problem now rather than alienating it because of its poor human rights record and other democracy deficits makes for a compelling argument. In the meantime, human rights concerns will not be forgotten, merely located appropriately within a comprehensive universe of pressing global concerns with shifting priorities. Responding to her human rights critics during a news conference with Chinese Foreign Minister Yang Jiechi, Clinton commented: "The promotion of human rights is an essential aspect of U.S. global policy" (Kessler, 2009). After the completion of Secretary Clinton's Asia tour, Todd Stern,

President Obama's special envoy for climate change, summed up the shifting human rights-global warming relationship:

> In our view, nothing is more important for dealing with [the global warming] threat than a U.S.–China partnership. There is no way to preserve a safe, livable planet unless China plays a very important role along with the [US]. This is not a matter of politics or morality or right or wrong. It is simply the unforgiving math of accumulating emissions. (Ibid.)

So, if neither a League nor a Concert of Democracies is a viable approach to global governance in the post-9/11 world, what about the remaining two options: Mark Leonard's (2005) concept of a "Union of Unions" or John McClintock's (2008) "Global Union of Democracies"? The "Union of Unions" represents an inductive approach to global governance: given that the EU has been proposed as a model of regional integration based on shared sovereignty, other regional actors (e.g., ASEAN, AU) would emulate the model and, at the end of the process, link up synergistically in an overarching "Union of Unions." By contrast, the "Global Union of Democracies" is more of a deductive approach: it would also employ the EU as a model, but create the Global Union at the outset, comprising the EU and other actors, primarily states, and not very powerful ones initially. Once it became clear that the Global Union was effective in addressing complex global problems such as global warming and poverty, other nations would follow suit. Once more than two nations joined from any one region, they would start to comprise a regional actor eventually analogous to the EU. The Global Union would then grow into something tantamount to a "Union of Unions."[5]

My own preference is to combine the inductive with the deductive – i.e., to advance the Global Union of Democracies as the ultimate objective. As Charles Sanders Peirce reminds us, we have to start "from where we are" (cited in Kaplan 1964, p. 86) and concentrate on regional integration as a basis for global governance. That way, we can creatively engineer responsible sovereignty into shared sovereignty. The Brooking Institution's Managing Global Insecurity project, therefore, seems to be an excellent platform for advancing the global governance component of President Obama's foreign policy agenda.

There is one critical point in Obama's foreign policy strategy that may derail much if not all of his carefully articulated plans for constructive change, globally and nationally: his policies for Afghanistan and Pakistan. A major "outlier" in his policy is his position that, as he draws down US troops in Iraq, he will send them to Afghanistan to deal with the resurrected Taliban insurgency there. Associated with this concern is that he has continued the Bush policy of launching Predator drone attacks on suspected Taliban targets in Pakistan. These began during his very first week in office, causing a number of casualties, perhaps including children (Reid, 2009). Far from reducing the number of such attacks, however, Obama has dramatically increased them (see Bergen and Tiedemann, 2009).[6]

These are real concerns but, if we examine President Obama's Afghan policy in the larger framework within which it has been articulated, they may be put to rest. This larger framework is compatible with the "three levels of conflict reality" introduced in chapter 2: (1) conflict-as-symptoms; (2) conflict-as-fractured-relationships that give rise to symptoms; and (3) conflict-as-underlying-deep-rooted-causes-and-conditions of the fractured relationships that give rise to symptoms.

Obama's framework for Afghanistan, which corresponds to his "three legs to the stool of American foreign policy" (Clinton, 2009) – defense, diplomacy, and development –

includes (1) more troops (defense) to deal with conflict as symptoms; (2) more diplomacy to deal with fractured relationships which give rise to the symptoms; and (3) more development to deal with the underlying deep-rooted causes and conditions of the fractured relationships. This reorientation of US policy reflects the sentiments of General David Petraeus, who heads US forces and the International Security Assistance Force (ISAF) in Afghanistan, and who co-wrote the US military's new guidelines on counter-insurgency, that "you can't kill or capture your way out of a complex, industrial-strength insurgency" (FP, 2009, p. 49).

What this means is that Obama's defense-based "surge" into Afghanistan (symptoms) must occur within a more comprehensive framework, inclusive, and not at the expense, of diplomacy (relationships) and development (deep-rooted causes). The balance of the shifting investments and prioritization across these three interrelated components of his foreign policy "stool" will determine whether his promise of constructive "change we can believe in" remains intact or comes under significant challenge. One way to manage the complex interplay among defense, diplomacy, and development is to maintain a continuous mapping in "real time" of symptoms, relationships, and underlying causes and conditions, perhaps by employing a conceptual device such as the comprehensive checklist or enhanced 3PF.

Moving beyond the challenge of Afghanistan, one approach to managing the complex interplay between inductive (Union of Unions) and deductive (Global Union of Democracies) approaches to EU-based global governance is to use the G20 as a point of departure for motivating the concerned international community to deal with other global problems as well. For John McClintock, architect of the idea of a Global Union of Democracies, global warming and global poverty would be dealt with first to generate momentum toward expansion of the Global Union (2008, chs. 12 and 13). Subsequently, global problem solvers would deal with such things as war and conflict, third world debt, the proliferation of nuclear weapons, and global pandemics. Although these pressing issues – part of a global zeitgeist calling for their solution (ibid., pp. 248–9) – are interrelated, development NGOs tend to treat them separately (Murray, 2009), thereby compounding the issue in each case.

Consider, for instance, the Brooking Institution's MGI project (2008a, p. 27), where the focus is on six global challenges: climate change, nuclear proliferation, threats to biological security, terrorism, conflict, and poverty and economic instability. An essential working hypothesis of the project, expressed persuasively by its co-director Carlos Pascual, is that all these issues are interrelated:

> What we . . . know is that these issues are deeply interconnected. . . . With the economic crisis, it is underscored on the one hand the need for open markets, to be able to create centers of growth and capital to be able to help take us out of this crisis, yet at the same time, investing in the poor who are suffering from the crisis.
>
> But this will come up against . . . a risk of protectionism that will derive from the fear of the future. It will be up to global leaders to actually push back on those protectionist tendencies, and in the Action Plan we begin to describe some ways in order to do that.
>
> The economic crisis is deeply linked to climate change and it will complicate those debates. On the one hand, it will create opportunities for an economic stimulus. But as we've heard from economists throughout the world, in order to solve the climate change problem, there needs to be a price that is put on carbon, and that will have an impact on industry such as steel and coal, and auto manufacturers, and will there be the political will to take [action] on those issues? In the Action Plan, we propose an approach that leads to a

phased international negotiation in order to be able to do this more effectively that leads to . . . international consensus. Climate change will exacerbate conflict, and as a result of that, we will see greater competition for resources of the nature that we see today in Congo, and hence the need for greater investment in peacekeeping and mediation and peacebuilding capabilities.

In the voids that we see after conflict, we have seen the capacity for terrorists to establish a base. And so we propose in the Action Plan how to begin thinking about the importance of investing in local capabilities for the rule of law and policing.

We have seen, as well, that . . . weak states . . .can become a threat for disease. And the positive side of, or the critical factor in, addressing that disease is technological innovation, yet the misuse of that technology becomes a risk in itself.

So we propose in the Action Plan ways in which scientists can begin working together to identify ways in which to regulate that technology, yet at the same time provide an incentive for its further development. And against all of these issues, we have to remember the specter of nuclear proliferation and the risks that that entails, because if terrorists, in fact, actually get their hands on these nuclear weapons, in an environment where there is conflict, that perhaps can become the biggest existential risk of all. And so one of the things I would underscore, in moving forward, is that we have to recognize the fact that there are interrelationships among all of these issues. (MGI, 2008b, pp. 13–15)[7]

Resistance to change

If we recognize these linkages but, for institutional or cognitive reasons, remain wedded to the dominant single-focus orientation, we risk operationalizing Karl Popper's (1972) "unintended" paradox that every problem solved leads to another problem – for Popper a source of new knowledge but for policymakers and practitioners a source of frustration and policy failure.[8]

One institutional *and* cognitive source of the endurance of the single-issue focus (as well as primacy of the single-factor explanation) is the way we organize knowledge into discrete disciplinary categories. On the one hand, theorists, researchers, and practitioners schooled in one discipline – which is still the norm (see Sandole, 2007a, ch. 2; Alger, 2007; Galtung, 2008) – must become proficient in multiple disciplines in order to capture the wide array of perspectives inherent in peacebuilding. But, on the other hand, how can they survive professionally in academic and other settings that continue to privilege unidisciplinary hegemony?

Returning to the four worlds' model (4WM) discussed in chapter 1, our tendency to bifurcate, to simplify, to stereotype – in general, to aim for an aesthetic norm of parsimony (Sandole, 1999, ch. 1) – has World 2 (mental) and World 4 (biological-physiological) as well as World 3 (human-made) origins. Quite simply, we seem to have difficulty entertaining more than one or a few ideas at a time, rendering us challenged in capturing the multidimensionality, nuance, nonlinearity, and flux of complex phenomena and processes that *are* the real world and, therefore, are essential to capture in the peacebuilding enterprise.

According to John Sexton (2010), president of New York University, "We have created a society that has . . . an allergy to nuance and complexity [characterized by] a kind of collapse into an intellectual relativism where opinions become fact and even knowledge and wisdom . . . It's a dangerous thing."[9] This is, in part, because the "allergy" has led to an "ingenuity gap": the breakdown between our increasingly complex social, economic, political, physical, and other problems and our ability to solve them (Homer-Dixon, 2000).

Our tendency to simplify may have made phylogenetic sense thousands of years ago when our ancestors' survival depended on quick reactions to environmental shocks, especially raids conducted by the "Other." This has been compounded by the stress of modern and postmodern life, in the latter case by technological advances that have enabled us to be wired globally, "24/7." There are now so many sources and kinds of information – and, for some, the need to be in touch with them at all times – that it is difficult to pay attention to more than one's own travails at any point in time, let alone genocide in a far-flung country or "abstract" problems such as global warming or poverty.

Even before the massive cognitive overload characteristic of the postmodern (e.g., post-9/11) period, however, researchers, for example in the multidisciplinary field of international relations, faced increasing stress in trying to manipulate variables that did not lend themselves to any kind or degree of control (e.g., historical memory), manage increasing amounts of data, or attempt to liaise with policymakers – all tending to push them (*and* policymakers) toward cognitive simplicity (Sandole, 1999, pp. 189–92). Much more challenging:

> There are real and specific reasons why politicians, planners, managers, and statesmen, as well as scholars and the public at large, tend to misjudge the behavior of large and complex social systems. . . . "It is my basic theme," wrote Jay W. Forrester a number of years back [1971], "that the human mind is not adapted to interpreting how social systems behave. Our social systems belong to the class called multi-loop, non-linear feedback systems." . . . [Consequently] a society may suffer a "growing sense of futility" as it repeatedly attacks deficiencies while the "symptoms continue to worsen." (North, 1975, p. 6)

These sentiments could have been articulated in response to any one component of the present global problematique, comprised of the financial and economic collapse, climate change, poverty, state failure, terrorism, WMD proliferation, pandemics, and the like, with complex interrelationships among them. Arguably, while the number of complex global problems and their interrelationships has increased during the past forty years, the human capacity for understanding and addressing them has not. Worse, that capacity may be under siege by the increase in stress-related cognitive overload, resulting, in part, in what World Bank president Robert Zoellick sees as a disconnect between rhetoric (calls for global solutions to global problems) and reality (regression to nationalist protectionism) (Giles and Barber, 2009).

Our inability to manage, if not reduce, the disconnect between the increasingly complex, interconnected, difficult-to-predict, and fast-paced developments in the man-made and natural environments, and our capacity to resolve problems in and among those domains, exists at a critical point in the evolution of our endangered species: if we don't get "it" right, then our continued journey into a turbulent future will be even more precarious than it has been thus far (see Homer-Dixon, 2000; Rifkin, 2009).

Capitalizing on Obama's Promise to Strengthen Global Problem Solving and Peacebuilding

In what sense can this volume end on a sanguine note about the capability of the concerned international community to deal effectively with peacebuilding not only in the post-[violent] conflict phase, where minimalist approaches have barely succeeded in achieving negative peace, often for brief periods, but also in long-term, pre-[violent] conflict peacebuilding, where violent conflict prevention is a primary objective but with few examples of success (e.g., UNPREDEP) from which to draw inspiration? When we consider that the main subject of this volume has been a subset of long-term peacebuilding – namely, the need to address the complex global problematique whose content and structure are among the origins and sources of sustenance of violent conflicts worldwide – then we may have more grounds to conclude on a hopeless than a confident note.

Nevertheless, there are glimmers of hope. Barack Obama, for example, has been trying to deal with many of these complex global problems at the same time, any one of which would normally be sufficient for the first term of any president. After a turbulent year during which even his most ardent supporters were concerned with the prospect of "premature closure" on his presidency, he has become newly emboldened and empowered, domestically with the passage of healthcare and financial regulatory reform legislation by the US Congress, and internationally, with the signing of a US–Russian agreement to slash their respective nuclear warheads and launchers by a third. Reflecting his experience and expertise as a community organizer, Obama has also increased his repertoire to include dealing directly with foreign leaders as well as their domestic constituents (see Wilson, 2010).

Against this background, President Obama convened the first-ever single-issue summit with the heads of state and government and other leaders of forty-seven countries to meet in Washington, DC, during 12–13 April 2010, to ensure the security of nuclear weapons and fissionable materials (Wilson, 2010; Nass, 2010, p. 1; Wilson and Sheridan, 2010). By implication, the ultimate objective of the nuclear security summit is to ensure that nuclear weapons do not fall into the hands of terrorists.

We may have here a model for addressing other, including multi-issue, problem areas. As newly energized leader of the "indispensable" nation, for example, Obama could, in conjunction with the UN Peacebuilding Commission, the EU, and the Brookings Institution, convene a three-day summit for leaders of the G20 to meet in Washington to discuss "Peacebuilding for the 21st Century: The Imperative to Realize Global Interest as National Interest." With necessary preparatory work done on either a funded or a voluntary basis by, among others, academics and their students in select courses and working groups, the summit could address the following interrelated themes:

1 enhancing the UN Peacebuilding Commission;
2 operationalizing the responsibility to protect (R2P), with implications for the "whole-of-government" and "whole-of-community" approaches to peacebuilding, the new European peace and security system (NEPSS), and the international humanitarian system within the context of the multi-track diplomacy framework;
3 identifying the complex interconnections among elements of the global problematique, paying special attention to constellations of interconnected/interdependent issues associated with any given single issue that should feature in complex problem-solving efforts;
4 assessing different approaches to regional and global governance;
5 distilling and synthesizing insights from themes 1–4 and applying them to "test runs" in Afghanistan, Iraq, and Haiti.

Let's look at these five themes in further detail to explore how in each case we might convert conceptual ideas into operational breakthroughs.

UN Peacebuilding Commission

The Peacebuilding Commission (PBC) was endorsed as an idea at the 2005 world summit and established in 2006 by resolutions of the General Assembly and Security Council (Evans, 2008, p. 172). Part of its genesis had to do with the shameful genocidal massacres that occurred in Rwanda during April–July 1994 and at Srebrenica in Bosnia-Herzegovina during mid-July 1995. The objective of the PBC is to establish "an *integrated peacebuilding strategy* to promote *greater strategic coherence* and *coordination* among regional and international organizations, donor agencies, non-governmental organizations, and operational actors working in countries on the Commission's agenda" (UN/PBSO, 2008, p. 4, emphasis added).

As a related entity, the Peacebuilding Support Office (PBSO) was established to act as the secretariat for the Peacebuilding Commission, plus actively to support "initiatives to document, collate, systematize, share and disseminate peacebuilding knowledge, *lessons learned, best practices* and research insights in various formats" (UN/PBSO, 2008, p. 5, emphasis added). The PBSO's efforts in this regard include the establishment, in March 2008, of an inter-agency Peacebuilding Community of Practice (PB CoP) to act as a "knowledge platform" for sharing lessons learned, best practices, and other information. Given its wide-ranging convening role, plus its responsibility to disseminate information on best practices and lessons learned, the PBSO is well positioned to assist in linking academic and policy research with the work of the UN and other actors involved in peacebuilding (ibid., p. 10). One approach to achieving this interlinkage is through a Peacebuilding Policy Research Consortium "that systematically supports the generation, validation, dissemination and utilization of policy-relevant research on peacebuilding," especially in conflict-habituated and developing countries with the active participation of relevant governmental and nongovernmental actors involved in the overall peacebuilding enterprise (ibid., p. 11).[10]

In part, on account of its relative "newness," the promise of the PBC and its affiliated offices to enhance the theory and practice of peacebuilding has not been met. Although initial skepticism about the viability of the new UN peacebuilding architecture during its first year of operation, from mid-2006 to mid-2007, was eclipsed by some "cautious optimism" by early 2008, "there is still much that needs to be done to make the PBC the central part of the landscape it has to be if there is to be a dramatic improvement in the exercise of the *responsibility to rebuild*" (Evans, 2008, pp. 172–4, emphasis added).

The proposed US-initiated summit could build upon the work completed thus far by the PBC in identifying and disseminating information about best practices and lessons learned in peacebuilding, especially those that "triangulate" with the lessons of UNPREDEP discussed in chapter 3. This objective could be pursued through efforts to convert R2P into an operational reality.

Operationalizing the responsibility to protect (R2P)

The responsibility to protect (R2P), which includes the responsibility to prevent, react, and to rebuild, was also embraced by the world summit in 2005 – again, in large part because of the shameful events that were allowed to occur in Rwanda and Srebrenica. Since R2P calls upon the concerned international community to save populations at risk, especially when the victims' own governments are the source of that risk, it represents one of the great conceptual innovations since the Westphalian treaties launched the modern state system and legitimized the sacrosanct concept of sovereignty over 350 years ago. As such, it incorporates long-term, pre-conflict (*preventive*), during conflict (*reactive*), and post-conflict peacebuilding (*rebuilding*) dimensions comprising political/diplomatic, economic/social, constitutional/legal, and security sector measures of both a direct and a structural nature (see Evans, 2008, chs. 4, 5 and 7).

Decisions to employ force to save threatened populations must be based on stringent criteria, such as considerations of (1) seriousness of harm, (2) proper purpose, (3) last resort, (4) proportional means, and (5) balance of consequences (Evans, 2008, ch. 6). Although these concerns reflect Christian "just war" theory, they also "resonate equally, and are not inconsistent, with the other major world religious and intellectual traditions" (ibid., p. 140; Warner and Giacca, 2009, pp. 296–7).

Among the challenges involved in implementing R2P is the absence of political will to translate it into an operational reality, especially among the veto-wielding members of the UN Security Council, Russia and China, for whom any effort to "violate" traditional sovereignty is anathema.[11] The fact that R2P calls for the use of force, under very specific conditions, to protect populations at risk when their own governments have failed them makes R2P for many an illusory dream of idealists.

An additional challenge is that R2P has been conflated with the US-led invasions and occupations of Iraq and Afghanistan, resulting in even more skepticism directed at the R2P concept than might otherwise be the case, rendering it even less likely that it would become a core component of any applied peacebuilding design (see Weiss, 2007, chs. 4–5). That the US is the primary actor driving this process puts into even sharper relief the unique role it plays in shaping international thinking and behavior.

These and other challenges notwithstanding, if R2P were "up and running" as a viable strategy, it would have significant implications for "whole-of-government" and "whole-of-community" approaches being incorporated into implemented peacebuilding designs. "Whole-of-government" approaches imply the coordination of the three stools of Obama's foreign policy orientation, the defense, diplomacy, and development sectors of government. "Whole-of-community" implies the coordination of governmental, intergovernmental, and non-governmental (civil society) sectors. Both of these inhere in the multi-track diplomacy approach discussed in chapter 2 (see Diamond and McDonald, 1996).

The multi-track approach is a major component of my effort to apply the three-pillar framework (3PF) to a design for post-Cold War security in Europe following the tragedy of the genocidal collapse of the former Yugoslavia during the Balkan wars of the 1990s. The objective of the 3PF-influenced new European peace and security system (NEPSS) is to ensure that anything like the virulent ethno-political violence that occurred in Srebrenica, Mostar, Sarajevo, Vukovar, and elsewhere in the former Yugoslavia would be a thing of the past (see Sandole, 2007a, ch. 3). NEPSS combines the descriptive with the prescriptive. Under the "descriptive," it makes use of existing institutions corresponding to the three "baskets" of the "Helsinki Final Act" (1975) of the Conference on Security and Cooperation in Europe (CSCE), which eventually became the Organization for Security and Cooperation in Europe (OSCE):

> *Basket 1*: political and military components of comprehensive security (NATO);
> *Basket 2*: economic and environmental components of comprehensive security (EU);
> *Basket 3*: human rights and humanitarian components of comprehensive security (Council of Europe [CoE]).

The descriptive component of NEPSS, which fine-tunes the interface between the OSCE, NATO, the EU and the CoE, is fine as far as it goes, but it does not go far enough to prevent "future Yugoslavias." The ethno-political violence that characterized the Balkan wars of the 1990s and that is likely to constitute the dominant form of hostilities in the future are the "new wars" (Kaldor, 2006). These occur between actors – often governments and secessionist groups – *within* states. Because the OSCE, NATO, the EU and the CoE deal primarily with relations *between* states, NEPSS would be incomplete without a dimension that addressed the new war phenomenon. Hence the "prescriptive dimension," which is structured primarily in terms of the multi-track framework, with local, societal, subregional, regional, and global levels of analysis as the vertical axis and actors corresponding to the nine tracks of the multi-track framework representing the horizontal axis. As a basis for increasing coordination among the various multi-level, multi-track processes in any given NEPSS intervention, a "map" for identifying and locating actors corresponding to each of the tracks for each level is presented in figure 5.1).

Based upon the assumption that all conflicts are local, then once some early warning system registers that a conflict is developing in a certain village or city, or any other location in a certain country at any point in time, track 1 to 9 resources from the local to global levels would be brought to bear on the event, if not at the same time then certainly in sequence.[12]

Track 1 Track 2 Track 3 Track 4 Track 5 Track 6 Track 7 Track 8 Track 9

Local	___	___	___	___	___	___	___	___	___
Societal	___	___	___	___	___	___	___	___	___
Sub-regional	___	___	___	___	___	___	___	___	___
Regional	___	___	___	___	___	___	___	___	___
Global	___	___	___	___	___	___	___	___	___

Figure 5.1   The structure of NEPSS

If diplomacy and development were held up by defense issues, then, under the clearly specified conditions mentioned with regard to R2P (see Evans, 2008, p. 141), force could be used to pull an attacker away from a besieged population. This use of *Realpolitik* would be a necessary (but *not* a sufficient) condition to achieve negative peace as a basis for moving eventually to positive peace, where the conditions for structural, cultural, and physical violence would be managed if not eliminated, achieving what John Burton (1990) calls "*provention.*"

A viable R2P would also have implications for fixing the international humanitarian system, which, again, according to Weiss (2007, ch. 5), is dysfunctional, if not broken (also see Polman, 2010). More than twenty years of major challenges have led to "a humanitarian enterprise in considerable flux – some would say in a full-blown identity crisis" – where members are not quite sure who they are, what they should do, how they should do it, or even whether their interventions have had a negative impact (Weiss, 2007, p. 143). The debates involve the "classicists," who advocate neutrality, impartiality, and consent, and the "solidarists," who advocate for the victims of oppression, even condoning on humanitarian grounds the use of force against violators of human rights (ibid., pp 144–7).

Under such circumstances, coordination among the increasing number of NGOs, especially, has become problematic, in part because of the spike in "new wars" and the task uncertainties associated with them, plus a fierce sense of proprietary independence among the actors and donor preferences for single issues (Murray, 2009). "Everyone is for coordination as long as it implies no loss of autonomy" (Weiss, 2007, p. 149). Just consider the situation in Haiti *before* the devastating 7.3 earthquake of 12 January 2010, when thousands of NGOs, national development organizations (e.g., USAID), and a UN peace operation were in the country, and it was a "failed state" *then*.[13] Words cannot adequately describe Haiti's status *now*, which raises the question of what – and how – the even larger post-earthquake international presence there will accomplish that it did not before.

Despite this disarray in the international humanitarian system, there have been improvements among the members, including increased interactions, an emphasis on specialized knowledge, and the development of a consciousness of "common undertaking." In addition, humanitarian action has started to become rationalized by the development of codes of conduct, norms to shape standardized responses, training programs, personnel exchanges, and procedures to enhance efficiency and "identify best practices and lessons learned" (Weiss, 2007, p. 151). Although Weiss concludes that, "If past is prelude, . . . the numerous moving parts of the international humanitarian system will continue to impede effectively aiding and protecting war victims" (ibid., p. 152), there is enough of an improvement on which to build further. For example, as part of the envisaged summit undertaken by President Obama, donors and members of the military, national development agencies, the UN system, NGOs, and the International Committee of the Red Cross could be brought together to work toward agreeing on a common framework of international humanitarian action, where each can clearly discern its relation to the others. Once the various governmental, intergovernmental, and nongovernmental players involved appreciate that they can succeed only if others do as well, enhanced coordination and overall mission success should be among the consequences.

Since international humanitarian intervention now involves much more than short-term emergency aid to war victims, such as human rights protection, democracy promotion, development, and peacebuilding (Weiss, 2007,

p. 144), viable R2P and international humanitarian systems should certainly enhance overall peacebuilding efforts on the ground.

The complex interconnections among elements of the global problematique

This is one of the "elephants in the room" of applied peace-building, as global problems and their complex interconnec-tions and interdependencies tend not to be factored into peacebuilding design and implementation, even though, par-adoxically, they may be driving the situation that peacebuild-ing is meant to address. In order for peacebuilding to be more effective, therefore, the impact of the global problematique on any given developing, existential, or post-conflict situation must be recognized, analyzed, and responded to in some fashion.

As indicated in chapter 1, Abbott et al. (2007) provide a useful listing of interconnected global problems: (1) climate change, (2) competition over resources, (3) marginalization of the majority world, and (4) global militarization. Just in terms of one of these components, marginalization of the majority world, the authors tell us that "A *complex interplay* of discrimination, global poverty, Third World debt, infectious disease, global inequality and deepening socio-economic divisions, together make for key elements of current global insecurity" (ibid., p. 44, emphasis added). By the time the authors reach their concluding chapter, they alter the order of these problem areas slightly and, given the effort and resources applied to the "Global War on Terror," add terror-ism as a fifth area (earlier subsumed under the marginaliza-tion of the majority world), with the following policy recommendations for achieving sustainable security (ibid., pp. 84–5):

1 *Competition over resources*
    Pursue comprehensive energy efficiency, recycling and resource conservation, and management policies and practices, plus seek large-scale funding for alternatives to oil.

2 *Climate change*
    Introduce a carbon tax and replace carbon-based energy sources by diverse local renewable sources as the primary base of the generation of future energy.

3 *Marginalization of the majority world*
    Reform the global trade system, plus provide aid and debt relief to transform poverty reduction into a global priority.

4 *International terrorism*
    Deal with legitimate political grievances and hopes of marginalized groups, plus implement intelligence-based counter-terrorism operations against violent groups and pursue dialogue with terrorist leadership whenever practical.

5 *Global militarization*
    Nuclear weapons states must take clear, bold steps to achieve nuclear disarmament, plus pursue non-proliferation measures and halt the development of new nuclear and biological weapons.

The overall approach for seeking sustainable security is an integrated strategy where, with coordination through a reformed UN system, governmental and other actors deal cooperatively with the root causes of the five threats, each of which negatively impacts the others – i.e., they "cure the disease," instead of what governments have tended to do, "attack the symptoms" (Abbott et al., 2007, p. 85). The problem, however, as Julian Baggini (2010) reminds us in his review of Tony Judt's new book *Ill Fares the Land*, critiquing life, inequality, and poverty in Western democracies, is that "few are able to get beyond the symptoms to identify causes and cures." We are, in other words, stuck at the level of conflict-as-symptoms, unable to navigate our way to conflict-as-underlying-causes-and-conditions. This lingering aspect of the human condition reflects the persistence of the "ingenuity gap" (Homer-Dixon, 2000) which, in turn, reinforces a "resilience-deficit" in our infrastructure (Flynn, 2007), further stressing our already beleaguered capacity for ingenuity.

Fortunately, there are signs that elements of the five interconnected threats are being addressed, each to some extent. In addition to slashing nuclear warheads and launchers by a third on each side, the new START treaty agreed to by the Russians and Americans in Prague on 8 April 2010 is intended to reinforce the nonproliferation regime by sending a message that the former Cold War nuclear rivals, who still control over 90 percent of the world's nuclear weapons, are intent on leading on nuclear disarmament by example. In addition, the US and others have been "talking with the enemy" in Iraq, Afghanistan, and Pakistan. Moreover, there is finally seriousness on the part of the US to address the grievances of the Palestinians *as well as* the security concerns of the Israelis. Further, despite (or perhaps because of) the near collapse of the UN climate change negotiations in Copenhagen in December 2009, there are signs that governments, including that of the US, are taking seriously global warming and the need to identify and locate renewable sources of energy.

These encouraging signs notwithstanding, we still have a long, long way to go. The summit proposed here could build upon these trajectories by establishing working groups for each of the five problem areas, chaired by eminent persons and peopled by well-paid, highly competent professionals who can see the "big picture" and the relationship between it and their particular area of expertise and experience. Through the use of relevant checklists championed by physician-philosopher Atul Gawande (2009), discussed in chapter 2, these working groups can strive to maximize their efficacy by noting what has worked in similar situations. For instance, in a study of seventy-five major US policy initiatives, in which the researchers looked for patterns and lessons learned from significant governmental successes and failures, William Eggers and John O'Leary (2010) discerned five principles that, if followed, could enhance policymaking success:

1 *Encourage disagreement*

As argued by John Stuart Mill ([1859] 1998) in his famous tract *On Liberty*, success (including the discovery of "truth") can occur only through debate – the competition of ideas – by traversing boundaries of ideology and expertise.

2 *Use lessons learned and best practices*

As a point of departure, it is better to use an approach that has worked in other research, business, or policy settings than to start entirely from scratch.

3 *Encourage public debate*

As President Harry Truman, General George Marshall, and others learned in successfully launching the Marshall Plan – "one of the greatest achievements in 20th-century US foreign policy" – (a) the public must be educated on the benefits of the project; (b) marketing of the project must be non-ideological; (c) the public must be persuaded to commit to the goals of the project; and (d) congressional discussion and hearings must be encouraged.

4 *Embrace failure*

Simple best-case scenarios tend to be absent of alternative "Plan B's" and realistic budgets and timelines.

5 *Encourage discussion among politicians and bureaucrats*

Critical to the success of projects is the "bridger," the rare leader who can move back and forth between the political and bureaucratic worlds, translating the language of one into the understanding of the other, especially when the policymakers are getting it wrong. Such persons, essential to enacting "history-making undertakings," tend to be undervalued when the process is ongoing. Only later are they and their critical roles appreciated.

To enhance policymaking further, there is, of course, the straightforward, simple-rational approach, where options are prioritized and costed (Lomborg, 2007). This has value for the linear "normal science" of Thomas Kuhn's (1970, ch. 3) "puzzle solving," where problems are selected in part because they are assumed to have solutions. By contrast, there is a counter-intuitive approach with more relevance for Kuhn's "problem solving": "It is no criterion of goodness in a puzzle that its outcome be intrinsically interesting or important. On the contrary, the really pressing problems, e.g., a cure for cancer or the design of a lasting peace, are often not puzzles at all, largely because they may not have any solution" (ibid., pp. 36–7).

"Problem solving" for Kuhn is a nonlinear process that advocates taking an indirect approach to achieving one's goal. According to John Kay, author of *Obliquity: Why our Goals are Best Achieved Indirectly* (2009):

> we often cannot solve problems directly because of their inherent complexity, the incompleteness of our knowledge, the interdependence of the actors and the environment, and the fact that most models designed to assist decision-making are highly imperfect descriptions of reality. So we may often get closest to our ultimate goal by pursuing intermediate objectives, or working towards some higher goal that may have the side-effect of delivering what we need, be it more profit, more market share, or success in politics or war. (Cited in Davies, 2010)

An example of a "higher goal" in Kay's framing of an indirect approach could be the "big picture" to which any of the five problem areas is related – e.g., the "sustainable security" that problem solving in all five areas is meant to achieve. Given that we need an integrated approach to achieve and maintain sustainable security:

> it is no longer enough to focus on environmental issues in isolation from the threat of socio-economic divisions and marginalization . . ... What we have argued is that all these issues are *interconnected*, and that governments must address environmental issues with reference to those of development and security (and vice versa). . . . measures are needed which simultaneously ensure environmental protection, sustainable development *and* global security. This calls for a *new approach*. (Abbott et al., 2007, p. 93, emphasis added)

In effect, Abbott and his colleagues are calling for an integrated approach to peacebuilding, with an emphasis on cosmopolitan conflict resolution (Ramsbotham et al., 2005) and *provention* (Burton, 1990), which is what this volume has been about and toward which President Obama could dedicate the summit proposed above.

Regional and global governance

Moving toward a world of sustainable security facilitated by an approach to comprehensive peacebuilding, with an emphasis on cosmopolitan conflict resolution and *provention*, could be enhanced by appropriate models of regional and global governance. Although the European Union continues to be battered by post-Lisbon developments and contradictions, including the Greek euro crisis, it remains the exemplar par excellence of Kant's peace system, a reason, no doubt, it features in the Brooking Institution's MGI project. Despite its manifold problems and high boredom factor, the EU's rankings on a variety of socio-economic indicators, especially in comparison with the US, make it the envy of the world (see Rifkin, 2004).

If the EU "good life" could be exported to the "bottom billion" (Collier, 2007a), the peacebuilding project will have reached what for now is clearly an unattainable zenith. Still, it could happen, or, at least, we could move closer to the goal, just as the new START treaty moves Russia, the US, and the world closer to President Obama's goal of the "global zero" option (Nass, 2010). As conflict resolution pioneer and economist Kenneth Boulding has argued with his "Boulding's First Law", "If it exists, then it is possible."[14]

As more and more countries start to experience reductions in socio-economic inequalities, driven in large part by the revolution in information communication technologies extending the central nervous system and connecting our species across time and space (Rifkin, 2009), there will be corresponding reductions in homicide, obesity, drug use, mental illness, anxiety, teenage pregnancies, high-school dropouts, playground bullying, long working hours, and large prison populations, plus an overall increase in life expectancy and community life (see Wilkinson and Pickett, 2009; Judt, 2010) – connections which are more causal than spurious. By implication, there will be fewer domestic tensions to be projected onto invented foreign enemies, thereby furthering the trajectory toward sustainable security, a realized Democratic Peace, some kind of Union of Democracies, and an Empathic Civilization where the new bottom line is a reinforced sense of community at all levels instead of a more "rugged" individual attempting to survive precariously in a progressively entrenched Hobbesian state of nature.

Afghanistan, Iraq, and Haiti as "test cases"

It is against this dynamic background that comprehensive peacebuilding, using the insights generated by the proposed summit from the four themes outlined above, could be implemented in high-visibility cases such as Afghanistan, Iraq, and Haiti, among many others among the "bottom billion" (e.g., nuclear-armed Pakistan). This would have practical value on at least two levels: (1) enhancing sustainable security within each of these countries and between each and its neighbors; and (2) demonstrating to conservative participants in the "Culture Wars," who tend to have a more visceral need for security at the personal level than do their liberal counterparts, that comprehensive peacebuilding as defined in this volume, which requires various kinds and degrees of regulation impacting the autonomy of the individual, does, in fact, enhance rather than erode personal security. Nevertheless, replacing a felt antipathy with cerebral support among conservatives worldwide for anything that can be framed as a violation of their personal autonomy will continue to be a daunting challenge for global problem solvers, as "fact" may not necessarily succeed in trumping "feeling" (as was clear during the vitriolic battle over health-care reform in the US).

Conclusion

Borrowing from Abbott et al. (2007, pp. 6–8):

> Our analysis may, at times, appear to be centered on the United States. This is necessary because recent U.S. approaches to foreign policy and multilateralism have severely hampered many of the efforts to address the problems covered in this book. In some instances U.S. policies have actually added to those problems. . . . Furthermore, the U.S. is now the most influential global actor and the only country with a truly global military reach, and this further increases its impact on the security and political issues we are exploring.[15]

Ditto!

In addition, it is strongly felt that Barack Obama, the "global community organizer par excellence," has the capacity to succeed in galvanizing global forces toward complex problem solving and comprehensive peacebuilding, a capacity which has been reinvigorated by congressional approval of health-care and financial regulatory reform and by a number of initiatives to control nuclear weapons and prevent them from falling into the hands of terrorists (see Rachman, 2010; Stephens, 2010). As one of Germany's premier journalists, Theo Sommer (2010), puts it, "Mr. President . . . The world needs you, your commitment, your leadership. There is no one else around who can do it."

But how can we expect Obama, sobered by protectionist tendencies at home, to influence international colleagues, more and more obsessed with "every man for himself," to "do the right thing" in the face of mounting political pressure to do the opposite. He must invoke William James's (1910) moral equivalent of war, discussed in chapter 4, so that, through cognitive dissonance (Festinger, 1962), policymaking elites and their constituents "feel" that global climate change trumps all other issues, including the specter of global economic collapse. Nevertheless, given the immediate threats posed by the global economic crisis, Obama can link this to global warming and other components of the global problematique at G20 and other meetings, until other policymakers are doing what he is doing: dealing with many issues simultaneously.

Probably the best way to focus the minds of his colleagues would be to emphasize the four to seven years which global policymakers have for turning global warming around, lest "species survivability" become a critical, tipping-point issue (see McKie, 2009; MGI, 2008b, pp. 27–8). While some ideologically charged critics of the existence of, or the urgency of dealing with, global warming still try to deny, disguise, or eliminate evidence of the problem – much like George W. Bush or his staff did – Obama can make the case, as did Benjamin Franklin and Sir Winston Churchill before him, that "We must hang together, or most assuredly we shall all hang separately." As *The Economist* (2010) puts it, the fact of uncertainties about climate change allows us to construct relatively benign futures, but it does not justify ignoring "futures in which climate change is large, and in some of which it is very dangerous indeed." For instance, research conducted by the US National Oceanic and Atmospheric Administration (NOAA) after the contentious report issued in 2007 by the UN Intergovernmental Panel on Climate Change clearly demonstrates that, of eleven indicators of climate examined, "each one pointed to a world that was warming owing to the influence of greenhouse gases" (Harvey, 2010). A subsequent report by the US Environmental Protection Agency (EPA) examined all documents related to the so-called climategate affair at the Climate Research Unit of East Anglia University in Britain, concluding that the information revealed "nothing that seriously discredits the scientific consensus on global warming" (WP, 2010b). So, even continuing to grant that the doubters are correct in asserting that uncertainties accompany the science, they are nevertheless wrong when they offer that as a reason for doing nothing. Then, assuming continuing validity of the proposition that "Nothing preoc-cupies the mind as much as the prospect of being hung," the use of comprehensive peacebuilding to enhance the survival of the planet, *homo sapiens*, and other species may become core elements of the "new" realism.

In this regard, President Obama's chief of staff, former Congressman Rahm Emanuel (2008), has commented that "The crisis we have today . . . is an opportunity to finally do what Washington for years has postponed and kicked down the road. . . . [We] cannot afford now to kick those down the

[road] any longer." One approach to taking advantage of the opportunities created by the manifold global crises is to combine synergistically the historical moment of Obama's presidency with the global zeitgeist and for the UN, the US, the EU, Japan, China, and others, initially within the G20, to design and launch a number of interconnected regional "Marshall Plans" in Asia, Africa, the Middle East, and the Balkans, where, as in the original model, the donors *as well as* the recipients would benefit in "win–win" (+5+5) fashion.

Such a global economic stimulus package would be compatible with, and encouraging of, long-term maximalist peacebuilding, which, if accompanied by strategies to privilege the local and "talk with the enemy," despite problems experienced thus far (e.g., with Iran), would likely be in full conformity with Obama's "Change that we can believe in!" If not now, when?

Epilogue

This volume now "stops" (rather than "ends") as a "work in progress about a work in progress" – as a set of conceptual insights, including creative checklists, to help policymakers (and researchers, academics, students, and others) navigate their way through a shifting terrain of increasing global "complex interdependence" (Clemens, 2004; Sandole, 2006d), where everything is insidiously related to everything else and where, consequently, any effort to deal with any one issue must deal with multiple issues, lest the law of unintended consequences trump all efforts to contain possible catastrophic disorder.

As this volume was nearing completion, in late September 2009, in only one week (22–6 September 2009), world leaders gathered in New York City for the annual meetings of the General Assembly of the United Nations; President Obama, on the first day of the UN meetings, hosted a meeting between Israel and Palestine "to break the Middle East stalemate after a troubled week for US diplomacy in the region" (Morris, 2009); the Clinton Global Initiative met in New York City, with leaders from government, business, and civil society discussing pressing global challenges; and leaders of the G20 met in Pittsburgh, for the third time in a year, to discuss how to prevent a repeat global economic crisis. Not to pass up on a great opportunity to generate even more momentum toward addressing the "commons," World Bank President Robert Zoellick recommended that the G20 agenda cover "responsible globalization," in which the participants link "efforts to promote more balanced growth with financial stability, development and climate change" (Guha, 2009).

Just one week before these meetings, President Obama cancelled Bush-era plans to deploy a missile defense system in two former Warsaw Pact countries, Poland and the Czech Republic. This planned deployment had outraged the Russians to such an extent that, along with NATO's expansion up to Russia's borders – to include Georgia and Ukraine – the resurrection of a new Cold War between the two former rivals seemed to be likely. With this "gratuitous irritant" out of the way, the Russians and Americans were able to hit the "reset button" in their relations and, among other issues of common concern (see Talbott, 2009), agree to a new START treaty in Prague on 8 April 2010.

Despite the potential auspicious trajectory of events in September 2009, the global problematique is still very active and threatening. Consider, for example, the fiasco of the post-Kyoto conference in Copenhagen in December 2009, which failed to deal effectively with global warming. Indeed, since then, one island has even disappeared. New Moore Island, claimed by both India and Bangladesh for more than thirty-five years, has "vanished almost as quickly as it came into existence":

> Disappearances like this could become much more common in South Asia over the next few years. The UN predicts that low-lying Bangladesh could lose almost one-fifth of its territory and see 20 million citizens displaced by 2050 if, as expected, sea levels rise by 3.3 feet. . . . five inhabited islands in the Sundarbans delta region, where New Moore once sat, could disappear in the next 10 years alone. (AP, 2010)

Nevertheless, efforts are being made to address these problems, and not unsuccessfully, in part because of the problem-solving momentum generated by Obama's success domestically with healthcare reform and his efforts internationally to undermine nuclear weapons proliferation, including the possibility of nuclear weapons or materials falling into the hands of terrorists.

As an ambitious possible assist, we have likened this volume to an updated version of *The Prince*, except that, in our case – assuming that national interest is, indeed, global interest and vice versa – the objective is to have many actors achieve their positive goals, and none at the expense of others. This throws a new light on "security," which is no longer a scarce resource to be pursued in zero-sum, ethnocentric terms. Accordingly, Machiavelli's prescriptions are no longer relevant to the "new" reality; instead, they are dangerously at odds with it. The need for a multi-paradigmatic "new realism" is clear.

As part of this "new security paradigm," the volume has framed peacebuilding as an example of John Burton's (1993) "Conflict Resolution as a Political Philosophy" in action. Again, this captures not only Burton's (1990) idea of conflict *provention* – the need to deal significantly with the sources of violent conflict, to the point of their elimination – but also Ramsbotham, Woodhouse, and Miall's (2005, pp. 251, 263–4) cosmopolitan conflict resolution, which reflects "the idea that the flourishing and well-being of human beings is a matter of concern to all. This applies to people equally, whoever they are, and it applies globally." Hence:

> the response to terrorism is one part of a response to a much larger set of global issues, which have to do not only with violence but also with human rights, opportunities for livelihood and free expression, and the life-chances of ordinary people. *It is attending to these sources of conflict, rather than launching military interventions, that preventive action is needed.* An opportunity is available to be seized, since there is a

genuine international consensus that terrorist methods are entirely abhorrent and unacceptable, but also that where associated political aspirations are legitimate they must be seen to be addressed with utmost seriousness. *Global injustices and the failure of existing institutions to recognize and respect political aspirations need remedying for their own sake. But in the process, there is hope of addressing the sources of humiliation, rage and despair that are the fuel of terrorism.* It faces many obstacles, but the cosmopolitan conflict resolution approach has a vital role to play. (Ibid., emphasis added)

Without claiming too much for the volume, a careful digestion of its contents would alert policymakers and others to what may be required in terms of regional and global infrastructure – including creative partnerships between the US, the EU, regional organizations, and NGOs – to avoid, say, another Yugoslav-type implosion into genocidal warfare.

The volume can also be helpful to the leader of the "indispensable nation," as Barack Obama and others involved in Afghanistan, Pakistan, and elsewhere in the global war on terror attempt to determine the optimal mix, sequence, and weightings among the "three D's" of his foreign policy orientation – defense, diplomacy, and development. These conditions are necessary for achieving sustainable security, which may, indeed, as predicted by the new head of the British army, Sir David Richards, take thirty to forty years (Dombey, 2009).

Finally, as one personal contribution to ensuring the participation of students in the comprehensive peacebuilding project, especially those who aspire to become policymakers or other types of global problem solvers, I have recently established a graduate course, "Global Governance and Complex Problem Solving in the Post-9/11 World" (CONF 695), as part of the MSc and PhD in conflict analysis and resolution at the Institute for Conflict Analysis and Resolution at George Mason University, for which this volume will be included among the required readings. One feature of the course is that the students are invited voluntarily to edit their final papers into a "Memo for the President," which we will then endeavor to send to the National Security Council, as well as to other relevant agencies of the US government, in the hopes that it might be read and "even" influence policy with a cosmopolitan conflict resolution and *provention* perspective.[1]

Notes

PROLOGUE

1 Notable examples of efforts to shape the thinking of policymakers include Albright (2008), Bacevich (2008), Brzezinski (2007), Fukuyama (2006), Kagan (2008), Mahbubani (2008), Nye (2004), Patten (2008), Sanger (2009), Shapiro (2008), Zakaria (2008).
2 This is in contrast to how political leaders should, *a priori*, behave, i.e., based upon compelling deductive logic.
3 See chapter 58 in Book I of *The Discourses*, on "The Multitude is Wiser and More Constant than a Prince" (Machiavelli, [1532] 1966).
4 See "cosmopolitan conflict resolution" in Ramsbotham et al. (2005), Part II.
5 A new edition of *The Prince* (2008, trans. Peter Constantine) was published at about the same time that Jeffrey Sachs and Secretary Albright's more comprehensive recommendations appeared, furthering the continuation of the clash of competing political paradigms – e.g., *Realpolitik* and *Idealpolitik* – in the postmodern world (see Sandole, 1999, pp. 110–13).

CHAPTER I PEACEBUILDING AND THE GLOBAL PROBLEMATIQUE

1 The Korean War "ended" in 1953 with an armistice that brought negative peace to relations between the US and North Korea, a fragile condition that has endured for more than half a century with little movement toward positive peace.
2 For a comprehensive analysis of the "ontology" of peace, see Richmond (2005, 2008).

3 This puzzle is an explicit entrée into the conceptually and operationally frustrating world of competing, overlapping, and unclear definitions of peacebuilding. Such "definitional debates" characterize other aspects of conflict analysis and resolution (CAR) as well – e.g., conflict, violence, aggression, mediation, conflict resolution, peace, and the like. For ease of expression, in general discourse, including in this volume, we tend to employ the "generic" term (which may, nevertheless, confound effective communication). Hence, for Anna Snyder (2009, p. 56, note 1):

> Peacebuilding is a term that continues to be defined in many ways in the field of peace and conflict studies. [Here] it is used in its broadest sense, including many types of peace activities rather than the narrower definition that homes in on post-conflict reconstruction and reconciliation. Peacemaking, which may also refer to a broad range of peace activities, here refers to mediation, negotiation, conciliation, and/or dialogue.

While frustrating, the existence of this problem is also a sign of the maturation ("growing pains") of CAR, and of peacebuilding in general, implying that the latter may be more effectively employed in practice and policy. For example, the clash between the generic use of the term and the narrow minimalist vs. maximalist forms of peacebuilding can assist researchers in determining which orientations, policies, and practices are more likely to conduce to one or the other forms, and to what extent getting to the minimalist form may be a prerequisite for achieving maximalist peacebuilding.

4 Minimalist peacebuilding "writ large" does not, by definition, advance as far as peacebuilding "writ small," achieving only up to peacekeeping or coercive peacemaking levels.

5 Some time later, again endeavoring to build on the earlier work of an illustrious predecessor – i.e., Albert Einstein – I used the 4WM as a basis for crafting a "Unified Field Theory of Conflict and Conflict Resolution" (see Sandole, 1999, ch. 8).

6 After the genocidal massacres in Rwanda during April–July 1994 and in Srebrenica (Bosnia-Herzegovina) during 12–18 July 1995, the "responsibility to protect" (R2P) norm, with respect to protecting populations from genocide, ethnic cleansing, war crimes and crimes against humanity, became for many a

Kantian "categorical imperative" (see ICISS, 2001; Weiss, 2007, ch. 4; and www.responsibilitytoprotect.org).

7 This is, admittedly, for "constructivists," a problematic statement (see Moses and Knutsen, 2007).

8 These findings are compatible with surveys that I conducted of CSCE/OSCE senior diplomats in Vienna, Austria, at four points in time (1993, 1997, 1999, and 2004). The findings indicate that, during the eleven-year period under study: "the world seemed to be developing in a less violent, more peaceful way [in part because] the CSCE/OSCE moved closer to a complex operating paradigm, with *Idealpolitik* as well as *Realpolitik* elements inclusive of a *culture of conflict resolution*" (Sandole, 2007a, p. 176).

9 "4+2" refers to the integration of the best from *Realpolitik*, *Idealpolitik*, Marxism and non-Marxist radical thought (NMRT), with confrontational as well as collaborative means for implementing these "best practices" (Sandole, 1993; 1999, ch. 6).

10 Strobe Talbott is president of the Brookings Institution, which co-directs the MGI Project (MGI, 2008a, 2008b), addressing these and other global threats. Hence, it is highly likely that his wisdom will be elicited to help shape President Obama's foreign policy agenda.

11 I sometimes use "post-[violent] conflict situations," instead of the more customary "post-conflict situations," to indicate that "conflict" does not necessarily end with the cessation of violence. We have only to consider Bosnia-Herzegovina, where, fifteen years after the imposition of "negative peace" by the Dayton peace process, conflict is still very much part of the political landscape.

CHAPTER 2 COMPLEX PROBLEM SOLVING
IN VIOLENT CONFLICTS

1 In her *Memo to the President-Elect*, former US Secretary of State Madeleine Albright (2008, pp. 6–7) makes the useful distinction between outlining global problems in need of solution (the "what"), which we attempted in chapter 1, and the greater challenge of indicating "how" such problems might be solved, which is the objective in this chapter.

2 Party I is the row chooser (horizontal; first number in each quadrant), while Party II is the column chooser (vertical, second number in each quadrant).

3 In the classic formulation of PD, two young men are apprehended by the police on grounds that they have committed a horrible crime. They are taken to police headquarters, separated, and interrogated incommunicado. Each is presented with the following options: "Confess and you go free, while we 'throw the book' at your partner. Remain silent and we get you both on a lesser charge (manslaughter)"! No matter how each frames and considers the issue, each winds up "defecting" (+10–10/–10+10) and, therefore, both lose (–5–5) (see Rapoport, 1964, p. 290, note 13).

4 "Cognitive dissonance" refers to an actor's sense of breakdown between an actual state of affairs and an expected state of affairs. Experienced emotionally as anxiety ("acute psychological distress"), it provides an opportunity to reachieve balance between expectation and reality or between personal beliefs and behavior (see Festinger, 1962).

5 In one rendering of this "game," two young men in their respective cars race toward each other on a single road, the objective being to determine who swerves from the potentially suicidal course first – i.e., who the "chicken" is. The problem is, if neither decides to avoid certain death, they crash, with their lives cut short in a fireball, possibly taking a number of onlookers with them.

6 The Russian–Georgian war over South Ossetia and resulting East–West crisis of August 2008 caused alarm among some observers that a "new" Cold War might be in the making (see Meier, 2008).

7 There seems to be a developing preference within the Obama administration to avoid any further reference to the GWOT (see Burkeman, 2009).

8 Lewis F. Richardson's (1939, 1960) seminal work on arms races is illustrative of earlier thinking on "self-stimulating/self-perpetuating violent conflict processes."

9 The 3Ds concept also reflects initiatives in the NGO community, such as the 3D Security Initiative, which specifically mentions "development, diplomacy, and defense" as constituent elements of its "system-wide approach to security" involving civilian and

military actors. See www.3dsecurity.org/ (accessed 2 September 2009).

10 An example of entry into conflict settings at the middle-range level is the Partnership for Peace (PfP) Consortium Study Group on Regional Stability in South East Europe, which deals with conflicts in the Balkans and elsewhere in Southeastern Europe. Its published proceedings are disseminated to government ministries and others, and then made available online (at www.bmlv.gv.at/wissen-forschung/publikationen/verlag.php?id=22). This enhances access by members of all leadership levels worldwide. For a different view on the utility of entry at the middle range level of leadership, see Ryan (2009, p. 306):

> [The Marxist approach] might . . . call into question the idea of compatible interests between elites and the grassroots, which challenges Lederach's influential idea of the conflict pyramid, part of an attempt to integrate strategic approaches to conflict resolution (Lederach, 1997). Here Lederach identifies a middle level of society that can act as a bridge between elites and the grassroots when working for peace. But Marxists might question if these three levels are mutually compatible and suggest that mobilization of the grassroots should lead to more conflict with elites.

11 Senator George Mitchell is a high-status member of the American political establishment with an impressive record as a third-party intervener in the Northern Irish peace process that led to the Good Friday Agreement.

12 See Davidson and Montville (1981–2), McDonald and Bendahmane (1987), Diamond and McDonald (1996), Mitchell and Banks (1996), and Reychler and Paffenholz (2001, chs. 5.1–5.2, 6.1–6.4, and 7.1–7.2).

13 For a comprehensive critique of track 2 problem-solving efforts, especially with regard to the Israeli–Palestinian conflict, see Rouhana (2000).

14 Of course, what von Clausewitz ([1832] 1968) said was that "War is politics by other means."

15 In its major study of violence worldwide, the World Health Organization utilizes Dugan's nested theory as a basis for its "ecological model for understanding violence" (WHO, 2002, p. 9, fig. 3), where:

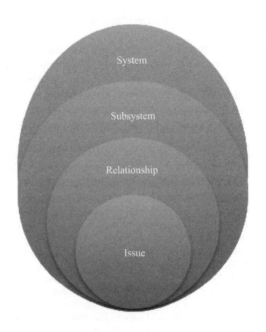

Systemic environment = Societal
Subsystemic environment = Community
Relationship
Issue = Individual

16 The exemplar of this growing phenomenon – greatly amplified
   by the Internet – is the Global Partnership for the Prevention of
   Armed Conflict (GPPAC); see www.gppac.net/page.php?id=1485
   (accessed 14 April 2009).
17 See Brown (1957); Deutsch (1971); and Thompson and Van
   Houten (1970, pp. 143–4).
18 The costly US invasion and occupation of Iraq from March 2003
   until the present time can be seen as a result of the lingering
   nonrealistic affect generated by the terrorist attacks of 11
   September 2001.
19 See Lerche and Said (1970, pp. 147–50); Kissinger (1964, p. 1
   [cited in Dougherty and Pfaltzgraff, 1997, pp. 78–80]); and
   Moore (1986, p. 27).

20 UNPREDEP is discussed in detail in chapter 3.

21 See Davidson and Montville (1981–2); McDonald and Bendahmane (1987); and Diamond and McDonald (1996).

22 The theme of the "intoxication" of warfare is explored in the film *The Hurt Locker*, directed by Katherine Bigelow, which won six Academy Awards in 2010, including for best director and best picture.

CHAPTER 3   IMPROVING THE RECORD

1 See Avruch and Black (1993); Bangura (2008); Richmond (2005, 2008); Rouhana (2000); Ryan (2009); Tschirgi (2004); and UN/PBSO (2008).

2 The "whole-of-government" and similar approaches (e.g., "whole-of-community") will be addressed in chapter 5.

3 This observation stands in sharp contrast to Call and Cousens's (2008) explicit preference for the minimalist approach to peacebuilding or, at most, something between minimalism (negative peace) – "the most readily visible indicator of success for efforts to consolidate peace" – and maximalism (positive peace): "the most ambitious measures . . . to redress *so-called* 'root causes' of conflict" (ibid., pp. 6, 7, emphasis added). Call and Cousens

> adopt a definition of peacebuilding that reflects the trend among scholars of armed conflict, as well as some practitioners, which is: actions undertaken by international or national actors to institutionalize peace, understood as the absence of armed conflict ("negative peace") and a modicum of participatory politics (a component of "positive peace") that can be sustained in the absence of an international peace operation. *If there is a trade-off between these goals, the immediate absence of conflict, in our view, should take priority if peacebuilding is the frame of reference*". (Ibid., p. 4, emphasis added)

4 Perhaps such findings should not be surprising, given that they have been generated by studies of attempted security and justice reforms in war-torn societies conducted by a "donor-fatigued" international community with limited resources, interventions of short duration, local conflict-resolution resistance, and other challenges, including low-esteem characterizations of "internationals" as either "missionaries, mercenaries, or misfits"

(personal communication by "international" member of the OSCE mission in Bosnia-Herzegovina).

5 Clearly, "privileging the local" can itself be problematic in a complex situation where conflict *among* "the locals" is what may have brought about state collapse and the need for international intervention. This is a challenge that must be addressed on a case-by-case basis to avoid violating the categorical imperative to "do no harm" (Anderson, 1999; Polman, 2010).

6 Sokalski implicitly makes this connection between UNPREDEP's "three-pillar" strategy and the "three levels of conflict reality":

> troop deployments (*peacekeeping*) and good offices (*peacemaking*) are highly visible and directed modalities to bring about peace and stability. The broader technique of fostering civil society through social and economic development (*peacebuilding*) is certainly more unobtrusive, but it is also a much more difficult method of trying to resolve economic and social inequalities, first and foremost because its scope is so wide: after all, how does a small UN mission try to set an entire society aright? (2003, p. 151, emphasis added)

7 UNPREDEP was terminated on 1 March 1999. The People's Republic of China vetoed its extension at a meeting of the UN Security Council on 25 February 1999, ostensibly because there was no longer any need for the mission. The "real" reason, apparently, was that the PRC was incensed that Macedonia and the "other" China, Taiwan, had entered into diplomatic relations (Sokalski, 2003, pp. 207, 211, 214–16). Shortly afterwards, NATO's 78-day bombing campaign against Serbia occurred, in response to Serb "ethnic cleansing" of Albanians in Kosovo. The subsequent empowerment of the Kosovar Albanians, the shared border between Kosovo and Macedonia, and the absence of UNPREDEP helped unleash six months of hostilities between the Macedonian government and ethnic Albanians during spring/summer 2001 (shortly before the events of 11 September 2001).

8 This may account, in part, for the deployment of "human terrain teams" to Afghanistan. HTTs are made up of anthropologists and social scientists, who work alongside soldiers to win the hearts and minds of the Afghan people (see Gezari, 2009).

9 In his seminal classic on the nature of "paradigms" (collective world views) and their maintenance and transformation, Thomas Kuhn tells us that

the new paradigm, or a sufficient hint to permit later articulation, emerges all at once, sometimes in the middle of the night, in the mind of a man deeply immersed in crisis. What the nature of that final stage is – how an individual invents (or finds he has invented) a new way of giving order to data now all assembled – must here remain inscrutable and may be permanently so. Let us here note only one thing about it. *Almost always the men who achieve these fundamental inventions of a new paradigm have been either very young or very new to the field whose paradigm they change.* . . . obviously these are the men who, being little committed by prior practice to the traditional rules . . . are particularly likely to see that those rules no longer define a playable game and to conceive another set that can replace them. (1970, p. 89–90; emphasis added)

10 In this regard, Sokalski mentions that "Organizations, programs, and agencies of the [UN] system are normally the first allies of action on behalf of peace. Yet at the field level, individual UN entities involved in operational activities all too often pursued their *programs independently and without sufficient regard to, or benefit from, one another's presence*" (2003, p. 176, emphasis added).

11 For a comprehensive account of the peacemaking activities of Max van der Stoel, the OSCE's very first high commissioner on national minorities, from 1 January 1993 until early 2001, see Kemp (2001).

12 For various perspectives on such a "continuum of action," see Fisher and Keashly (1991), Fisher (1997, ch. 8), and Lund (1996, ch. 2).

13 In other words, UNPREDEP was deprived of funding in the critical areas of conflict reality levels 2 and 3, dealing with relationships and the underlying causes and conditions of why relationships become fractured.

14 Russian "peacekeepers" have been protecting the South Ossetians and Abkhaz since the end of hostilities in both breakaway regions in the early 1990s. After ministers announced at the NATO Bucharest summit in April 2008 that Ukraine and Georgia could be invited to become NATO members, Russia issued passports to the South Ossetians and Abkhaz, thereby transforming them into "Russian citizens," worthy of Russia defense from any future Georgian or other aggression.

15 Personal communication with Prof. Dr Lyudmila Harutyunyan, director of the Center for Regional Integration and Conflict

Resolution, and chair, Department of Sociology, Yerevan State
University, Armenia, 17 September 2008.

16 On 3 March 2010, against the expressed wishes of the Obama
administration, the Foreign Affairs Committee of the US House
of Representatives voted 23 to 22 to adopt a nonbinding measure
on "the systemic and deliberate annihilation of 1,500,000
Armenians" during the Ottoman era. It called on President
Obama to "characterize [the atrocities] as genocide" when he
addressed the issue during the annual presidential statement in
April 2010. This vote so infuriated the Turkish government that
it recalled its ambassador to Washington "for consultation,"
warning that the decision "could adversely affect [Turkish and
US] cooperation on a wide common agenda" (Sheridan, 2010a).

17 The Caucasus platform was inspired by the European Union's
Stability Pact for South Eastern Europe (which was succeeded on
27 February 2008 by the Regional Cooperation Council). The
pact was designed to prepare the states emerging out of the
implosion of Yugoslavia for EU membership, so that
Southeastern Europe would never again be a source of genocidal
conflict (see Kardas, 2008; Regional Cooperation Council,
2008). This, plus the fact that the platform builds on the EU's
European Neighbourhood Policy for the region (see European
Commission, 2008; Leonard, 2005, pp. 106–10) and that Turkey
is currently negotiating entry into the EU, is a powerful hint that
it calls for some kind of integration within the region, which
would dampen tensions that might otherwise escalate the
secessionist conflicts that have characterized it until now.

18 At the forty-fifth Munich Security Conference on 7 February
2009, US Vice President Joseph Biden asserted President
Obama's objective of improved relations with Russia, to which
Russia responded with "cautious optimism" (see Blitz and Peel,
2009). President Obama's subsequent meeting with Russian
President Dmitry Medvedev, one day before the G20 summit in
London on 1 April 2009, was far more positive, resulting in
offers to restart nuclear arms talks to replace the Strategic Arms
Reduction Treaty (START) due to expire on 5 December 2009,
plus an invitation for Obama to visit Moscow in July to discuss
remaining issues before the December signing of the new treaty
(Borger, 2009). On 8 April 2010, Obama and Medvedev
concluded a new START treaty to slash their respective nuclear

warheads and launchers by one-third (WP, 2010a; Cienski and Dombey, 2010). According to Senator Richard G. Lugar (R-Ind.), "a key supporter of arms control, . . . the administration [planned] to have the [signing] ceremony . . . in Prague, where Obama first laid out the arms-control agenda that helped win him the Nobel Peace Prize" (Sheridan and Pan, 2010). The *Financial Times* (FT, 2010) heralds this agreement as one of the two biggest achievements of Obama's presidency (the other being the passage of healthcare reform).

19 For a critique of the Marshall Plan "metaphor," articulated one month following the devastating earthquake in Haiti, see Beehner (2010).

20 According to Lund (2009, p. 291), ad hoc prevention consists of "actions directed at specific countries [e.g., Macedonia] facing imminent conflicts." By contrast, *a priori* prevention includes the actions of global and regional organizations [e.g., the UN and EU, respectively], premised on "legal conventions or other normative standards, such as in human rights and democracy . . . that whole classes of states are expected to stay within." In either case, preventive action may be direct and/or structural, the former dealing with "conflict-as-symptoms" and the latter with "conflict-as-relationships" and/or "conflict-as-underlying-causes-and-conditions" (ibid., pp. 289–91).

CHAPTER 4   PEACEBUILDING AND THE "GLOBAL WAR ON TERROR"

1 According to Zartman (2005, pp. 2–3):

> Absolute terrorism . . . expresses the frustration of the "suicider" with the situation and his inability to change it by any other means. Suiciders . . . are beyond negotiation, even beyond dissuasion. . . . Within the category, however, total (or revolutionary) absolutes can be distinguished from conditional absolutes. Total absolutes have nothing to negotiate about: they have nothing to negotiate with, and any attempt to negotiate with them only encourages them . . . It is notoriously difficult even to contact them and to talk them out of their act while they are up in the air or even on the street heading toward their target. . . . Conditional absolutes are suiciders who use the same tactics but for finite, dividable, exchangeable goals, even though their act itself is as self-contained and absolute as that of any other

suiciders. They do have something to negotiate about – territory,
independence, conditions – even if their suicide tactics are
absolute. . . . Contingent or instrumental terrorism refers mainly to
hostage-taking and covers much of the literature of the past century
on negotiating with terrorists. Its violence is not definitive or
absolute; . . . Contingent terrorists seek negotiations, to exchange
their victims for something – publicity, ransom, release of their
friends.

See also Faure and Zartman (2010).

2 Needless to say, "who" members of a certain minority group are
   may imply commission or omission of certain objectionable acts;
   nevertheless, despite the unavoidable linkage, the emphasis in
   the definition of structural violence is on "who" rather than
   "what."

3 The Working Group produced two volumes (Moore, 2002,
   2004), both published by the US Defense Threat Reduction
   Agency (DTRA). (In addition, see Sandole, 2002c, 2004; Sandole
   et al., 2004.)

4 In contrast to the impression perhaps inadvertently given that
   "all Muslims are the same," it is useful to observe that the
   concept of a "clash of civilizations" certainly exists in the minds
   of its inventor, Princeton's Sir Bernard Lewis (Mamdani, 2004),
   its primary popularizer, Harvard's Samuel Huntington (1993,
   1996), and certainly Osama bin Laden (Whitlock, 2008). It does
   not, however, seem to be reality for the 601 journalists in
   thirteen Arab countries in North Africa, the Levant, and the
   Arabian peninsula surveyed in 2007 by Lawrence Pintak, Remy
   Ginges, and Nicholas Felton (2008). While the majority of the
   journalists clearly found fault with US policy in general,
   especially on the Middle East, they just as clearly appreciate
   Americans and American values on political reform, human
   rights, poverty, and education. The survey results trump rhetoric
   with reality, "shatter[ing] many of the myths upon which
   American public diplomacy strategy has been based." The results
   remind us that, while the pernicious civilizational clash can
   always become a self-fulfilling reality, as it has for some in the
   post-9/11 world, it need not be a permanent feature of global
   affairs in the twenty-first century.

5 For some salutary developments in this regard, see Economist
   (2008c).

6 Morton Deutsch at the John Jay conference during 21–3 March 2002, in a comment attributed to Frantz Fanon.

7 Psychiatrist and conflict resolution pioneer Vamik Volkan (1997, p. 68) uses the metaphor of "psychological DNA" to refer to the tenacity with which traumatic historical events exercise a hold over people's perceptions, thinking, and actions, often for centuries after the initial events occurred.

8 In asymmetric warfare, under-resourced nonstate actors use whatever limited, nontraditional means to which they have access in order to cause injury, damage, or destruction to much more powerful, (usually) state governmental enemies, who would easily defeat them in a conventional military exchange.

9 The comments by the suspects in this trial clearly confirm Robert Pape's (2005) thesis that, in this particular case, the objective of the "new" (i.e., suicide) terrorism is to force the infidel, "Crusader" occupier to withdraw from the lands of Islam.

10 A more recent and strident demonstration of US displeasure toward the Israeli settlements policy was expressed by Dr Rice's successor, Hillary Rodham Clinton, reprimanding Prime Minister Binyamin Netanyahu for his government's plans to build 1,600 new homes in occupied East Jerusalem. The plan was announced when Vice President Joseph Biden, who was equally condemnatory, was in the country to support "proximity talks" between Israelis and Palestinians (see Dombey, 2010; Kessler, 2010; Zacharia, 2010).

11 The classic example of this counter-intuitive experience can be found in the *Realpolitik* maxim that "the best way to prevent war is to prepare for war" ("*Sic vis pacem, para bellum*"). This proposition made sense in antiquity, and into the modern period, until, with progressive technological development, it "catastrophically shifted," making war *more*, rather than less likely.

12 The withdrawal of foreign forces by July 2010, a year before Obama's planned date for pulling out US forces, was a key ingredient of Hezb-i-Islami's fifteen-point plan for ending the war in Afghanistan (Riechmann, 2010).

13 According to Pakistani journalist Ahmed Rashid (2008), Bommer's ambitious plan may now be more necessary than ever, if not too late:

Relations between the U.S. military and the Pakistani army, critical allies in the "war on terror," are at their worst point since Sept. 11, 2001, senior Western military officers and diplomats [in Kabul] say, as Pakistani troops withdraw from several tribal areas bordering Afghanistan that are home to Taliban and al-Qaeda leaders and thousands of their fighters. Gen. Ashfaq Kiyani, chief of the Pakistani army, has told U.S. military and NATO officials that he will not retrain or reequip troops to fight the counterinsurgency war the Americans are demanding on Pakistan's mountainous western border. . . . More than 80 percent of the $10 billion in U.S. aid to Pakistan since the Sept. 11 attacks has gone to the military; much of it has been used to buy expensive weapons systems for the Indian front rather than the smaller items needed for counterinsurgency. . . . Taliban attacks from Pakistan into Afghanistan have risen dramatically this spring; in April, incidents spiked to more than 100 a week, up from 60 a week in March. Attacks probably rose in May, according to NATO officials, who report a sharp increase in the number of Pakistanis, Arabs and those of other nationalities fighting alongside the Taliban in Afghanistan.

Since President Obama's inauguration, Pakistani authorities have worked more closely with the US in advancing American objectives in Pakistan with regard to Afghanistan, including participating in joint operations with the US to apprehend or kill "high-value" Taliban. As of this writing, General David Petraeus's image of a "whole-of-government" approach has been applied to developing a partnership with Pakistan.

14 Three of the accused were convicted, on 7 September 2009, of plotting "to kill thousands of people using liquid bombs on transatlantic flights" (Michael Peel, 2009).

CHAPTER 5 THE US AND THE FUTURE OF PEACEBUILDING

1 On evaluation of peacebuilding interventions, see Gürkaynak et al. (2009). On the design and implementation of research, see Sandole (2009a).

2 This is clearly a sentiment with which former President Bush's chief of staff Karl Rove does not agree (see Rove, 2010).

3 As of this writing, the Pakistani government is seeking to reopen its probe into Dr Khan's WMD-related activities. For his part, Khan – who is accompanied "everywhere by security personnel and generally prohibited from meeting with foreigners or traveling abroad" – claims that the Pakistani government not only knew but approved of his transactions with North Korea and Iran (see R. Jeffrey Smith, 2010).

4 The isolation of China is less likely for the Concert than for the League. According to the former's architects, Anne-Marie Slaughter and John Ikenberry,

> a Concert of Democracies that included southern as well as northern democracies would insist on including China in any expansion of the G8. That fact highlights the contrast between our Concert and Senator McCain's proposal of a League of Democracies, together with the expulsion of Russia from the G8. Democracies understand the need to have effective global institutions that include *all* important powers" (2008, emphasis added).

Although Robert Kagan (2008, pp. 97–105) refers to both "Concert" and "League," and his formulation is similar in many respects to that of Slaughter and Ikenberry, he is nevertheless much closer to McCain's vision of a League which envisages a "balance of power" between democratic and autocratic countries, with China and Russia remaining in the latter category for some time to come.

5 As to whether a Global Union of Democracies might also alienate China, given that members must be democracies, McClintock (2008, p. 206) indicates that China (as well as Russia) "would have to become less authoritarian and to be prepared to better accommodate the wishes of ordinary people in the decisions of the state." Despite its troublesome human rights record, evident even during the Beijing Olympics, China has made great strides in achieving one component of an *eventual* democracy: economic growth. In this regard World Values Survey and European Values Study researchers Ronald Inglehart and Christian Welzel (2009, p. 48) point out that: "Beneath China's seemingly monolithic political structure, the social infrastructure of democratization is emerging, and it has progressed further than most observers realize. China is now

approaching the level of mass emphasis on self-expression values at which Chile, Poland, South Korea, and Taiwan made their transitions to democracy."

6 According to Peter Bergen and Katherine Tiedemann (2009) of the New America Foundation, by the middle of October 2009 there had been forty-three strikes in Pakistan (two while Bush was still in office), compared with thirty-four during the whole of 2008.

7 Clearly, the quantity and quality of these interrelationships are such that, through fear of invoking the "law of unintended consequences," they could lead to decision-making paralysis. Hence, Ambassador Pascual's caveat that, "if we say that everything is related to everything else, and you have to solve everything to make progress, we create an untenable situation where we cannot make progress. And so we have to recognize those linkages, draw on the opportunities, yet not handcuff ourselves in the process" (MGI, 2008b, pp. 15–16).

8 See Popper's P1 – TT – EE – P2 – i.e.:

> we start from some problem P1, proceed to a tentative solution or tentative theory TT, which may be (partly or wholly) mistaken; in any case it will be subject to error-elimination, EE, which may consist of critical discussion or experimental test; at any rate, new problems P2 arise from our own creative activity; and these new problems are not in general intentionally created by us, they emerge autonomously from the field of new relationships which we cannot help bringing into existence with every action, however little we intend to do so. (Popper, 1972, p. 119)

9 A study conducted by Craig Burnett, Elizabeth Garrett, and Matthew McCubbins, "The Dilemma of Direct Democracy," found "no support for the expectation that better informed voters . . . are likely to make reasoned decisions than those who are . . . uninformed." They observed that "Knowledge does not matter," as participants in their study cast their votes "in a manner consistent with their own underlying preferences" (cited in Lozada, 2010).

10 For further information on the UN's new peacebuilding architecture, including the Peacebuilding Fund, whose role is to provide "sustained support to countries emerging from conflict . . . at a time when other funding mechanisms may not yet be available" (UN/PBSO, 2008, p. 5), see UN/PBC (2009) and the Stanley Foundation (2009).

11 See Gareth Evans's (2008, ch. 10) instructive comments on "mobilizing political will."

12 Again, the nine tracks are: Track 1: diplomacy; Track 2: professional conflict resolution; Track 3: commerce; Track 4: personal involvement; Track 5: learning; Track 6: advocacy; Track 7: faith in action; Track 8: providing resources; and Track 9: information (see Diamond and McDonald, 1996).

13 According to Bryan Schaaff (2010, p. 6), Haiti has been referred to as the "Republic of NGOs," with perhaps as many as 6,000 private agencies serving a population of 9 million. Sheridan (2010b) puts the figure as high as 10,000.

14 Communicated to me by my colleague Dr Maire Dugan.

15 This global influence of the US remains significant despite the impact on it of the global financial and economic crisis (see Mandelbaum, 2010).

EPILOGUE

1 To peruse the syllabus for this course, go to http://icar.gmu.edu/ ICAR_Courses_09FA.html.

References

Abbott, Chris, Paul Rogers and John Sloboda (2007) *Beyond Terror: The Truth about the Real Threats to our World*. London: Rider.

ABC (2008) "Australia Calls for North East Security Structure," 1 April, www.abc.net.au/ra/programguide/stories/200804/s2205306.htm (accessed 21 November 2008).

Abu-Nimer, Mohammed (2003) *Nonviolence and Peace Building in Islam: Theory and Practice*. Gainesville: University Press of Florida.

Albright, Madeleine (2008) *Memo to the President Elect: How We Can Restore America's Reputation and Leadership*. New York: HarperCollins.

Alexander, Michelle (2010) *The New Jim Crow: Mass Incarceration in the Age of Colorblindness*. New York: New Press.

Alger, Chadwick F. (2007) "Peace Studies as a Transdisciplinary Project," in *A Handbook of Peace and Conflict Studies*, ed. Charles Webel and Johan Galtung. London and New York: Routledge.

Anastasiou, Harry (2007) "The EU as a Peace Building System: Deconstructing Nationalism in an Era of Globalization," *International Journal of Peace Studies*, 12(2): 31–50.

Anderson, Mary B. (1999) *Do No Harm: How Aid Can Support Peace – or War*. Boulder, CO: Lynne Rienner.

AP (2010) "Rising Sea Swallows Contested Island," Associated Press, 25 March, www.aolnews.com/world/article/climate-change-erases-contested-island/19414020 (accessed 25 March 2010).

Applebaum, Anne (2002) "Europe, Not Sure What to Make of Itself," *Washington Post*, 5 May, pp. B1, B5.

Avruch, Kevin (2009) "Culture Theory, Culture Clash, and the Practice of Conflict Resolution," in *A Handbook of Conflict Analysis and Resolution*, ed. Dennis J. D. Sandole, Sean Byrne, Ingrid Sandole-Staroste, and Jessica Senehi. London and New York: Routledge.

Avruch, Kevin, and Peter W. Black (1993) "Conflict Resolution in Intercultural Settings: Problems and Prospects," in *Conflict Resolution Theory and Practice: Integration and Application*, ed.

Dennis J. D. Sandole and Hugo van der Merwe. Manchester: Manchester University Press; New York: St Martin's Press.

Axelrod, Robert (1984) *The Evolution of Cooperation*. New York: Basic Books.

Bacevich, Andrew J. (2008) *The Limits of Power: The End of American Exceptionalism*. New York: Metropolitan Books.

Baggini, Julian (2010) "Divided We Fall: An Unequal Society is Bad for Rich and Poor Alike: Review of *Ill Fares the Land*, by Tony Judt," *Financial Times*, 3 April, "Life and Arts,"p. 15.

Baker, Peter (2002) "Attacks on Foreigners Rising in Russia: Frequency of Violence, Recruiting by Fascist Groups Alarm Kremlin," *Washington Post*, 11 August, pp. A1, A21.

Bangura, Abdul Karim (2008) *African Peace Paradigms*. Dubuque, IA: Kendall/Hunt.

Barash, David P. (2002) "Evolution, Males, and Violence," *Chronicle of Higher Education*, 24 May http://chronicle.com/free/v48/i37/37b00701.htm (accessed 9 June 2008).

Barber, Tony (2008) "Russia Agrees to Pull Back Forces in Georgia," *Financial Times*, 9 September.

Bawer, Bruce (2006) *While Europe Slept: How Radical Islam is Destroying the West from Within*. New York: Doubleday.

Baxter, Sarah (2004) "He Predicted the Clash of Civilisations," *Sunday Times*, 23 May, "News Review," p. 8.

BBC (2007) "Transcript: BBC Taleban Interview," BBC News, 21 June, http://news.bbc.co.uk/1/hi/world/south_asia/6224990.stm (accessed 9 June 2008).

Beehner, Lionel (2010) "Opinion: 'Too Many Marshall Plans,'" *AOL News*, 8 February, www.aolnews.com/opinion/article/opinion-too-many-marshall-plans/19347455 (accessed 16 March 2010).

Behrman, Jere R., Harold Alderman, and John Hoddinott (2007) "Hunger and Malnutrition," in *Solutions for the World's Biggest Problems: Costs and Benefits*, ed. Bjørn Lomborg. Cambridge and New York: Cambridge University Press.

Bekker, Vita, and Heba Saleh (2008) "Israel and Hamas Agree to Ceasefire: Egypt Mediation Leads to Truce. Gaza Crossings Might Be Opened," *Financial Times*, 18 June, p. 5.

Benedek, Wolfgang (ed.) (2006) *Civil Society and Good Governance in Societies in Transition*. Belgrade: Belgrade Center for Human Rights.

Bennhold, Katrin (2008) "Giving Young French Muslims a Close Look at the US," *New York Times*, 8 June, http://www.nytimes.

com/2008/06/08/world/europe/08clichy.html?_r=1&oref=slogin (accessed 9 June 2008).

Bergen, Peter, and Katherine Tiedemann (2009) "Revenge of the Drones: An Analysis of Drone Strikes in Pakistan," 19 October, www.peterbergen.com/articles/details.aspx?id=409 (accessed 4 April 2010).

Bertelsmann Stiftung (2010) *Culture and Conflict in Global Perspective: The Cultural Dimensions of Conflicts from 1945 to 2007.* Gütersloh: Bertelsmann Stiftung.

Bildt, Carl (1998) *Peace Journey: The Struggle for Peace in Bosnia.* London: Weidenfeld & Nicolson.

Bilefsky, Dan (2009) "War's Lingering Scars Slow Bosnia's Economic Growth," *New York Times*, 8 February, www.nytimes.com/2009/02/08/world/europe/08bosnia.html?_r=1&emc=eta (accessed 8 February 2009).

Biller, Dan (2007) "The Economics of Biodiversity Loss," in *Solutions for the World's Biggest Problems: Costs and Benefits*, ed. Bjørn Lomborg. Cambridge and New York: Cambridge University Press.

Blitz, James, and Tobias Buck (2007) "US Criticizes Israel over Settlements: Rare US Attack on Israeli Policy. Rice Emphasizes Need to Build Trust," *Financial Times*, 7 December, p. 2.

Blitz, James, and Quentin Peel (2009) "Moscow Warms to Biden's Overture," *Financial Times*, 9 February, p. 4.

Bloom, Mia (2005) *Dying to Kill: The Allure of Suicide Terror.* New York: Columbia University Press.

Bommer, Ashley (2008) "Hearts and Minds on the Durand Line: A Tribal Fund for the Pakistan–Afghanistan Border Is Critical to Winning the War on Terror," *Washington Post*, 18 February, p. A17.

Borger, Julian (2009) "Barack Obama and Dmitry Medvedev Promise Nuclear Arsenal Deal by End of Year," *The Guardian*, 1 April, www.guardian.co.uk/world/2009/apr/01/us-russia-nuclear-deal (accessed 20 April 2009).

Botes, Johannes (1997) "Media Roles in Conflict and Conflict Resolution: A Comparison between Television Moderators and Conventional Mediators," unpubd PhD dissertation, Institute for Conflict Analysis and Resolution, George Mason University.

Botes, Johannes (2003) "Public Affairs Television and Third Party Roles: The *Nightline* Debates in South Africa (1985) and Israel (1988)," *Peace and Conflict Studies*, 10(2): 1–19.

Botes, Johannes (2004) "Television Debates as a Form of Pre-Negotiation in Protracted Conflicts: *Nightline* in South Africa (1985) and Israel (1988)," *International Negotiation Journal*, 9(1): 161–91.

Boulding, Kenneth E. (1956) *The Image: Knowledge in Life and Society*. Ann Arbor: University of Michigan Press.

Boutros-Ghali, Boutros (1992) *An Agenda for Peace: Preventive Diplomacy, Peacemaking and Peace-keeping*. New York: United Nations.

Brandt, Willy (1980a) *North–South: A Programme for Survival*. London: Pan [report of the Brandt Commission].

Brandt, Willy (1980b) "A Plea for Change: Peace, Justice, Jobs – an Introduction," in *North–South: A Programme for Survival*. London: Pan.

Brewer, John, and Albert Hunter (2006) *Foundations of Multimethod Research: Synthesizing Styles*. Thousand Oaks, CA, and London: Sage.

Brown, Judson S. (1957) "Principles of Intrapersonal Conflict," *Journal of Conflict Resolution*, 1(2): 135–53; repr. in *Conflict Resolution: Contributions of the Behavioral Sciences*, ed. Clagett G. Smith. Notre Dame and London: University of Notre Dame Press, 1971.

Brulliard, Karin (2010) "In Pakistan, a Bid to Show Child Fighters Another Life," *Washington Post*, 28 March, pp. A1, A11.

Brzezinski, Zbigniew (2007) *Second Chance: Three Presidents and the Crisis of American Superpower*. New York: Basic Books.

Burkeman, Oliver (2009) "Obama Administration Says Goodbye to 'War on Terror,'" *The Guardian*, 25 March, www.guardian.co.uk/world/2009/mar/25/obama-war-terror-overseas-contingency-operations (accessed 12 April 2009).

Burton, John W. (1979) *Deviance, Terrorism and War: The Process of Solving Unsolved Social and Political Problems*. New York: St Martin's Press; Oxford: Martin Robertson.

Burton, John W. (1990) *Conflict: Resolution and Prevention*. London: Macmillan; New York: St Martin's Press.

Burton, John W. (1993) "Conflict Resolution as a Political Philosophy," in *Conflict Resolution Theory and Practice: Integration and Application*, ed. Dennis J. D. Sandole and Hugo van der Merwe. Manchester: Manchester University Press; New York: St Martin's Press.

Burton, John W. (1997) *Violence Explained*. Manchester: Manchester University Press; New York: St Martin's Press.

Caldwell, Christopher (2009) *Reflections on the Revolution in Europe: Immigration, Islam, and the West.* New York: Doubleday.

Call, Charles T. (ed.) (2007) *Constructing Justice and Security after War.* Washington, DC: United States Institute of Peace Press.

Call, Charles T., and Elizabeth M. Cousens (2008) "Ending Wars and Building Peace: International Responses to War-Torn Societies," *International Studies Perspectives,* 9(1): 1–21.

Cannon, Walter B. (1939) *The Wisdom of the Body.* Rev. edn, New York: W. W. Norton.

Carpenter, Ami (2008) "Rendering Idea to Practice: Development Assistance and Conflict Prevention in Guatemala," unpubd doctoral dissertation, Institute for Conflict Analysis and Resolution, George Mason University.

Castle, Stephen (2008). "EU Proposes Deeper Ties to 6 ex-Soviet Nations," New York Times, 3 December; www.nytimes.com/2008/12/03/world/europe/03iht-union.4.18373607.html?_r=1&scp=5&sq=stephen%20castle%203%20december%202008&st=cse (accessed 28 July 2010).

Çelik, Betül Ayşe, and Bahar Rumelili (2006) "Necessary but Not Sufficient: The Role of the EU in Resolving Turkey's Kurdish Question and the Greek–Turkish Conflicts," *European Foreign Affairs Review,* 11: 203–22.

Cienski, Jan, and Daniel Dombey (2010) "US and Russia Sign Nuclear Treaty: Obama Hails Deal to Reduce Warheads," *Financial Times,* 9 April, p. 6.

Clarke, Richard A., and Robert K. Knake (2010) *Cyber War: The Next Threat to National Security and What to Do about It.* New York: Ecco.

Clausewitz, Carl Philipp Gottfried von ([1832] 1968) *On War,* ed. Anatol Rapoport. Harmondsworth: Penguin.

Clemens, Walter, C., Jr. (2004) *Dynamics of International Relations: Conflict and Mutual Gain in an Era of Global Interdependence.* 2nd edn, Lanham, MD, and Oxford: Rowman & Littlefield.

Clinton, Hillary Rodham (2009) "Arrival at the Department of State: Remarks to Department Employees at Welcome Event," US Department of State, 22 January, www.state.gov/secretary/rm/2009a/01/115262.htm (accessed 23 February 2009).

CNN (2006) "Chavez: Bush 'devil'; US 'on the way down,'" 21 September, www.cnn.com/2006/WORLD/americas/09/20/chavez.un/index.html (accessed 26 January 2009).

Collier, Paul (2007a) *The Bottom Billion: Why the Poorest Countries are Failing and What Can be Done about It*. Oxford and New York: Oxford University Press.

Collier, Paul (2007b) "Conflicts," in *Solutions for the World's Biggest Problems: Costs and Benefits*, ed. Bjørn Lomborg. Cambridge and New York: Cambridge University Press.

Corn, David (2008) "McCain in NH: Would Be 'Fine' to Keep Troops in Iraq for 'A Hundred Years,'" 3 January, www.motherjones.com/mojoblog/archives/2008/01/67 (accessed 29 July 2008).

Corner, Mark (2008) *Towards a Global Sharing of Sovereignty*. London: Federal Trust for Education and Research.

Coser, Lewis A. (1956) *The Functions of Social Conflict*. New York: Free Press; London: Collier-Macmillan.

Coxhead, Ian, and Ragnar Øygard (2007) "Land Degradation," in *Solutions for the World's Biggest Problems: Costs and Benefits*, ed. Bjørn Lomborg. Cambridge and New York: Cambridge University Press.

Dallaire, Romeo (2004) *Shake Hands with the Devil: The Failure of Humanity in Rwanda*. New York: Carroll & Graf.

Davidson, William D., and Joseph V. Montville (1981–2) "Foreign Policy According to Freud," *Foreign Policy*, 45: 145–57.

Davies, Howard (2010) "Diversionary Tactics: In Business as in the Rest of Life, the Path to Success is Rarely Straight: Review of John Kay's *Obliquity: Why our Goals are Best Achieved Indirectly*," *Financial Times*, 6 March, "Life & Arts," p. 16.

Dehghanpisheh, Babak (2008) "The Great Moqtada Makeover," *Newsweek*, 28 January, pp. 44–5.

Deibert, Ronald J., and Rafal Rohozinski (2010) "Risking Security: Policies and Paradoxes of Cyberspace Security," *International Political Sociology*, 4(1): 15–32.

Deutsch, Morton (1971) "Conflict and its Resolution," in *Conflict Resolution: Contributions of the Behavioral Sciences*, ed. Clagett G. Smith. Notre Dame and London: University of Notre Dame Press.

Deutsch, Morton (1973) *The Resolution of Conflict: Constructive and Destructive Processes*. New Haven, CT: Yale University Press.

Deutsch, Morton (2003) "Cooperation and Conflict: A Personal Perspective on the History of the Social Psychological Study of Conflict Resolution," in *International Handbook of Organizational Teamwork and Cooperative Working*, ed. M. A. West, D. J. Tjosvold, and K. G. Smith. New York: John Wiley.

Diamond, Louise (1997) "Training in Conflict-Habituated Systems: Lessons from Cyprus," *International Negotiation*, 2: 353–80.

Diamond, Louise, and John W. McDonald, Jr. (1996) *Multi-Track Diplomacy: A Systems Approach to Peace*. 3rd edn, West Hartford, CT: Kumarian Press.

Dollard, J., L. W. Doob, N. E. Miller, O. H. Mowrer, and R. R. Sears (1939) *Frustration and Aggression*. New Haven, CT: Yale University Press; abridged edn repr. in *The Dynamics of Aggression: Individual, Group, and International Analyses*, ed. Edwin I. Megargee and Jack E. Hokanson. New York and London: Harper & Row, 1970.

Dombey, Daniel (2009) "Afghan Victory 'in a Few Years,'" *Financial Times*, 14 August, p. 2.

Dombey, Daniel (2010) "Survival of Israel is at Stake, Says Clinton," *Financial Times*, 23 March, p. 6.

Dougherty, James E., and Robert L. Pfaltzgraff, Jr. (1997) *Contending Theories of International Relations: A Comprehensive Survey*, 4th edn, New York: Longman.

Dugan, Maire (1996) "A Nested Theory of Conflict," *Women in Leadership*, no. 1: 9–20.

Dunne, J. Paul (2007) "Arms Proliferation," in *Solutions for the World's Biggest Problems: Costs and Benefits*, ed. Bjørn Lomborg. Cambridge and New York: Cambridge University Press.

Economist (2007a) "Reforming Jihadists: Preachers to the Converted," *The Economist*, 15 December, p. 71.

Economist (2007b) "Public Repentance: A Jihadist Recants," *The Economist*, 15 December, p. 72.

Economist (2008a) "Diplomacy: Speaking to the Enemy: Sometimes it Makes Sense; Sometimes it Doesn't; Sometimes Not Talking Can be Appeasement," *The Economist*, 24 May, p. 19.

Economist (2008b) "Israel, Syria and the Palestinians: Two-track Tango: Peace on the Horizon? Or Just a Mirage?" *The Economist*, 24 May, p. 68.

Economist (2008c) "Islam and the West: When Religions Talk. Religious Leaders, Scholars and Business People are Meeting all Over the World to Argue about Free Speech and Islamic Sensibilities: How Much Does this Achieve?" *The Economist*, 14 June, pp. 74–5.

Economist (2009) "Turkish–Armenian Relations: Football Diplomacy," *The Economist*, 5 September, pp. 55–6.

Economist (2010) "The Clouds of Unknowing: There are Lots of Uncertainties in Climate Science, but that Does Not Mean that it is Wrong," *The Economist*, 20 March, pp. 83–6.

Eggers, William D., and John O'Leary (2010) "The Marshall Plan. Iraq. Health Care? Why Our Greatest Ambitions Succeed – or Fail," *Washington Post*, 21 March, pp. B1, B2.

Eilperin, Juliet (2008) "Gore Launches Ambitious Advocacy Campaign on Climate," *Washington Post*, 31 March, p. A4.

Emanuel, Rahm (2008) Interview with Bob Schieffer, *CBS News' Face the Nation*, 9 November, www.cbsnews.com/htdocs/pdf/FTN_110908.pdf (accessed 2 March 2009).

Eralp, Doga Ulas (2009) "The Effectiveness of the EU as a Peace Actor in Post-Conflict Bosnia Herzegovina: An Evaluative Study," unpubd PhD dissertation, Institute for Conflict Analysis and Resolution, George Mason University.

Eralp, Doga Ulas, and Nimet Beriker (2005) "Assessing the Conflict Resolution Potential of the EU: The Cyprus Conflict and Accession Negotiations," *Security Dialogue*, 36(2): 175–92.

EU (2008) "Peacekeeping Close to Home: Paving the Way to EU Membership in the Western Balkans," *EU Focus*, November, p. 6; www.eurunion.org/News/eunewsletters/EUFocus/2008/EUFocus-Peacekeeping-Nov08.pdf (accessed 28 July 2010).

European Commission (2008) "European Neighborhood Policy," 19 July, http://ec.europa.eu/world/enp/index_en.htm (accessed 1 November 2008).

European Council (1993) "Presidency Conclusions, Copenhagen European Council, 21–22 June 1993," www.europarl.europa.eu/enlargement/ec/pdf/cop_en.pdf (accessed 31 October 2008).

Evans, Gareth (2008) *The Responsibility to Protect: Ending Mass Atrocity Crimes Once and for All*. Washington, DC: Brookings Institution Press.

Fanon, Frantz (1968) *The Wretched of the Earth*. New York: Grove Press.

Faure, Guy Olivier, and I. William Zartman (eds) (2010) *Negotiating with Terrorists: Strategy, Tactics, and Politics*. London and New York: Routledge.

Festinger, Leon (1962) *A Theory of Cognitive Dissonance*. Stanford, CA: Stanford University Press.

Fisher, Ronald J. (1997) *Interactive Conflict Resolution*. Syracuse, NY: Syracuse University Press.

Fisher, Ronald J., and Loraleigh Keashly (1991) "The Potential Complementarity of Mediation and Consultation within a Contingency Model of Third Party Intervention," *Journal of Peace Research*, 28(1): 29–42.

Flynn, Stephen (2007) *The Edge of Disaster: Rebuilding a Resilient Nation*. New York: Random House.

Folmer, Henk, and G. Cornelis van Kooten (2007) "Deforestation," in *Solutions for the World's Biggest Problems: Costs and Benefits*, ed. Bjørn Lomborg. Cambridge and New York: Cambridge University Press.

FP (2009) "The General's Next War: The FP Interview with Gen. David H. Petraeus," *Foreign Policy*, January/February, pp. 48–50.

FP (2010) "The Failed States Index: 2010 Rankings," *Foreign Policy*, July/August, p. 76; www.foreignpolicy.com/articles/2010/21/the_failed_states_index_2010 (accessed 2 August 2010).

Frankel, Glenn, and Tamara Jones (2005) "In Britain, a Divide over Racial Profiling: Mistaken Killing by Police Sets off Debate," *Washington Post*, 27 July, pp. A1, A18.

Frankl, Viktor E. (1959) *Man's Search for Meaning*. New York: Simon & Schuster.

Frantz, Douglas, and Catherine Collins (2007) *The Nuclear Jihadist: The True Story of the Man who Sold the World's Most Dangerous Secrets . . . and How We Could Have Stopped Him*. New York: Twelve.

Freizer, Sabine (2009) "The EU–Turkey–Cyprus Triangle: 'Football Diplomacy,'" 15 October, www.crisisgroup.org/home/index. cfm?id=6348&l=1 (accessed 16 March 2010).

FT (2007) "Brown in Appeal to Taliban Fighters," *Financial Times*, 13 December, "News Digest," p. 4.

FT (2010) "Obama Makes the World a Safer Place: Nuclear Deal with Russia is an Important Achievement," *Financial Times*, 29 March, "Editorial," p. 8.

Fukuyama, Francis (2006) *America at the Crossroads: Democracy, Power, and the Neoconservative Legacy*. New Haven, CT, and London: Yale University Press.

Fukuyama, Francis (2008) "Russia and a New Democratic Realism," *Financial Times*, 3 September, p. 11.

Galtung, Johan (1964) "A Structural Theory of Aggression," *Journal of Peace Research*, 1: 95–119; repr. in *Conflict Resolution: Contributions of the Behavioral Sciences*, ed. Clagett G. Smith. Notre Dame and London: University of Notre Dame Press, 1971.

Galtung, Johan (1969) "Violence, Peace and Peace Research," *Journal of Peace Research*, 6(3): 167–91.

Galtung, Johan (1996) *Peace by Peaceful Means: Peace and Conflict, Development and Civilization*. London and Thousand Oaks, CA: Sage.

Galtung, Johan (2008) "Toward a Conflictology: The Quest for Transdisciplinarity," in *A Handbook of Conflict Analysis and Resolution*, ed. Dennis J. D. Sandole, Sean Byrne, Ingrid Sandole-Staroste, and Jessica Senehi. London and New York: Routledge.

Gawande, Atul (2009) *The Checklist Manifesto: How to Get Things Right*. New York: Metropolitan Books.

Gezari, Vanessa M. (2009) "Rough Terrain," *Washington Post Magazine*, 30 August, pp. 16–23, 28–9.

Ghani, Ashraf, and Clare Lockhart (2008) *Fixing Failed States: A Framework for Rebuilding a Fractured World*. Oxford and New York: Oxford University Press.

Giles, Chris, and Lionel Barber (2009) "Zoellick Urges Global Response," *Financial Times*, 19 February, p. 2.

Gladwell, Malcolm (2002) *The Tipping Point: How Little Things Can Make a Big Difference*. New York: Basic Bay Books.

Gleick, James (1988) *Chaos: Making a New Science*. New York and London: Penguin Books.

Gopin, Marc (2000). *Between Eden and Armageddon: The Future of World Religions, Violence and Peacemaking*. Oxford and New York: Oxford University Press.

Gopin, Marc (2002) *Holy War, Holy Peace: How Religion can Bring Peace to the Middle East*. Oxford and New York: Oxford University Press.

Gopin, Marc (2004) *Healing the Heart of Conflict: 8 Crucial Steps to Making Peace with Yourself and Others*. New York: Rodale Books.

Gore, Al (2006) *An Inconvenient Truth: The Planetary Emergency of Global Warming and What We Can Do About It*. New York: Rodale Books.

Greenwood, Michael J. (2007) "Population: Migration," in *Solutions for the World's Biggest Problems: Costs and Benefits*, ed. Bjørn Lomborg. Cambridge and New York: Cambridge University Press.

Guha, Krishna (2009) "Global Challenges Have to be Tackled," *Financial Times*, 21 September, p. 4.

Gürkaynak, Esra Çuhadar, Bruce Dayton, and Thania Paffenholz (2009) "Evaluation in Conflict Resolution and Peacebuilding," in *A*

Handbook of Conflict Analysis and Resolution, ed. Dennis J. D. Sandole, Sean Byrne, Ingrid Sandole-Staroste, and Jessica Senehi. London and New York: Routledge.

Gurr, Ted Robert (1970) *Why Men Rebel*. Princeton, NJ: Princeton University Press.

Haass, Richard N. (2009). *War of Necessity, War of Choice: A Memoir of Two Iraq Wars*. New York: Simon & Schuster.

Hamburg, David A. (2002) *No More Killing Fields: Preventing Deadly Conflict*. Lanham, MD, and Oxford: Rowman & Littlefield.

Harvey, Fiona (2010) "Climate Change is Undeniable Says Study," *Financial Times*, 20 July, p. 1.

Hedges, Chris (2002) *War is a Force that Gives Us Meaning*. New York: Public Affairs.

Henry, Peter Blair (2007) "Financial Instability," in *Solutions for the World's Biggest Problems: Costs and Benefits*, ed. Bjørn Lomborg. Cambridge and New York: Cambridge University Press.

Herz, John H. (1950) "Idealist Internationalism and the Security Dilemma," *World Politics*, 5(2): 157–80.

Hewitt, J. Joseph (2010a) "The Peace and Conflict Instability Ledger: Ranking States on Future Risks," in *Peace and Conflict 2010*, ed. J. Joseph Hewitt, Jonathan Wilkenfeld, and Ted Robert Gurr. Boulder, CO: Paradigm.

Hewitt, J. Joseph (2010b) "Trends in Global Conflict, 1946–2007," in *Peace and Conflict 2010*, ed. J. Joseph Hewitt, Jonathan Wilkenfeld, and Ted Robert Gurr. Boulder, CO: Paradigm.

Hewitt, J. Joseph, Jonathan Wilkenfeld, and Ted Robert Gurr (eds) (2008) *Peace and Conflict 2008*. Boulder, CO: Paradigm.

Hewitt, J. Joseph, Jonathan Wilkenfeld, and Ted Robert Gurr (eds) (2010) *Peace and Conflict 2010*. Boulder, CO: Paradigm.

Hoeffler, Anke (2010) "State Failure and Conflict Recurrence," in *Peace and Conflict 2010*, ed. J. Joseph Hewitt, Jonathan Wilkenfeld, and Ted Robert Gurr. Boulder, CO: Paradigm.

Holbrooke, Richard (1998) *To End a War*. New York: Random House.

Holsti, Ole R., Robert C. North, and Richard A. Brody (1968) "Perception and Action in the 1914 Crises," in *Quantitative International Politics: Insights and Evidence*, ed. J. David Singer. New York: Free Press; London: Collier-Macmillan.

Homer-Dixon, Thomas F. (1999) *Environment, Scarcity, and Violence*. Princeton, NJ: Princeton University Press.

Homer-Dixon, Thomas F. (2000) *The Ingenuity Gap*. New York: Alfred A. Knopf.

Homer-Dixon, Thomas F. (2008) " 'Straw Man in the Wind': Symposium on 'The World Is Not Enough,' " *National Interest*, no. 93, January/February, pp. 26–8.

Honig, Jan Willem, and Norbert Both (1996) *Srebrenica: Record of a War Crime*. London and New York: Penguin Books.

HSRP (Human Security Report Project) (2005) *Human Security Report: War and Peace in the 21st Century*. Oxford: Oxford University Press; www.humansecurityreport.info.

Hudson, Rex A., and the staff of the Federal Research Division of the Library of Congress (1999) *Who Becomes a Terrorist and Why: The 1999 Government Report on Profiling Terrorists*. Guilford, CT: Lyons Press.

Huntington, Samuel P. (1993) "The Clash of Civilizations?" *Foreign Affairs*, 72(3): 22–49.

Huntington, Samuel P. (1996) *The Clash of Civilizations and the Remaking of World Order*. New York: Simon & Schuster.

Huth, Paul, and Benjamin Valentino (2008) "Mass Killing of Civilians in Time of War, 1945–2000," in *Peace and Conflict 2008*, ed. J. Joseph Hewitt, Jonathan Wilkenfeld, and Ted Robert Gurr. Boulder, CO: Paradigm.

Hutton, Guy (2007a) "Air Pollution," in *Solutions for the World's Biggest Problems: Costs and Benefits*, ed. Bjørn Lomborg. Cambridge and New York: Cambridge University Press.

Hutton, Guy (2007b) "Unsafe Water and Lack of Sanitation," in *Solutions for the World's Biggest Problems: Costs and Benefits*, ed. Bjørn Lomborg. Cambridge and New York: Cambridge University Press.

ICISS (International Commission on Intervention and State Sovereignty) (2001) *The Responsibility to Protect*. Ottawa: International Development Research Centre.

Ignatius, David (2007) "Portents of a Nuclear Al-Qaeda," *Washington Post*, 18 October, p. A25.

Ignatius, David (2008) "Backing Georgia, Quietly," *Washington Post*, 10 September, p. A15.

IHT (2008) "Text of President Bush's Speech to the Israeli Parliament," *International Herald Tribune*, 15 May, www.iht.com/articles/ap/2008/05/15/news/Bush-Mideast-Text.php (accessed 16 May 2008).

Inglehart, Ronald, and Christian Welzel (2009) "How Development Leads to Democracy," *Foreign Affairs*, March/April, pp. 33–48.

James, William (1910) "The Moral Equivalent of War," *McClure's Magazine*, August, pp. 463–8.

Jamison, Dean T. (2007) "Disease Control," in *Solutions for the World's Biggest Problems: Costs and Benefits*, ed. Bjørn Lomborg. Cambridge and New York: Cambridge University Press.

Johnson, Douglas H. (2003) *The Root Causes of Sudan's Civil Wars*. Bloomington: Indiana University Press.

Judt, Tony (2010) *Ill Fares the Land*. London: Allen Lane.

Kagan, Robert (2008) *The Return of History and the End of Dreams*. New York: Alfred A. Knopf.

Kaldor, Mary (2006) *New and Old Wars: Organized Violence in a Global Era*. 2nd edn, Cambridge: Polity.

Kant, Immanuel ([1795] 1983) "Perpetual Peace: A Philosophical Sketch," chapter 6 in *Perpetual Peace, and Other Essays on Politics, History, and Morals*, trans. Ted Humphrey. Indianapolis: Hackett.

Kant, Immanuel ([1785] 1993) *Grounding for the Metaphysics of Morals: On a Supposed Right to Lie Because of Philanthropic Concerns*, 3rd edn, trans. James W. Ellington. Indianapolis: Hackett.

Kaplan, Abraham (1964) *The Conduct of Inquiry: Methodology for Behavioral Science*. San Francisco: Chandler.

Kaplan, Robert D. (2001) *Sense of the Tragic: Developmental Dangers in the Twenty-First Century*, Jerome E. Levy Occasional Papers No. 2. Newport, RI: US Naval War College Press.

Kardas, Saban (2008) "Turkey's Push for Caucasus Stability and Cooperation Platform," *Azerbaijan in the World*, 1(14–15), http://ada-edu-az.outsourceinformationsystems.com/biweekly/articles.aspx?id=71 (accessed 14 September 2008).

Kay, John (2010) *Obliquity: Why our Goals are Best Achieved Indirectly*. London: Profile Books.

Kemp, Walter A. (ed.) (2001) *Quiet Diplomacy in Action: The OSCE High Commissioner on National Minorities*. The Hague, London and Boston: Kluwer Law International.

Kessler, Glenn (2009) "US, China to Focus on Slump, Climate: Long-Standing Human Rights Concerns Put on Back Burner During Clinton Trip," *Washington Post*, 22 February, p. A14.

Kessler, Glenn (2010) "Clinton Upbraids Netanyahu over Housing Plans," *Washington Post*, 13 March, pp. A1, A8.

Kimmel, Michael (2002) "Gender, Class, and Terrorism," *Chronicle of Higher Education*, 48(22): B11–B12.

Kissinger, Henry A. (1964) *A World Restored – Europe after Napoleon: The Politics of Conservatism in a Revolutionary Age*. New York: Grosset & Dunlap.

Klare, Michael T. (2008) "'Clearing the Air': Symposium on 'The World Is Not Enough,'" *National Interest*, no. 93, January/February, pp. 28–31.

Knutson, Jeanne N. (1981) "Social and Psychodynamic Pressures toward a Negative Identity," in *Behavioral and Quantitative Perspectives on Terrorism*, ed. Yonah Alexander and John M. Gleason. New York: Pergamon Press.

Knutson, Jeanne N. (1984) "Toward a United States Policy on Terrorism," *Political Psychology*, 5(2): 287–94.

Kohut, Heinz (1971) *The Analysis of the Self: A Systematic Approach to the Psychoanalytic Treatment of Narcissistic Personality Disorders*. New York: International Universities Press.

Kuhn, Thomas S. (1970) *The Structure of Scientific Revolutions*. 2nd edn, Chicago: University of Chicago Press.

LaFree, Gary, Laura Dugan, and Susan Fahey (2008) "Global Terrorism and Failed States," in *Peace and Conflict 2008*, ed. J. Joseph Hewitt, Jonathan Wilkenfeld, and Ted Robert Gurr. Boulder, CO: Paradigm.

LaFree, Gary, Laura Dugan, and R. Kim Cragin (2010) "Trends in Global Terrorism, 1970–2007," in *Peace and Conflict 2010*, ed. J. Joseph Hewitt, Jonathan Wilkenfeld, and Ted Robert Gurr. Boulder, CO: Paradigm.

Leatherman, Janie, and Nadezhda Griffin (2009) "Ethical and Gendered Dilemmas of Moving from Emergency Response to Development in 'Failed' States," in *A Handbook of Conflict Analysis and Resolution*, ed. Dennis J. D. Sandole, Sean Byrne, Ingrid Sandole-Staroste, and Jessica Senehi. London and New York: Routledge.

Lederach, John P. (1997) *Building Peace: Sustainable Reconciliation in Divided Societies*. Washington, DC: United States Institute of Peace Press.

Leonard, Mark (2005) *Why Europe Will Run the 21st Century*. New York: Public Affairs.

Lerche, Charles O., Jr., and Abdul A. Said (1970) *Concepts of International Politics*. 2nd edn, Englewood Cliffs, NJ: Prentice-Hall.

Lerner, Jonathan (2002) "I Was a Terrorist," *Washington Post Magazine*, 24 February, pp. 24, 26–8, 38–40.

Linotte, Daniel (2007) "Terrorism," in *Solutions for the World's Biggest Problems: Costs and Benefits*, ed. Bjørn Lomborg. Cambridge and New York: Cambridge University Press.

Linzer, Dafna (2004) "The World after 9/11: The Nuclear Threat. Nuclear Capabilities May Elude Terrorists, Experts Say," *Washington Post*, 29 December, pp. A1, A6.

Little, Allan (2008) "Karadzic's Broken Bosnia Remains," 17 September, http://news.bbc.co.uk/2/hi/europe/7621649.stm (accessed 8 February 2009).

Lloyd, John (2009) "The War on Terrorism without Inhibitions," *Financial Times*, 3 August, p. 6.

Lomborg, Bjørn (ed.) (2007). *Solutions for the World's Biggest Problems: Costs and Benefits*. Cambridge and New York: Cambridge University Press.

Lozada, Carlos (2010) "What's the Big Idea? Do Informed Voters Make Better Choices?" *Washington Post*, 4 April, p. B5.

Lund, Michael S. (1996) *Preventing Violent Conflicts: A Strategy for Preventive Diplomacy*. Washington, DC: United States Institute of Peace Press.

Lund, Michael S. (2009) "Conflict Prevention: Theory in Pursuit of Policy and Practice," in *The Sage Handbook of Conflict Prevention*, ed. Jacob Bercovitch, Victor Kremenyuk, and I. William Zartman. Thousand Oaks, CA: Sage.

Machiavelli, Niccolò ([1532] 1966) *The Prince and Selected Discourses*, trans. Daniel Donno. New York: Bantam Books.

Machiaveli, Niccolò ([1532] 1998) *The Prince*, trans. W. K. Marriott, www.fordham.edu/halsall/basis/machiavelli-prince.html#CHAPTER%20XIV (accessed 31 July 2008).

Machiavelli, Niccolò ([1532] 2008) *The Prince*, trans. Peter Constantine. New York: Modern Library.

Mack, Andrew (2005) "Peace on Earth? Increasingly, Yes," *Washington Post*, 28 December, p. A21.

Mahbubani, Kishore (2008) *The New Asian Hemisphere: The Irresistible Shift of Global Power to the East*. New York: Public Affairs.

Mamdani, Mahmood (2004) *Good Muslim, Bad Muslim: America, the Cold War, and the Roots of Terror*. New York: Pantheon Books.

Mandelbaum, Michael (2010) *The Frugal Superpower: America's Global Leadership in a Cash-Strapped Era.* New York: Public Affairs.

Mao Tse-tung (1961) *Mao Tse-Tung on Guerrilla Warfare,* trans. Samuel B. Griffith. New York: Praeger.

Marks, Susan Collin (2000) *Watching the Wind: Conflict Resolution during South Africa's Transition to Democracy.* Washington, DC: United States Institute of Peace Press.

Marshall, Monty G., and Ted Robert Gurr (2005) *Peace and Conflict 2005: A Global Survey of Armed Conflicts, Self-Determination Movements, and Democracy.* College Park: Center for International Development and Conflict Management, University of Maryland; www.cidcm.umd.edu/inscr/peace.htm.

McClintock, John (2008) *The Uniting of Nations: An Essay on Global Governance.* 2nd edn, New York and Oxford: Peter Lang.

McDonald, John W., Jr., and Diane B. Bendahmane (eds) (1987) *Conflict Resolution: Track Two Diplomacy.* Washington, DC: US Department of State, Foreign Service Institute.

McKie, Robin (2009) "President 'Has Four Years to Save Earth': US Must Take the Lead to Avert Eco-Disaster," *The Observer,* 18 January, www.guardian.co.uk/environment/2009/jan/18/jim-hansen-obama (accessed 2 March 2009).

McMahon, Patrice C., and Jon Western (2009) "The Death of Dayton: How to Stop Bosnia from Falling Apart," *Foreign Affairs,* September/ October, pp. 69–83.

Meier, Andrew (2008) "Let Russia Join NATO: The West Has Pushed Back against Moscow's Repeated Attempts to Establish Closer Ties," *Los Angeles Times,* 20 August; www.latimes.com/news/printedition/opinion/la-oe-meier20-2008aug20,0,2858433.story.

MGI (Managing Global Insecurity) (2008a) *A Plan for Action: A New Era of International Cooperation for a Changed World.* Washington, DC: Brookings Institution; www.brookings.edu/reports/2008/11_action_plan_mgi.aspx (accessed 16 February 2009).

MGI (Managing Global Insecurity) (2008b) *A Plan for Action: Renewed American Leadership and International Cooperation for the 21st Century.* Washington, DC: Brookings Institution; www.brookings.edu/events/2008/~/media/Files/events/2008/1120_mgi/20081120_mgi.pdf (accessed 16 February 2009).

Mian, Zia, R. Rajaraman, and Frank von Hipel (2002) "Nuclear Role Models," *Washington Post,* 6 August, p. A15.

Mill, John Stuart ([1859] 1998) *On Liberty and Other Essays*. Oxford and New York: Oxford University Press.

Miron, Jeffrey A. (2007) "Drugs," in *Solutions for the World's Biggest Problems: Costs and Benefits*, ed. Bjørn Lomborg. Cambridge and New York: Cambridge University Press.

Mitchell, Christopher, and Michael Banks (1996) *Handbook of Conflict Resolution: The Analytical Problem-Solving Approach*. London: Pinter.

Moore, Christopher W. (1986) *The Mediation Process: Practical Strategies for Resolving Conflict*. San Francisco and London: Jossey-Bass.

Moore, R. Scott (ed.) (2002) *Terrorism: Concepts, Causes, and Conflict Resolution*. Fort Belvoir, VA: US Defense Threat Reduction Agency.

Moore, R. Scott (ed.) (2004) *Apocalyptic Terrorism: Understanding the Unfathomable*. Fort Belvoir, VA: US Defense Threat Reduction Agency.

Morris, Benny (2008a) *1948: A History of the First Arab–Israeli War*. New Haven, CT: Yale University Press.

Morris, Benny (2008b) "Using Bombs to Stave Off War," *New York Times*, 18 July; www.nytimes.com/2008/07/18/opinion/18morris. html (accessed 3 August 2008).

Morris, Harvey (2009) "Obama Will Chair Mideast Talks to Tackle Stalemate," *Financial Times*, 21 September, p. 2.

Moselle, Tyler (2010) "Tackling Insurgents is Not Enough for America," *Financial Times*, 19 March, p. 9.

Moses, Jonathon W., and Torbjørn L. Knutsen (2007) *Ways of Knowing: Competing Methodologies in Social and Political Research*. Basingstoke and New York: Palgrave Macmillan.

Mrkic, Goran (2009) "New Outbreak of Violence Possible in B-H," *Dnevni list* [Mostar, Bosnia-Herzegovina], 26 January; available at www.bbcmonitoringonline.com/mmu/ (accessed 3 February 2009).

Mueller, John (1989) *Retreat from Doomsday: The Obsolescence of Major War*. New York: Basic Books.

Murray, Sarah (2009) "World in Need of Dual Approach," *Financial Times*, 3 February, p. 8.

Myrdal, Gunnar (1962) *An American Dilemma: The Negro Problem and Modern Democracy*, 2 vols. New York: Pantheon Books.

Nan, Susan Allen (2003) "Intervention Coordination," Conflict Information Consortium, University of Colorado, www. beyondintractability.org/m/intervention_coordination.jsp (accessed 6 June 2008).

Nass, Matthias (2010) "Reaching for Global Zero: Barack Obama's Campaign for a World without Nuclear Weapons," *Atlantic Times*, April, pp. A1, A6; www.atlantic-times.com/archive_detail. php?recordID=2121.

North, Robert C. (1975) "Some Paradoxes of War and Peace," *Peace Science Society (International), Papers*, 25: 1–14.

North, Robert C. (1990) *War, Peace, Survival: Global Politics and Conceptual Synthesis*. Boulder, CO, and Oxford: Westview Press.

Nye, Joseph S., Jr. (2004) *Soft Power: The Means to Success in World Politics*. New York: Public Affairs.

Obama, Barack ([1995] 2004) *Dreams from my Father: A Story of Race and Inheritance*. New York: Three Rivers Press.

Obama, Barack (2007) "Renewing American Leadership," *Foreign Affairs*, 86(4): 2–16.

Obama, Barack (2008) "Obama's Remarks on Iraq and Afghanistan," *New York Times*, 15 July; www.nytimes.com/2008/07/15/us/ politics/15text-obama.html?_r=1 (accessed 16 February 2009).

Orazem, Peter F. (2007) "Lack of Education," in *Solutions for the World's Biggest Problems: Costs and Benefits*, ed. Bjørn Lomborg. Cambridge: Cambridge University Press.

Paffenholz, Thania (2009a) "Understanding the Development– Conflict Nexus and the Contribution of Development Cooperation to Peacebuilding," in *A Handbook of Conflict Analysis and Resolution*, ed. Dennis J. D. Sandole, Sean Byrne, Ingrid Sandole–Staroste, and Jessica Senehi. London and New York: Routleage.

Paffenholz, Thania (2009b) *Summary of Results for a Comparative Research Project: Civil Society and Peacebuilding*, CCDP Working Paper 4. Geneva: Graduate Institute of International and Development Studies, Centre on Conflict, Development and Peacebuilding.

Paffenholz, Thania (ed.) (2010) *Civil Society and Peacebuilding: A Critical Assessment*. Boulder, CO, and London: Lynne Rienner.

Paffenholz, Thania, and Luc Reychler (2007) *Aid for Peace: A Guide to Planning and Evaluation for Conflict Zones*. Baden-Baden: Nomos.

Pape, Robert A. (2005) *Dying to Win: The Strategic Logic of Suicide Terrorism*. New York: Random House.

Pate, Amy (2010) "Trends in Democratization: A Focus on Minority Rights," in *Peace and Conflict 2010*, ed. J. Joseph Hewitt, Jonathan Wilkenfeld, and Ted Robert Gurr. Boulder, CO: Paradigm.

Patrinos, Harry Anthony (2007) "Living Conditions of Children," in *Solutions for the World's Biggest Problems: Costs and Benefits*, ed.

Bjørn Lomborg. Cambridge and New York: Cambridge University Press.

Patten, Chris (2008) *What Next?: Surviving the Twenty-First Century.* London and New York: Penguin.

Pearce, Fred (2010) *Peoplequake: Mass Migration, Ageing Nations and the Coming Population Crash.* St Austell, Cornwall: Eden Project.

Peel, Michael (2009) "British Islamists Convicted of Liquid Bomb Aircraft Plot," *Financial Times,* 8 September, p. 5.

Peel, Quentin (2009) "EU Champion Takes Fright in Flight to Protectionism," *Financial Times,* 27 February, p. 4.

Phillips, Melanie (2006) *Londonistan: How Britain is Creating a Terror State Within.* London: Gibson Square.

Pielke, Roger A., Jr. (2007) "Vulnerability to Natural Disasters," in *Solutions for the World's Biggest Problems: Costs and Benefits,* ed. Bjørn Lomborg. Cambridge and New York: Cambridge University Press.

Pierre, Robert E. (2002) "Fear and Anxiety Permeate Arab Enclave Near Detroit," *Washington Post,* 4 August, p. A3.

Pintak, Lawrence, Remy Ginges, and Nicholas Felton (2008) "Arab Media: Misreading the Messenger," *International Herald Tribune,* 26 May, p. 8.

Polman, Linda (2010) *War Games: The Story of Aid and War in Modern Times.* New York: Viking Press.

Popper, Karl R. (1972) *Objective Knowledge: An Evolutionary Approach.* Oxford: Clarendon Press.

Powell, Jonathan (2008) *Great Hatred, Little Room: Making Peace in Northern Ireland.* London: Bodley Head.

PPD (2006) "Ping-Pong Diplomacy Spearheaded US–Chinese Relations," *eJournal USA,* 1 April, http://usinfo.state.gov/journals/itps/0406/ijpe/pingpong.htm (accessed 1 November 2008).

Pruitt, Dean G. (1987) "Creative Approaches to Negotiation," in *Conflict Management and Problem Solving: Interpersonal to International Applications,* ed. Dennis J. D. Sandole and Ingrid Sandole-Staroste. London: Frances Pinter; New York: New York University Press.

Pruitt, Dean G. (2006) "Negotiation with Terrorists," *International Negotiations,* 11: 371–94.

Prunier, Górard (2005) *Darfur: The Ambiguous Genocide.* Ithaca, NY: Cornell University Press.

Rachman, Gideon (2008) "The Battle for Food, Oil and Water," *Financial Times,* 28 January; www.ft.com/cms/s/0/d3cde844-cdb7-11dc-9e4e-000077b07658.html (accessed 30 July 2008).

Rachman, Gideon (2010) "Obama's Victory Changes the World," *Financial Times*, 23 March, p. 9.

Ramadan, Tariq (2010) *The Quest for Meaning: Developing a Philosophy of Pluralism*. London and New York: Allen Lane.

Ramsbotham, Oliver, Tom Woodhouse, and Hugh Miall (2005) *Contemporary Conflict Resolution: The Prevention, Management and Transformation of Deadly Conflicts*. 2nd edn, Cambridge: Polity.

Rapoport, Anatol (1960) *Fights, Games, and Debates*. Ann Arbor: University of Michigan Press.

Rapoport, Anatol (1964) *Strategy and Conscience*. New York and London: Harper & Row.

Rapoport, Anatol (1974) *Conflict in Man-Made Environment*. Harmondsworth: Penguin.

Rashid, Ahmed (2008) "Pakistan's Worrisome Pullback," *Washington Post*, 6 June, p. A19.

Rashid, Ahmed (2010) "We Divide Afghanistan at our Peril," *Financial Times*, 4 August, p. 7.

Ray, Charles G. (2008) "Using Information Technology to Meet the Challenges of Evidence-Based Practices," *Open Minds Circle*, www.openminds.com/circlehome/circle/peibhiray.htm (accessed 16 February 2009).

Regional Cooperation Council (2008) *Stability Pact for South Eastern Europe*, www.stabilitypact.org/default.asp (accessed 1 November 2008).

Reid, Tim (2009) "President Obama 'Orders Pakistan Drone Attacks,'" *The Times*, 23 January; www.timesonline.co.uk/tol/news/world/us_and_americas/article5575883.ece (accessed 23 February 2009).

Reychler, Luc, and Thania Paffenholz (eds) (2001) *Peacebuilding: A Field Guide*. Boulder, CO, and London: Lynne Rienner.

Richardson, Lewis F. (1939) *Generalized Foreign Politics: A Study in Group Psychology*. Cambridge: Cambridge University Press.

Richardson, Lewis F. (1960) *Arms and Insecurity*. Chicago: Quadrangle Books.

Richmond, Oliver P. (2005) *The Transformation of Peace*. London and New York: Palgrave Macmillan.

Richmond, Oliver P. (2008) "Reclaiming Peace in International Relations," *Millennium: Journal of International Studies*, 36(3): 439–70.

Riechmann, Deb (2010) "13 Die in Afghanistan Amid Calls for Peace with Militants: Vice President is Hopeful about Talks as Insurgents Lay Out Terms," *Washington Post*, 22 March, p. A8.

Rifkin, Jeremy (2004) *The European Dream: How Europe's Vision of the Future is Quietly Eclipsing the American Dream*. Cambridge: Polity; New York: Tarcher.

Rifkin, Jeremy (2009) *The Empathic Civilization: The Race to Global Consciousness in a World in Crisis*. Cambridge: Polity; New York: Tarcher.

Rohde, David (1997) *Endgame: The Betrayal and Fall of Srebrenica, Europe's Worst Massacre since World War II*. New York: Farrar, Straus & Giroux.

Rose-Ackerman, Susan (2007) "Corruption," in *Solutions for the World's Biggest Problems: Costs and Benefits*, ed. Bjørn Lomborg. Cambridge and New York: Cambridge University Press.

Rouhana, Nadim N. (2000) "Interactive Conflict Resolution: Issues in Theory, Methodology, and Evaluation," in *International Conflict Resolution after the Cold War*, ed. Paul C. Stern and Daniel Druckman. Washington, DC: National Academy Press.

Rove, Karl (2010) *Courage and Consequence: My Life as a Conservative in the Fight*. New York: Threshold.

Ryan, Stephen (2009) "Conflict Transformation: Reasons to Be Modest," in *A Handbook of Conflict Analysis and Resolution*, ed. Dennis J. D. Sandole, Sean Byrne, Ingrid Sandole-Staroste, and Jessica Senehi. London and New York: Routledge.

Sachs, Jeffrey (2008) *Economics of a Crowded Planet*. London and New York: Penguin.

Sageman, Marc (2008) "Get Ready: The Homegrown Young Radicals of Next-Gen Jihad," *Washington Post*, 8 June, pp. B1, B4.

Sandole, Dennis J. D. (1984) "The Subjectivity of Theories and Actions in World Society," in *Conflict in World Society: A New Perspective on International Relations*, ed. Michael Banks. New York: St Martin's Press; Brighton: Wheatsheaf.

Sandole, Dennis J. D. (1987) "Conflict Management: Elements of Generic Theory and Practice," in *Conflict Management and Problem Solving: Interpersonal to International Applications*, ed. Dennis J. D. Sandole and Ingrid Sandole-Staroste. London: Frances Pinter; New York: New York University Press.

Sandole, Dennis J. D. (1993) "Paradigms, Theories, and Metaphors in Conflict and Conflict Resolution: Coherence or Confusion?" in *Conflict Resolution Theory and Practice: Integration and Application*, ed. Dennis J. D. Sandole and Hugo van der Merwe. Manchester: Manchester University Press; New York: St Martin's Press.

Sandole, Dennis J .D. (1998a) "A Comprehensive Mapping of Conflict and Conflict Resolution: A Three Pillar Approach," *IAPTC Newsletter* [International Association of Peacekeeping Training Centres], 1(5): 7–8.

Sandole, Dennis J. D. (1998b) "A Comprehensive Mapping of Conflict and Conflict Resolution: A Three Pillar Approach," *Peace and Conflict Studies*, 5(2): 1–30; www.gmu.edu/academic/pcs/sandole.

Sandole, Dennis J. D. (1999) *Capturing the Complexity of Conflict: Dealing with Violent Ethnic Conflict in the Post-Cold War Era*. London and New York: Pinter.

Sandole, Dennis J. D. (2002a) "The Balkans Stability Pact as a Regional Conflict Management and Prevention 'Space': An Evaluation," in *The Stability Pact for South East Europe – Dawn of an Era of Regional Co-operation?*, ed. Predrag Jurekovic, Ernst Felberbauer, and Andreas Wannemacher. Vienna: National Defence Academy.

Sandole, Dennis J. D. (2002b). "Virulent Ethnocentrism: A Major Challenge for Transformational Conflict Resolution and Peacebuilding in the Post-Cold War Era," *Global Review of Ethnopolitics*, 1(4): 4–27; www.ethnopolitics.org.

Sandole, Dennis J. D. (2002c) "The Causes of Terrorism," in *Terrorism: Concepts, Causes, and Conflict Resolution*, ed. R. Scott Moore. Fort Belvoir, VA: US Defense Threat Reduction Agency.

Sandole, Dennis J. D. (2003) "A Typology," in *Conflict: From Analysis to Intervention*, ed. Sandra Cheldelin, Daniel Druckman, and Larissa Fast. London and New York: Continuum International.

Sandole, Dennis J. D. (2004). "The 'New' Terrorism: Causes, Conditions and Conflict Resolution," *Wiener Blätter zur Friedensforschung*, no. 121, December, pp. 43–56.

Sandole, Dennis J. D. (2005a) "Hurting Stalemate in the Middle East: Opportunities for Conflict Resolution?" *ICAR News* [Institute for Conflict Analysis and Resolution, George Mason University], Spring, pp. 1, 6–9; www.gmu.edu/departments/icar.

Sandole, Dennis J. D. (2005b). "The Western–Islamic 'Clash of Civilizations': The Inadvertent Contribution of the Bush Presidency," *Peace and Conflict Studies*, 12(2): 54–68.

Sandole, Dennis J. D. (2006a) "Traditional 'Realism' versus the 'New' Realism: John W. Burton, *Conflict Provention*, and the Elusive 'Paradigm Shift,'" *Global Society*, 20(4): 543–62.

Sandole, Dennis J. D. (2006b) "Identity under Siege: Injustice, Historical Grievance, Rage, and the 'New' Terrorism," in *Identity, Morality, and Threat: Studies in Violent Conflict*, ed. Daniel Rothbart and Karina Korostelina. Lanham, MD: Lexington Books.

Sandole, Dennis J. D. (2006c) "The 'Fog of War' on Terrorism: US Policy, Deception, and the Continuing Slide into the 'Clash of Civilizations,'" *ILSA Journal of International and Comparative Law*, 13(1): 149–70.

Sandole, Dennis J. D. (2006d) "Complexity and Conflict Resolution," in *Complexity in World Politics: Concepts and Methods of a New Paradigm*, ed. Neil E. Harrison. Albany: State University of New York Press.

Sandole, Dennis J. D. (2007a). *Peace and Security in the Postmodern World: The OSCE and Conflict Resolution*. New York and London: Routledge.

Sandole, Dennis J. D. (2007b) "Challenges of Co-operative Security in a Post [Violent] Conflict Space," in *Approaching or Avoiding Cooperative Security? The Western Balkans in the Aftermath of the Kosovo Settlement Proposal and the Riga Summit*, ed. Ernst M. Felberbauer, Predrag Jureković, and Frédéric Labarre. Vienna: National Defense Academy.

Sandole, Dennis J. D. (2009a) "Critical Systemic Inquiry (CSI) in Conflict Analysis and Resolution: The Essential Bridge between Theory and Practice," in *A Handbook of Conflict Analysis and Resolution*, ed. Dennis J. D. Sandole, Sean Byrne, Ingrid Sandole-Staroste, and Jessica Senehi. London and New York: Routledge.

Sandole, Dennis J. D. (2009b) "Turkey's Unique Role in Nipping in the Bud the 'Clash of Civilizations'," *International Politics*, 46(3): 636–55.

Sandole, Dennis J. D., Kimberly Dannels Ruff, and Evis Vasili (2004) "Identity and Apocalyptic Terrorism," in *Apocalyptic Terrorism: Understanding the Unfathomable*. Fort Belvoir, VA: US Defense Threat Reduction Agency.

Sanger, David E. (2009) *The Inheritance: The World Obama Confronts and the Challenges to American Power*. New York: Harmony Books.

Sargsyan, Serzh, and Arthur Baghdasaryan (2008) "Moving Forward in Armenia," *Washington Post*, 17 March, p. A17.

Sarkozy, Nicolas (2010) Speech on Regulation, presented at Columbia University, 29 March, cited in *Washington Post*, 30 March 2010, p. A16.

Saunders, Harold H. (2005) *Politics is about Relationship: A Blueprint for the Citizens' Century*. Basingstoke and New York: Palgrave Macmillan.

Schaaf, Bryan (2010) "USIP Report: Haiti after the Earthquake," *Haiti Innovation: Choice, Partnership, Community*. Washington, DC: United States Institute of Peace; www.haitiinnovation.org/en/2010/01/31usip-report-haiti-after-earthquake (accessed 22 February 2010).

Schmelzle, Beatrix, and Martina Fischer (2009) "Introduction" *Peacebuiding at a Crossroads? Dilemmas and Paths for Another Generation*. Berlin: Berghof Research Center for Constructive Conflict Management.

Sexton, John (2010) Interview with Bill Moyers on *The Journal*, 12 March, www.pbs.org/moyers/journal/03122010/watch.html (accessed 2 August 2010).

Shapiro, Robert J. (2008) *Futurecast: How Superpowers, Populations, and Globalization Will Change the Way You Live and Work*. New York: St Martin's Press.

Sheehan, James J. (2008). *Where Have All the Soldiers Gone? The Transformation of Modern Europe*. Boston and New York: Houghton Mifflin.

Sheridan, Mary Beth (2010a) "Over Turkish Protests, House Panel Calls Killing of Armenians 'Genocide,'" *Washington Post*, 5 March, p. A8.

Sheridan, Mary Beth (2010b) "In Aid Plan for Haiti, US to Rebuild from Government Outward: New Approach Relies More on Statecraft, Less on Web of NGOs," *Washington Post*, 31 March 2010, p. A8.

Sheridan, Mary Beth, and Philip P. Pan (2010) "US, Russia Reach Nuclear-Arms Deal," *Washington Post*, 25 March, pp. A1, A6.

Sherif, Muzafer (1967) *Group Conflict and Cooperation: Their Social Psychology*. London: Routledge & Kegan Paul.

Simmel, Georg (1955) *Conflict and the Web of Group-Affiliations*, trans. Kurt H. Wolff and Reinhard Bendix. New York: Free Press; London: Collier-Macmillan.

Slaughter, Anne-Marie, and John Ikenberry (2008) "Democracies Must Work in Concert," *Financial Times*, 10 July; www.ft.com/cms/s/0/fd9e2fdc-4e7f-11dd-ba7c-000077b07658.html (accessed 1 March 2009).

Smith, David (2010) *The Age of Instability: The Global Financial Crisis and What Comes Next*. London: Profile Books.

Smith, R. Jeffrey (2010) "Pakistani Scientist Could Face Inquiry: Islamabad Seeks to Reopen Nuclear Proliferation Probe," *Washington Post*, 23 March, p. A11.

Snyder, Ann (2009) "Gender Relations and Conflict Transformation among Refugee Women," in *A Handbook of Conflict Analysis and Resolution*, ed. Dennis J. D. Sandole, Sean Byrne, Ingrid Sandole-Staroste, and Jessica Senehi. London and New York: Routledge.

Söderbaum, Fredrik, and Patrik Stålgren (eds) (2009) *The European Union and the Global South*. Boulder, CO: Lynne Rienner.

Sokalski, Henryk J. (1999) "Lessons Learned from UNPREDEP," paper presented at "Perspectives on the Role of Prevention in Europe," Berlin, 9–11 June; www.wilsoncenter.org/subsites/ccpdc/german/sokalp.htm (accessed 27 January 2009).

Sokalski, Henryk J. (2003) *An Ounce of Prevention: Macedonia and the UN Experience in Preventive Diplomacy*. Washington, DC: United States Institute of Peace Press.

Sommer, Theo (2010) "Welcome Back, Mr President," *Atlantic Times*, April, p. A3; www.atlantic-times.com/archive_detail.php?recordID=2128.

Sorkin, Andrew Ross (2009) *Too Big to Fail: The Inside Story of How Wall Street and Washington Fought to Save the Financial System – and Themselves*. New York: Viking.

Soros, George (1998) *The Crisis of Global Capitalism: Open Society Endangered*. New York: Public Affairs.

Sprinzak, Ehud (1991) "The Process of Delegitimation: Towards a Linkage Theory of Political Terrorism," in *Terrorism Research and Public Policy*, ed. Clark McCauley. London: Frank Cass.

Srulevitch, Andrew (2005) "In Larger Freedom: Kofi Annan's Reform Proposal," Conference of Presidents of Major American Jewish Organizations, www.conferenceofpresidents.org/media/user/images/unreform.pdf (accessed 27 March 2010).

Stanley Foundation (2009) *Peacebuilding Following Conflict*. Muscatine, IA: Stanley Foundation [conference proceedings].

Stephens, Philip (2009) "Wanted: Leaders to Confront the Demons of Europe's Past," *Financial Times*, 20 February, p. 9.

Stephens, Philip (2010) "Suddenly Obama Looks like a President with an Endgame," *Financial Times*, 9 April, p. 9.

Stern, Jessica (2010) "How to Deradicalize Islamic Extremists," *Foreign Affairs*, January/February, pp. 95–108.

Strauss, Delphine, Dan Dombey, and Isabel Gorst (2009) "Turkey–Armenia Breakthrough Welcomed," *Financial Times*, 2 April, p. 5.

Sullivan, Kevin (2008) "Alleged Plot to Blow up Airliners: British Jury in Terror Case Shown 'Martyrdom Tapes,'" *Washington Post*, 5 April, p. A10.

Talbott, Strobe (2008a) *The Great Experiment: The Story of Ancient Empires, Modern States, and the Quest for a Global Nation*. New York: Simon & Schuster.

Talbott, Strobe (2008b) "Trouble Ahead," *Financial Times*, 4 January; www.ft.com/cms/s/0/1a06557c-b8c7-11dc-893b-0000779fd2ac. html (accessed 1 August 2008).

Talbott, Strobe (2009) "A Better Base for Cutting Nuclear Weapons," *Financial Times*, 21 September, p. 11.

Tenet, George, with Bill Harlow (2007) *At the Center of the Storm: My Years at the CIA*. New York: HarperCollins.

Thom, René (1989) *Structural Stability and Morphogenesis: An Outline of a General Theory of Models*, trans. D. H. Fowler. Redwood City, CA: Addison-Wesley.

Thomas, K. (1975) "Thomas–Kilmann Conflict Mode Instrument," in *The Handbook of Industrial and Organizational Psychology*, ed. M. Dunnett. Chicago: Rand McNally.

Thomas, W. I. (1923) *The Unadjusted Girl*. Boston: Little, Brown.

Thompson, J. D., and D. R. Van Houten (1970) *The Behavioral Sciences: An Interpretation*. Reading, MA, and London: Addison-Wesley.

Thucydides (1951) *The Peloponnesian War*. New York: Modern Library.

Toch, Hans (1966) "The Social Psychology of Violence," address delivered to the American Psychological Association, September; abridged in *The Dynamics of Aggression: Individual, Group and International Analyses*, ed. Edwin I. Megargee and Jack E. Hokanson. New York and London: Harper & Row.

Toft, Monica Duffy, and Stephen M. Saideman (2010) "Self-Determination Movements and their Outcomes," in *Peace and Conflict 2010*, ed. J. Joseph Hewitt, Jonathan Wilkenfeld, and Ted Robert Gurr. Boulder, CO: Paradigm.

TRC (2003) *Truth and Reconciliation Commission of South Africa Report*. Pretoria: South African Government Information, 21 March, www.info.gov.za/otherdocs/2003/rc/ (accessed 3 June 2008).

Tschirgi, Neclâ (2004) *Post-Conflict Peacebuilding Revisited: Achievements, Limitations, Challenges.* New York: International Peace Academy; Geneva: WSP International.

UN/PBC (2008) "Synthesis Report and Summary of Discussions: Key Insights, Principles, Good Practices and Emerging Lessons in Peacebuilding," Working Group on Lessons Learned, Special Session, United Nations Peacebuilding Commission, New York, 12 June.

UN/PBC (2009) "United Nations Peacebuilding Commission," February, www.un.org/peace/peacebuilding (accessed 16 February 2009).

UN/PBSO (2008) "Expanding the Dialogue: Research and Policy Networks on Peacebuilding," paper presented at the Peacebuilding Roundtable, International Development Research Centre, Ottawa, 10–11 December.

Van Creveld, Martin (1991) *The Transformation of War.* New York: Free Press.

Vasquez, John A. (1993) *The War Puzzle.* Cambridge and New York: Cambridge University Press.

Victor, David G. (2006) "Recovering Sustainable Development," *Foreign Affairs*, January/February, pp. 91–103.

Viswanathan, Brinda (2007) "Living Conditions of Women," in *Solutions for the World's Biggest Problems: Costs and Benefits*, ed. Bjørn Lomborg. Cambridge and New York: Cambridge University Press.

Volkan, Vamik (1997) *Bloodlines: From Ethnic Pride to Ethnic Terrorism.* Boulder, CO: Westview Press.

Waldrop, M. Mitchell (1992) *Complexity: The Emerging Science at the Edge of Order and Chaos.* New York and London: Simon & Schuster.

Waltz, Kenneth N. (1959) *Man, the State, and War: A Theoretical Analysis.* New York: Columbia University Press.

Warner, Daniel, and Gilles Giacca (2009) "The Responsibility to Protect," in *Post-Conflict Peacebuilding: A Lexicon*, ed. Vincent Chetail. Oxford and New York: Oxford University Press.

Wehr, Paul, and John Paul Lederach (1991) "Mediating Conflict in Central America," *Journal of Peace Research*, 28(1): 85–98.

Weiss, Thomas G. (2007) *Humanitarian Intervention: Ideas in Action.* Cambridge: Polity.

Wenger, Andreas, and Daniel Möckli (2003) *Conflict Prevention: The Untapped Potential of the Business Sector.* Boulder, CO, and London: Lynne Rienner.

White, Josh (2008) "Gates Sees Terrorism Remaining Enemy no. 1," *Washington Post*, 31 July, p. A1.

Whitlock, Craig (2008) "Al-Qaeda's Growing Online Offensive," *Washington Post*, 24 June, pp. A1, A12; www.washingtonpost.com/wp-dyn/content/article/2008/06/23/AR2008062302135.html?nav=emailpage.

Whitlock, Craig (2009a) "Serbian Officials Say Mladic is 'Within Reach,'" *Washington Post*, 30 July, p. A10.

Whitlock, Craig (2009b) "Old Troubles Threaten Again in Bosnia: 14 Years after War, Leaders Suggest US Should Step in to Rewrite Treaty," *Washington Post*, 23 August; www.washington post.com/wp-dyn/content/article/2009/08/22/AR2009082202234.html (accessed 16 July 2010).

WHO (2002) *World Report on Violence and Health: Summary.* Geneva: World Health Organization; www.who.int/violence_injury_prevention/violence/world_report/en/summary_en.pdf.

Wilkenfeld, Jonathan (2008) "Unstable States and International Crises," in *Peace and Conflict* 2008, ed. J. Joseph Hewitt, Jonathan Wilkenfeld, and Ted Robert Gurr. Boulder, CO: Paradigm.

Wilkinson, Richard, and Kate Pickett (2009) *The Spirit Level: Why More Equal Societies Almost Always Do Better.* London: Allen Lane.

Williams, Abiodun (2000) *Preventing War: The United Nations and Macedonia.* Lanham, MD, and Oxford: Rowman & Littlefield.

Wilson, Scott (2010) "Obama's Focus Abroad Shifts from the People to their Leaders," *Washington Post*, 29 March, pp. A1, A15.

Wilson, Scott, and Mary Beth Sheridan (2010) "Obama Leads Summit's Nuclear Security Efforts: Challenge is in Persuading Others," *Washington Post*, 11 April, p. A6.

Witte, Griff (2008) "Rice Urges Israel to Desist on Settlements: Despite Expansion, Secretary Sees 'Chance' for Peace Deal in '08," *Washington Post*, 16 June, p. A15.

WP (2002) "US Congress Votes in Support of Sharon's Military Action," *Washington Post*, 3 May, p. A18.

WP (2010a) "Russia: US Says Arms Deal is Expected 'Soon,'" *Washington Post*, 14 March, p. A10.

WP (2010b) "The Truth about Global Warming: More Evidence from Respected Sources," *Washington Post*, 2 August, p. A12.

Yohe, Gary (2007) "Climate Change," in *Solutions for the World's Biggest Problems: Costs and Benefits*, ed. Bjørn Lomborg. Cambridge and New York: Cambridge University Press.

Zacharia, Janine (2010) "Biden Condemns Move by Israel. East Jerusalem Announcement: New Housing Approval Comes at Awkward Time," *Washington Post*, 10 March, p. A10.

Zakaria, Fareed (2007) "Beyond Bush: What the World Needs is an Open, Confident America," *Newsweek*, 11 June, pp. 22–9.

Zakaria, Fareed (2008) *The Post-American World*. New York: W. W. Norton.

Zakaria, Fareed (2009) "Time to Deal in Afghanistan," *Washington Post*, 14 September, p. A15.

Zartman, I. William (1989) *Ripe for Resolution: Conflict and Intervention in Africa*. Rev. edn, London and New York: Oxford University Press.

Zartman, I. William (2005) "Negotiating with Terrorists," *PIN Points Newsletter*, no. 25, pp. 2–4; www.iiasa.ac.at.

Index